TURNER
AND THE
SOCIOLOGY
OF THE
FRONTIER

The Sociology of American History
RICHARD HOFSTADTER *and* SEYMOUR MARTIN LIPSET,
editors

TURNER
AND THE
SOCIOLOGY
OF THE
FRONTIER

Edited by *Richard Hofstadter*
and
Seymour Martin Lipset

❦ ❦ ❦

Basic Books, Inc., *Publishers*

New York   London

Contents

TURNER
AND THE
SOCIOLOGY
OF THE
FRONTIER

Richard Hofstadter

INTRODUCTION

It is now almost three quarters of a century since Frederick Jackson Turner, then not yet thirty-two, delivered at a meeting of the American Historical Association in Chicago the most famous and influential paper in the history of American historical writing, his essay on "The Significance of the Frontier in American History." The moment was propitious for his argument: it was 1893; the revolt of the western farmers which was to culminate a few years later in the Bryan campaign was growing; the Populists were hard at work and the cry for free silver was filling the air. Among others there was also rising a more quiet but equally determined cultural revolt, a protest against the cultural dominance of the East and against its patronizing attitudes. The very presence of the historians at Chicago, which had outbid the older cities of the East for the privilege of holding a World's Fair to celebrate the four hundredth anniversary of Columbus's discovery, was a token of the success of this protest.

As an expression of this rising western self-consciousness, Turner's paper was intended to challenge some of the notions of the dominant eastern historians. The first was associated with the name of Turner's former teacher at Johns Hopkins, Herbert Baxter Adams; it was the assumption that American democracy and local self-government had come, by way of England, from remote Anglo-Saxon political institutions that could be traced back to the forests of Germany. The other was the implicit assumption that the significance of the American experience hung basically upon the slavery question and its effects on the American Constitution and the federal system—an assumption which Turner identified particularly with the then influential volumes of the historian Hermann von Holst. In effect Turner's answer to the first was that American democracy came not from the German but the American forest, and to the second that the slavery controversy was only an "incident," though admittedly an important one, in the real history of America, which could be found in the development of the American West.

Turner's essay, whose force was increased by its repetition and elaboration in a number of other works, contained a series of essential propositions. The central one was that "the existence of an area of free land, its continuous recession, and the advance of American settlement westward explain American development." Associated with this was Turner's belief that since there was no longer a frontier line, the frontier period was over, and that this marked the end of "the first period of American history." It was the frontier that had produced American democracy and individualism, that had been the main source of American opportunity. ("So long as free land exists, the opportunity for a competency exists, and economic power secures political power.") The frontier, which was also "the line of the most rapid and effective Americanization," had "promoted the formation of a composite nationality for the American people." It had taken European man, stripped him of most of his cultural baggage, subordinated him to the discipline of the wilderness, and finally imposed upon him a set of new habits and institutions. It was, indeed, the frontier that developed the essentially American traits—coarseness and strength, acuteness, inventiveness, restless energy, a "masterful grasp of material things, lacking in the artistic but powerful to effect great ends." These essential propositions were supplemented by others. Turner ascribed much of the impact of the frontier to the fact that it was a process of perpetual rebirth: civilization began over and over again on the edge of the wilderness, putting successive generations through the same transforming discipline. "American social development has been continually beginning time and time again on the frontier." The essay also illustrated how the frontier thesis might be applied to particular problems or phases of our history: the advance of the frontier decreased our dependence on England, forged the legislation that developed the powers of the national government, strengthened loose construction of the Constitution, and shaped the democracy of Jefferson and Jackson.

Turner's paper created no sensation when it was first delivered, but his ideas were not long in having a strong impact both inside and outside the historical profession. Much of their appeal can be attributed to their congeniality with the increasing disposition of midwestern intellectuals to develop their own sectional pride, and much too to Turner's remarkable effectiveness as a seminar teacher. His own pupils in time carried out a strikingly large portion of the projected scheme for American historiography that he laid out in his early essays. But no doubt his influence also owed something to a quality in his work that is particularly relevant to the sociology of American history. Turner was probably the first American historian—and certainly the first of wide influence—to see that if the peculiar configuration of American history and the American character is to be understood, one must have recourse to certain repetitive sociological and economic processes that have refashioned men and institutions in the American environment. He thought he had found the essential site of such processes on the frontier, and its essential character in the perpetual "rebirth," as he called it, forced by primitive conditions. Over and over again Americans had reverted on the frontier to primitive forms of existence; over and over they had re-created the materials of a more complex civilization. It was this process that had fashioned this new creature, the American man, with his distinctive individualism and his own variant of democracy.

During Turner's lifetime most of the criticism of the frontier thesis came from cultural critics like Van Wyck Brooks and Lewis Mumford, who incorporated the frontier idea only to take issue with frontier values. At bottom they fully agreed with Turner that the frontier was of vital importance in forging American characteristics, but to it they attributed the harshness, violence, and intellectual and artistic sterility of American life. A few historians also took issue with Turner's claims for the frontier during his lifetime, but it was only after his death in 1932 that a veritable avalanche of criticism descended on the Turnerian structure, precipitated in large degree by the new ideological currents set in motion by the Great Depression.

Much of the criticism of Turner, as represented by George

Pierson's essay (Chapter 3), hung on matters of definition, of meaning, of logic and internal consistency. Precision had never been Turner's forte, and historians were not wanting to argue that his insights, though not devoid of truth, were rendered more or less useless by their elliptical statement. Even the frontier was not clearly and steadily defined; "the West" was vaguely and inconsistently used. Nor was it clear precisely what qualities Turner had in mind when he spoke of individualism, or how he defined democracy. Other avenues of attack bore on his version of the frontier process itself. Was frontier life, Mody C. Boatright among others asked (Chapter 4), any more individualistic than it was collective, or any more individualistic than the life of other parts of the country? Many critics questioned how democracy could have developed on the frontier if it was not brought there in the first place. Outstanding students of the history of American agriculture pointed out that the social structure of the frontier rather quickly came to resemble that of other rural areas—that it had its full complement of large estates, farm laborers, and tenants (Chapter 7). Repeatedly students of the frontier process insisted that what happened on the frontier was very largely a product of the cultural habits that were brought to it. Others insisted that Turner had considered the American frontier too much in isolation, and questioned whether other frontiers produced similar institutional developments. (Chapters 6 and 9.) Still others developed alternative views of American historical development, arguing for the primacy of material abundance or physical mobility. Neither, of course, is unrelated to the frontier itself; but with respect to American mobility (Chapter 5) it was possible to argue that the frontier process was simply a special case of a more general process of movement, embracing not only the movement westward, but the movement from country to city, the influx of immigrants, and the American habit of residential change, all of which persisted long after the disappearance of the frontier.

One of the most prominent lines of attack on Turner's theories has been directed against a view which in fact holds a surprisingly small place in his essays—the view that the frontier constituted a kind of safety valve of opportunity which prevented America from developing class consciousness and acute class struggles. A great deal of this literature focused rather narrowly on showing—

with considerable success—how rare it was for discontented eastern workmen to go west and establish farms. In what once seemed
the climactic statement of the attack on the labor-safety-valve
theory, Fred A. Shannon went so far as to argue that the frontier
had not even served as a safety valve for farmers, and insisted the
rapid growth of the cities in the late nineteenth century should
instead be regarded as an effective safety valve for rural discon-
tents (Chapter 10). This had the merit of directing attention to
the normal flow of the surplus rural population to the cities. But
Shannon's reasoning and his calculations have not gone unchallenged, and in recent years writers particularly interested in the
phenomenon of economic growth (Chapters 11 and 12) have substantially reargued, and in the eyes of many writers, successfully
rehabilitated the safety-valve idea. The inability of eastern wage-
earners to remove to the frontier and make farms for themselves
is not, in the view of these writers, a decisive fact, if we can establish that the general effects of the westward movement and the
new resources and opportunities it fed into the economy were to
raise real wages, enhance optimism, and blunt social conflicts.

It is not only the safety-value hypothesis that has been reargued. Stanley Elkins and Eric McKitrick (Chapter 8), ingeniously
using modern sociological community studies as an explanatory
analogy, have tried to show how the frontier process might
have affected democratic institutions at the local level. Turner,
they point out, was not trying to account for democracy in general, as a political theorist; he was merely trying to show how
certain features of *American* democracy may have become differentiated. And they contend that the fluid frontier situation, operating on a relatively homogeneous population, and confronting it
with a vast flow of new and unpredictable problems, while at the
same time depriving it of the benefits of a pre-established way of
settling them, stimulated innovation, brought about multiple leadership, and opened a variety of social opportunities. For them
popular participation on a considerable scale was the key to American democracy at the local level.

It has become plain, as the literature of Turner criticism has
mounted in the past twenty years, that the Turner thesis is bound
to remain controversial. It has spurred an immense amount of investigation, much of it on the difficult but interesting terrain that

lies between history and sociology. In this respect Turner's imprecision has not been all to his disadvantage, for it has implied open-endedness. He seized upon a hitherto rather neglected fact —the great importance of the West in American development— and expounded upon it with suggestive but provocatively elliptical essays that stimulated both criticism and research. Today it is easy to believe that historians will still be arguing over and pursuing the implications of his ideas at their hundredth anniversary in 1993.

❧ 2 ❧

Seymour Martin Lipset

THE TURNER THESIS IN
COMPARATIVE PERSPECTIVE:
AN INTRODUCTION

The general thesis laid down by Frederick Jackson Turner concerning the impact of the frontier on various characteristics of American society has led to a number of efforts to test it in the context of other frontier societies such as Canada, parts of Latin America, and Australia,[1] which are discussed in the paper in this volume by Marvin W. Mikesell. Presumably it might be argued if various elements in the experience of colonizing a frontier land resulted in individualism, egalitarianism, and high political participation in the United States, similar consequences should have occurred in other pioneer settlement countries. Students of the Australian frontier, however, have pointed to the fact that their frontier experience was quite different from that of both North American countries. In America, each individual attempted to find his own plot of land. The Australian agricultural frontier, on the other hand, was much less hospitable in terms of climate, and family agriculture was less practical. Many of the frontier enterprises involved large-scale cattle and sheep grazing, both of which required considerable capital if the enterprise was to be worthwhile. "The typical Australian frontiersman in the last century was a wage-worker who did not usually expect to become anything else."[2]

There are, of course, other differences which have been suggested to account for the varying nature and influences of the Australian and American frontiers. Thus the absence of strong aboriginal resistance in Australia as compared with the Indian wars in the United States may have weakened the need for strong

9

local community life in Australia.[3] And the frontier, regardless of the institutions and values which it fostered, necessarily had much less impact on Australia than on the United States, since the relative size of the frontier population as compared to the urban one was much less in the former because of geographic factors.[4]

Although frontier geographic conditions in the two North American states were quite comparable, these frontiers also differed greatly in large part for reasons derivative from their varying political histories.[5] Inasmuch as Canada had to be on constant guard against the expansionist tendencies of the United States, it could not leave its frontier communities unprotected or autonomous. "It was the established tradition of British North America that the power of the civil authority should operate well in advance of the spread of settlement."[6] Law and order in the form of the centrally controlled North West Mounted Police moved into the frontier before and along with the settlers. This contributed to the establishment of a much greater tradition of respect for the institutions of law and order on the Canadian frontier, as compared with the American, meant the absence of vigilante activity in Canada, and enabled Canada to avoid the Indian Wars which were occurring south of the border, since the Canadian government kept its word to the Indians and the Mounties prevented "renegade whites" from upsetting the Indians.

The pervasiveness of the government legal controls on the Canadian frontier seriously weakened the development of an excessive emphasis on individualism which characterizes the United States. There had been no particular glorification of the frontiersman in Canadian writing as there has been in the United States.[7]

The development of the Canadian frontier, in fact, did not simply follow on population movements impelled by natural social pressures, as occurred in the United States. Rather the Canadian government felt the need to deliberately plan for the settlement of the West. As the Canadian sociologist S. D. Clark has put it:

Canada maintained her separate political existence but only by resisting any movement on the part of her population which had the effect of weakening the controls of central political authority. The claims to the interior of the continent were staked not by advancing frontiersmen, acting on their own, but by advancing armies and police forces, large corporate enterprises and ecclesiastical organizations, supported by the state. The Canadian political temper, as a result, has run sharply counter to the American. Those creeds of American political life— individual rights, local autonomy, and limitation of executive power— which have contributed so much to the political strength of the American community have found less strong support within the Canadian political system.[8]

An effort to explain why Brazil, the largest, most populous, and most richly endowed of the Latin American states has done so much more poorly than the United States, also emphasized the varying nature of frontier settlement in the Americas. Vianna Moog points to the differences between "bandeirantes" and "pioneers" as a key source of the varying patterns of development in his native Brazil and the United States. As Adolf Berle summarizes his thesis:

"Bandeirantes" ("flag-bearers") were the explorers and settlers of the interior of Brazil, as "pioneers" were the conquerors and colonizers of the great unoccupied heartland of the United States. The difference lies in their motives and ideals. The Brazilian bandeirantes were perhaps the last wave of colonial conquistadores. The American pioneers, though of all kinds, were predominantly Reformation settlers. The resulting civilizations set up by the two groups of wilderness-conquerors were therefore quite different, despite many elements common to both.[9]

Moog relates the varying nature of the Brazilian and United States frontiers to the fact that for three centuries in Brazil the main motive for going to the frontier was to get rich quickly, to find gold or other precious minerals, and that labor whether in urban or rural occupations was denigrated as fit only for slaves, while the English and later American settlers looked for new homes based on their own work.[10] These differences were linked to varying cultural traits and motives for seeking new opportunity on the frontier. In Brazil the bandeirante is credited with the geographic enlargement of the country, much as the pioneer is in the United States. "In the United States a thing, to be capable of arousing enthusiasm, must bear the label of pioneer; in Brazil . . . it must merit the epithet of bandeirante." [11]

The history of Argentina offers yet another example of the way in which the social structure of an American frontier was determined by the predominant structure and values established in colonial times. Values and structures endemic in the settlement of an open frontier did not either serve to influence the social organization of the rural community or help shape a national democratic outlook. Argentine agriculture developed much like that of Australia with large cattle and sheep ranches which used many workers either as hired help or as tenants, and preserved a hierarchical status system. After Independence various efforts to encourage small landholding failed because of the power of the large landowners. And subsequently in the latter part of the nineteenth century, it proved to be impossible to apply meaningful homestead legislation to Argentina, although there was a general belief among Argentine experts that United States prosperity and development was attributable to its policy of encouraging land settlement in the form of family homesteads. The Argentine pampas, which closely resembled the prairies of the United States and Canada, remained in the hands of a small class of large landowners. "Churches, schools, and clubs did not develop in rural Argentina for the simple reason that settlement was dispersed and often temporary." [12] And as in Australia, the urban centers, particularly Buenos Aires, became the focus for immigrant settlement. "Rather than a frontier, Argentina had a city." [13]

The argument that the varying characters of the Brazilian, Argentine, Canadian, and American frontiers flow from differences in their early history assumes the perspective taken by Max Weber which stresses the role of core values in influencing the institutional structure of a nation. As applied here, it suggests the need to modify the assumptions of many historians who accept variants of the Turner thesis, that the frontier experience was the major determinant of American egalitarian values. Rather, the comparisons with Brazil, Argentina, and Canada would suggest that the egalitarian character of the American frontier was in some part determined by the values derived from the revolutionary political origins and the Calvinist work ethos. The thesis that the basic values which were fostered by the success of the American Revolution, the departure of Tory supporters, and the victory of the Jeffersonians shaped the frontier society has, of course, been advanced by a number of historians. Thus Henry Nash Smith has sought to show how the rural frontier settlements established in the West on the Great Plains reflected not only the physical environment but also "the assumptions and aspirations of a whole society." [14] He has argued that revisions in the Homestead Act, which would have permitted large farms and a more economical use of arid lands, as in Australia, were opposed by the new settlers because *they believed in the ideal of the family farm.*

It should be clear that efforts to evaluate the causal significance of macroscopic factors in influencing the historical pattern of a nation's development should, wherever possible, be evaluated in comparative perspective. Looking at the way in which other overseas settler societies with open frontiers handled their frontiers points to major elements in the American experience, which could be ignored by simply analyzing internal developments. In many ways, the other nations of the Americas and Australasia offer a comparative laboratory for the historians and social scientists primarily interested in the United States. History, like the social sciences generally, must become more comparative, and the debates about the frontier thesis point up this need.

Notes

NOTE: For an expanded treatment of the comparative approach, see C. Vann Woodward, ed., *The Comparative Approach to American History* (New York: Basic Books, Inc., 1967).

1. See Walker V. Wyman and Clifton B. Kroeber, *The Frontier in Perspective* (Madison: University of Wisconsin Press, 1957); Paul F. Sharp, "Three Frontiers: Some Comparative Studies of Canadian, American, and Australian Settlement," *Pacific Historical Review*, XXIV (1955), 369–377; Herbert Heaton, "Other Wests than Ours," *Tasks of Economic History*, Supplement VI to *Journal of Economic History* (December 1946), pp. 50–62, and the various references in the Mikesell paper (Chapter 9).

2. Russel Ward, *The Australian Legend* (New York: Oxford University Press, 1959), p. 226. See also Carter Goodrich, "The Australian and American Labour Movements," *The Economic Record*, IV (1928), 206–207; Jeanne Mackenzie, *Australian Paradox* (London: Macgibbon and Kee, 1962), p. 106; Brian Fitzpatrick, *The British Empire in Australia, An Economic History* (Melbourne: Melbourne University Press, 1941); Fred Alexander, *Moving Frontiers: An American Theme and Its Application to Australian History* (Melbourne: Melbourne University Press, 1947).

3. Ward, *op. cit.*, p. 36; G. V. Portus, "Americans and Australians," *The Australian Quarterly*, XIV (June 1942), 30–41; and Archibald G. Price, *White Settlers and Native Peoples: An Historical Study of Racial Contacts between English-Speaking Whites and Aboriginal Peoples in the United*

States, Canada, Australia, and New Zealand (Melbourne: Melbourne University Press, 1949).

4. Ward, *op. cit.*, p. 30.

5. See S. M. Lipset, "Revolution and Counter-Revolution: The United States and Canada," *Revolution and Counterrevolution* (New York: Basic Books, Inc., 1968), pp. 31–63.

6. Edgar W. McInnis, *The Unguarded Frontier* (Garden City, N.Y.: Doubleday, 1942), pp. 306–307.

7. Claude T. Bissell, "A Common Ancestry: Literature in Australia and Canada," *University of Toronto Quarterly*, XXV (1956), 133–134.

8. S. D. Clark, *The Canadian Community* (Toronto: University of Toronto Press, 1962), p. 214. Clark also points out that the reform sentiments which did emerge in the Canadian West had much less impact on the rest of the country for geographic reasons. "The larger Canadian cities were more sheltered than were American cities from any undesirable influence the West might have exerted; the Great Lakes and Precambrian Shield (a thousand miles of rock between Manitoba and the settled portions of Ontario) provided an effective barrier to close and constant intercourse" (p. 103).

9. Adolf A. Berle, "Introduction" to Vianna Moog, *Bandeirantes and Pioneers* (New York: Braziller, 1964), p. 9; see also Charles Wagley, *An Introduction to Brazil* (New York: Columbia University Press, 1963), pp. 74–75.

10. Moog, *op. cit.*, pp. 119–121.

11. *Ibid.*, p. 171.

12. James R. Scobie, *Argentina* (New York: Oxford University Press, 1964), p. 124. For a discussion of the way in which efforts to encourage farming on the North American pattern were defeated, see pp. 78–81 and 121–130.

13. *Ibid.*, p. 130. The impetus for the "growth of cities, which would eventually make the Argentines Latin America's most urbanized people . . . came from (the extensive) agricultural exploitation of the pampas. The immigrants who were drawn to Argentina in the late nineteenth century found the land already controlled by *estancieros* (large landlords) and speculators. With the ownership of land largely beyond their reach, the newcomers accumulated in Argentina's port cities, especially in Buenos Aires."

14. Henry Nash Smith, *Virgin Land: The American West as Symbol and Myth* (Cambridge: Harvard University Press, 1950), pp. 124. For similar points of view see George W. Pierson, "The Frontier and American Institutions," chapter 3, this volume, p. 38; and W. W. Rostow, "The National Style," in E. E. Morison, ed., *The American Style: Essays in Value and Performance* (New York: Harper and Brothers, 1958), pp. 247, 259.

George Wilson Pierson

THE FRONTIER AND AMERICAN INSTITUTIONS: A CRITICISM OF THE TURNER THEORY

How much of Frederick Jackson Turner's frontier hypothesis is reliable and useful today? This problem has begun to trouble economists, sociologists, geographers, and most of all the teachers of graduate students in the field of American history.

For how shall we account for the industrial revolution by the frontier? Do American music and architecture come from the woods? Did American cattle? Were our religions born of the contemplation of untamed nature? Has science, poetry, or even democracy, its cradle in the wilderness? Did literature grow fertile with innovation in the open spaces? Above all, what happens to intellectual history if the environment be all?

The predicament of the scholar, who has been living in a comfortable frontier philosophy, is beginning to attract some attention. Nor may we comfort ourselves with the assurance that ours is a purely academic debate. For frontier legends of one kind or another have now so permeated American thought as to threaten drastic consequences. Have not our most influential journalists and statesmen for some time been ringing *pessimistic* changes on the theme of "lost frontier," "lost safety-valve," "lost opportu-

George W. Pierson is Larned Professor of History at Yale University. He is the author of *Tocqueville and Beaumont in America*, *Yale College: An Educational History, 1871–1921*, and *Yale, The University College: 1921–1937*. He has also written a series of essays on American mobility.

Reprinted from *New England Quarterly*, XVI (June 1942), 224–255, by permission of the author and the publisher.

nity"? [1] Such convictions can lead to legislation. In Congress the underlying issue could be: was there but one economic frontier, was it really a "safety-valve," and are both now gone? The cultural historian meanwhile asks: is it true that the frontier was "the line of most rapid and effective Americanization"? More particularly, since we are now trying to define and safeguard the "American way of life," what share did the "frontier" have in its creation, and to what cultural influences must we henceforth look for its preservation?

No matter how phrased, these questions are fundamental. They suggest a serious re-study of our premises. And the place to begin, the present writer has concluded, is with Professor Turner's own theories in the matter: that is, with his celebrated and influential essays on the significance of the American frontier.[2]

My proposal is, therefore, first to re-examine, and then overhaul, what Professor Turner wrote on the relation of the frontier to American institutions. For his brilliant papers have been the bible, and today still constitute the central inspiration, of an extraordinary and widely-held faith. That such an investigation may lead us to question, or in particular abandon entirely, the doctrine once taught us by a beloved man is unfortunately only too obvious. But that this autopsy is necessary is the argument of the considerations advanced above, and the theme of much that follows.

How was it then—according to the essays—that the frontier affected American institutions?[3] What really was Turner's theory in this matter—and what examples did he give to support his theory? Finally, is this part of his doctrine a reasonable and useful guide to students of American history today?

The Theory of How the "Frontier" Affected American Institutions

First of all, a careful study of Turner's thirteen essays makes it plain that in theory he recognized, as all of us must do, the European origins of New World society. To the "germ theory" school of Johns Hopkins he readily conceded this much: that the first germs of things now American had (two or three centuries before) been European. "In the settlement of America we have to observe how European life entered the continent," he wrote in 1893. ". . . Our early history is the study of European germs developing in an American environment" (p. 3).

Again, Turner was willing to make two further concessions to Old World influence. In the late nineteenth century, immigrants and institutions could still be observed, pouring into the Ohio Valley and the frontier areas farther West. Of these outsiders, some were from the East, but many were obviously coming straight from Europe. Hence resulted, as Turner himself insisted, a foreign accretion to frontier society—and a sort of rural melting-pot. In the second place, the Atlantic seaboard meanwhile had remained steadily subject to the influence and suggestions of the Old World (pp. 294–295). In the East there was an obvious "tendency to adjust to a European type" (pp. 282, 68, *et passim*).

Notwithstanding such concessions, of course, Turner stated and restated many times a conviction that these Old World germs were not the really significant factors in our national evolution. Even in the shaping of social institutions they were merely the roots, the remote background, the undistinguished platform from which a new departure could be taken. And here it was that the frontier entered. For in Turner's view the frontier was the most important single influence in effecting that new departure. It turned European things into American things. The longer it operated, and the farther the frontier got from the Atlantic Coast, the more overwhelming became its influence. "Too exclusive attention has been paid by institutional students to the Germanic origins, too little to the American factors," Turner insisted.

The frontier is the line of most rapid and effective Americanization. The wilderness masters the colonist. It finds him a European in dress, industries, tools, modes of travel, and thought. . . . It strips off the garments of civilization. . . . It puts him in the log cabin . . . and runs an Indian palisade around him. . . . Little by little he transforms the wilderness, but the outcome is not the old Europe, not simply the development of Germanic germs. . . . The fact is, that here is a new product that is American. . . . Thus the advance of the frontier has meant a steady movement away from the influence of Europe, a steady growth of independence on American lines (pp. 3–4).

And the grand proposal winds up with the conclusion that the novelties in American civilization finally became so successful and powerful as to react on the seaboard and on Europe itself.

By what *means* did the frontier exert so powerful a force upon society? How did it grasp an institution, tear it apart, and remold it so effectively? In his esssays Turner never formulated his interpretation very succinctly. Rather he was inclined to exploit a whole congeries of explanations, shifting the burden of proof as circumstances seemed to warrant. A fair summary of his views can perhaps be organized under two heads.

First of all, as demonstrated in my analysis of his "frontier" and "frontiersmen," Turner thought of the frontier as a physical, even a savage, environment.[4] At the frontier this environment was "at first too strong" for the institution, even as for the man. In a word, the wilderness "mastered" the European germs by forcing the pioneer to abandon civilized ways entirely and start completely over. "American social development has been continually beginning over again on the frontier" (p. 2). On the other hand, whenever total elimination was not achieved, the frontier changed old ways by modifying them: that is, by forcing at least some adjustments to new physical conditions. Again, as previously stated, a new product was sometimes created through the amalgamation of populations coming from diverse countries, by a sort of rural melting-pot process (pp. 22–23). In the fourth place, the constant repetition of exposure to the New World environment had a cumulative effect. Finally, it seems that sheer movement and migration, particularly the repetition of the pioneer business of picking up and moving on, resulted in the loss of cultural baggage on the road.

By way of a first, parenthetical criticism, it may be pointed out that this last explanation goes rather far afield. At least, it illustrates the shifting character of Turner's concept of the frontier, and raises the serious question whether the woods and migration belong in the same definition, or can have engendered identical results. If so, how are we to regard internal population movements (such as that from farm to city) that had nothing to do with the frontier? Again, what of the other great colonial migrations, to Canada, South America, and the East? Did the vast population drifts of the Mediterranean regions, or the expansion of the Norse to Iceland and the coasts of Europe, have effects comparable to those claimed for the American frontier? And are we to describe the tremendous migration of the Chinese to Manchuria in recent years in language out of Turner's essays?[5]

Clearly we have here the problem of how travel or movement affects group discipline and culture. What scholars need is less emphasis on the concept "frontier" and a deeper comparative study of migrations around the earth. Meanwhile, it may fairly be suggested that not all migrations that we have known, even in our own history, have had similar cultural effects. If movement into the Ohio Valley was distintegrating, the journey of the Pilgrims and the march of the Mormons must have been disciplinary, integrating experiences of the severest sort. But let us return to our exposition.

Thus far, Turner may be said to have been thinking of the frontier primarily in terms of nature, of geography, of physical environment. Accordingly his hypothesis postulates a kind of geographic or environmental determinism. He had not fully developed this interpretation, however, before he intruded into his definition of "frontier"—and so into his whole hypothesis—certain moral or social meanings. As I have demonstrated elsewhere, the frontier was not merely *place* and *population*, that is to say a savage wilderness and a sparse society of trappers, herders, and pioneers. It was also *process*, or more specifically the processes of conquering the continent, of moving westward, of changing from Europeans into Americans. Whether such irregularity in definition can any longer be tolerated in our use of the hypothesis is a question which has been raised before[6] and will be recurred to. At this point, let it suffice to note that, in contrast to the geographic or natural explanations already listed, this wider concept of "frontier" introduced social and psychological reasons to account for the transformation of our institutions. Principally, the settling business affected European germs by first affecting the germ-carriers. First the wilderness process altered the character and attitudes of the men, then the men inevitably changed their institutions.

Thus, the differentiation and the Americanization of our society took place because European men, in the course of westward migration, took on the qualities that Turner chose to regard as distinctively American. Perhaps a brief recapitulation of "Americanisms" may clarify this point. Engulfed in the onward rushing torrent, fur traders, herders, and pioneers, middle- and far-westerners, changed: i.e., they became individualistic, optimistic, and democratic, courageous and aggressive, energetic and ambitious, rough and ready and careless of niceties, nervous and restless and adventurous, volatile and changeful, practical and materialistic; best of all, idealistic.[7] Obviously, so great a human transformation could not but have a profound influence on the societal organism. The frontier force was operating indirectly, perhaps, but none the less powerfully. From geographic determinism, therefore, the argument had passed, by deceptively easy stages, over to a determinism of a decidedly different sort. Whether or not he fully realized the fact, Turner tended increasingly to rely for his explanations on propositions based on a sort of social psychology.

Of the two major means or forces this postulated, now one could be detected in obvious operation on the body of inherited institutions, now another. More often the frontier as place and the frontier as social process were entangled and intertwined. Whether alone or together, however, these two forces had in theory certain clear-cut and ascertainable effects. They produced novelty or Americanism in our institutions along general and common lines. Let us ourselves pass, therefore, from cause and from means to an analysis of frontier results.

First of all, the essays put overwhelming theoretical emphasis on what might be called the *idealistic improvement* that the frontier introduced into our institutions. In part, as already hinted, improvement came from deliberate elimination of what was old, oppressive, and unwanted. The American wilderness enabled European peoples to leave behind aristocracies, privileges, monopolies, and vested interests of all kinds. Hence, automatically, an increase in equality and individual opportunity. In fact, so much that was frozen and institutional was intentionally abandoned that society tended to become "atomic," and individual man once more could match his stature against the strength of his institutions—the persistent enslaving systems—that he or his fathers had organized.[8]

Idealistic improvement came also from the simplification or reduction of many of these institutions which were not deliberately left behind. Others were pruned or modified. Finally, by sheer invention of devices calculated to promote a happier society, the new men of the New World moved forward toward the creation of a new and better civilization (better, in the author's opinion, because more free). Turner was apparently so confident that the results of our frontier experience were liberating, and on the whole beneficent, that the very language of his essays in dealing with this subject took on a warm and almost lyric quality. He urged American historians to study "this advance"; he sang the epic of the "imperial domain"; he returned again and again to the confident theory that idealism and innovation and democracy and opportunity flourished on the frontier as nowhere else in the United States. "From the time the mountains rose between the pioneer and the seaboard, a new order of Americanism arose" (p. 18).[9]

So much for the main line of development, the line of improvement. The reader comes now to the fact that under the pressure of the frontier there had also to be some loss. Turner himself admitted that one of the effects of our experience with so vast and rich a continent was to make men a little careless and wasteful, a little materialistic and anti-intellectual. At the same time the raw and savage wilderness could not but be unfriendly to the delicacies and refinements of civilization, to certain higher arts, and to the skills of the more populous and cultivated regions. Hence a kind of unplanned loss. If not positively hostile to morality and the social decencies, the westerner was often indifferent to much that would have enriched his life and his new society. And if not indifferent, then he was all too frequently helpless.

Yet the essays hardly overemphasize such defects. They are admitted as a modest balance in a thesis that on the whole attributes an extraordinary amount of influence, and an extraordinary number of beneficial results, to a partly geographic, partly sociological, frontier.

So much for pure theory. If, in the interest of a fair summary, we now postpone detailed criticism, and pass directly to a restatement of Turner's supporting evidence, one observation may nevertheless be intruded. Apparently the optimism, the buoyant localism, and the anti-European nationalism are as strong in Turner's institutional genetics as in his treatment of western character.[10] Whether such preferences can be justified in sociological theory, or maintained by historical evidence, is of course another question.

The Practical Results for Social Institutions

Let us examine next the specific proofs of illustrations advanced by Turner in the demonstration of his hypothesis. What examples did he give in his essays; what signs of frontier influence on American institutions are we advised to see?

Taking the effects in inverse order of importance, and gathering the scattered proofs together so as to bring them to bear at the appropriate points, we have first of all a series of statements indicating loss: a necessary or deliberate *abandonment*. Specifically, the material and psychological forces of the frontier are stated as having eliminated from our social inheritance the highest arts and skills. In these essays, it should be noted, Turner tended to repeat his examples, instead of elaborating or adding to them. So we find repeated statements that fine arts, literature, science, social niceties, and even the higher skills in government were necessarily sacrificed.[11] "Art, literature, refinement, scientific administration, all had to give way to this Titanic labor," he wrote in 1896 in his essay on "The Problem of the West" (p. 211). Again, in 1901, in applying his hypothesis to the Middle West, it seemed to him that "if the task of reducing the Province of the Lake and Prairie Plains to the uses of civilization should for a time overweigh art and literature, and even high political and social ideals, it would not be surprising" (p. 156). Again in 1910, Turner found himself urging the state university to call forth the individualism of the pioneer for finer uses: the state university "must honor the poet and painter, the writer and the teacher, the scientist and the inventor, the musician and the prophet of righteousness—the men of genius in all fields who make life nobler" (p. 288).[12] In particular, it sometimes seemed to him that frontier democracy had "destroyed the ideals of statesmanship" (p. 216). It refused to recognize the value or need of specialization, training, or experience in the business of government (p. 357). It substituted rotation in office and the spoils system. It even destroyed or disregarded the codes of social and business morality (p. 32).

Needless to say, consequences of this sort rather disturbed the champion of the frontier. Yet, as several of the foregoing extracts indicate, he was able to regard the losses as forced more by circumstance than by character, and as a temporary evil in any case. When the forest was felled, and soil and freedom were won, then the refinements of life would once again be possible. Turner's essays rank him clearly among those who defend the "cultural" shortcomings of the American people on the ground of want of time. The finer arts had simply been postponed. "As we turn from the task of the first rough conquest of the continent, there lies before us a whole wealth of unexploited resources in the realm of the spirit" was his optimistic way of recognizing the problem (p. 309).[13] Such confidence is soothing and encouraging. Yet one may be forgiven for noticing the gulf that at this point opened before Turner's feet. If his essays mean what they appear to mean, then the doctrine is that we were most American just when we were least cultivated.[14]

To put the case a little more generously, it may perhaps be arguable that it was the novelties—not the (temporary) losses—that spelled Americanism. Yet if so, how were these innovators to remain "American," and still by and by begin to import the special skills and higher arts from Europe? Turner did not say. Rather, one suspects, the answer is to be found in the fact that the refinements, present or absent, constituted for him a very small proportion of what was fundamentally important. His definition of "culture" was perhaps not unlike what we often think of as the typical nineteenth-century American definition. A cultivated, progressive society had four parts and only four: government, business, education, and religion. And the essence of these was freedom.

In the second place, according to the essays, under the pressure of the frontier our ancestral institutions and ways showed signs of *partial disintegration* and simplification. Such effects were especially noticeable in religion, finance, the law, agriculture, and group discipline.

In the field of religion, the frontier encouraged the explosion of

the Protestant Church into sects and hampered religious organization. It led the pioneers out beyond the reach of all but the most
indefatigable Eastern missionary. At the same time it made what
worship there was a more emotional and less intellectual performance (pp. 36, 112, 165). In the field of business and finance, the
pioneer developed a debtor-class psychology, a grudge against
banks, and a relaxed notion of business integrity. Paper-money
agitation and wild-cat banking were strong in the interior and
agricultural regions (pp. 32, 210, 249). As for the law and the
courts, Turner "refrained from dwelling on the lawless characteristics of the frontier, because they are sufficiently well known." He
did mention the squatter, also (once each) the gambler and the
desperado, the rustler and the lumber thief, and on one occasion
he even called them "types of that line of scum that the waves of
advancing civilization bore before them" (pp. 32–33, 272–273).
Generally, however, it seemed to him sufficient to stress the frontiersman's impatience of restraints, his notion of the personality of
the law, and particularly "the growth of spontaneous organs of
authority" in the shape of regulators and vigilantes "where legal
authority was absent" (pp. 33, 212, 254, *et passim*). Squatter sover-
eignty, noted Turner, was a "favorite Western political idea" (p.
140). Finally, in the social and economic organization of the people there was a very obvious decentralization and simplification.
Civilization became atomic. "Complex society is precipitated by
the wilderness into a kind of primitive organization based on the
family. The tendency is anti-social" (p. 30). The tendency was
also toward ethical crudity, toward ruthlessness. "The back-
woodsman was intolerant of men who split hairs, or scrupled over
the method of reaching the right" (p. 254).

Thus far our analysis has relisted the destructive and regretta-
ble results of the long and repeated exposure to primitive conditions. It is now in order to remind ourselves that Turner in his
essays treated such tendencies as incidental, as unfortunate by-
products of a much larger and sounder process. For the frontier
could be *creative and transforming*, as well as hostile to social
institutions. By what we today might call selection and cross-
breeding, by psychological suggestion, even by direct material
command, important *changes* were wrought in our institutions.

In the field of education, for example, despite initial handicaps.

great novelties were achieved. The state universities of the Middle West, Turner thought, had been "shaped under pioneer ideals," and from them had come "the fuller recognition of scientific studies, and especially those of applied science devoted to the conquest of nature; the breaking down of the traditional required curriculum; the union of vocational and college work in the same institution; the development of agricultural and engineering colleges and business courses . . ." (p. 283).[15] In a later passage, Turner likewise credited the democratic state universities with becoming "coeducational at an early date" (p. 354).

More extensive and notable were the influences exercised by the frontier on our economy, and through our economy on our whole way of life. The continent determined the successive economic occupations. And as the hunter gave way to the herder, the cattleman to the pioneer, the unskilled pioneer to the intensive farmer, this farmer finally to the manufacturer, "the evolution of each into a higher stage has worked political transformations" (pp. 11–12). As Indian trails grew into turnpikes and railroads, so the Indian villages—likewise located by nature—gave way to trading posts, and these to cities (p. 14). The land systems of the first Piedmont frontier—or "Old West"—set the precedents for the trans-Allegheny West, and so led to the national land policy, the preëmption acts, and finally, the Homestead Act (pp. 122, 170). The same back-country area in the Colonial Period "began the movement of internal trade," developed markets, and so started the slow diminution of the dependence of the Colonies on England, just as later the salt springs of the Ohio Valley freed the pioneers from dependence on the coast (pp. 108, 18, 24). The frontier, particularly as it moved away from the coast, first forced the Eastern states to fear for their population, next drew the seaports into a rivalry for its trade, and finally lured the city men from the sea into attempts to master the interior (pp. 24, 190). The crossing of the mountains put fire into Eastern veins. The problems and opportunities of the Ohio Valley proved "a tonic to this stock" (p. 166). The "imperial resources of the great interior" engaged "the most vital activities of the whole nation" (pp. 179, 178). At last the Great Plains handed the individualist farmer his first defeat; and the Mississippi Valley became "the inciting factor in the industrial life of the nation" (pp. 147, 194). Meanwhile, the competition of the cheap lands and the drainage of the labor supply "meant an upward lift to the Eastern wage earner"; and if the mining and industrial opportunities produced a division between employer and employed, the frontier provided a safety-valve. As Turner put this matter, "the sanative influences of the free spaces of the West were destined to ameliorate labor's condition, to afford new hopes and new faith to pioneer democracy, and to postpone the problem" (pp. 193, 275, 303). Again, it was from the Piedmont and interior areas that the opposition to slavery always came (pp. 122, 173). Finally, in distinct disagreement with the North *versus* South school of interpretation of the antebellum period, Turner insisted that "the legislation which most developed the power of the national government, and played the largest part in its activity, was conditioned on the frontier" (p. 24).

At this point, certain fundamental objections can no longer be postponed. In the first place, whatever may be decided as to the Piedmont (hence frontier?) origins of our land survey and sale policies, of our preëmption acts and Homestead Act, a crucial problem remains. If, as the hypothesis suggests, those first policies set precedents, if also "the squatters of Pennsylvania and the Carolinas found it easy to repeat the operation on another frontier" (pp. 122–123), what happens to the principle of originality? Here, on a small scale, we stumble into a persistent difficulty. The frontier offered novel problems, hence novelty. On the other hand, the influence of the frontier was strengthened because the exposure to it was repeated: hence copying—especially as copying was so "easy." In this instance, ought not the sale of land in rigid squares and sections—(a most awkward device in rough country)—to have yielded to some new and happier invention? And this, in turn, perhaps to a third, as the frontier moved westward? The implications of such questions are rather arresting.

A second far-reaching doubt arises over Turner's "imperial resources." For here, once again, we have the "frontier" being stretched to cover the whole West, and this West being defined in terms of resources. If salt, and coal, and oil, and the wealth of the continent were really the causes of institutional change, ought we not to separate them out from the frontier concept? [16]

Most dubious of all, perhaps, is the statement about the sanative and ameliorating influences of the free spaces. Granted that the exact influence and duration of the frontier as safety-valve are still under dispute, nevertheless, one conclusion seems to me inescapable. What really mattered was whether the frontier and its free land *seemed* to offer an escape, a chance to start over again. We could have had—and probably did have—land to burn, and it would have done us no good if the average man no longer saw any attraction in it. When cars, movies, and radios become essentials of the accepted standard of living, subsistence farming is repugnant even to the starving. Measured, therefore, against this concept of a changing fashion or standard of living, it may be suggested that the lure of the land began in Tudor England, before there was any available, and ceased in the United States before the available supply gave out.[17]

Returning to our exposition, it is now in order to recall the tremendous emphasis and enthusiasm that Turner's hypothesis puts into the *political aspects* of frontier influence. For if our experience with the wilderness forced alterations in religion and education, in laws and in economy, it positively transformed our public administration, policies, and theory of government.

To begin, the frontier (mainly as a compelling geography) is regarded as having created and fostered sectionalism. In the Colonial Period this frontier-as-geography divided New England from Virginia, and the Middle Region from both. Later it accentuated the disharmony between North and South and set the East off from the new West. Even within the West there came to be regions whose special interests were soon reflected in industry and politics. "Indeed, the United States is, in size and natural resources, an empire, a collection of potential nations, rather than a single nation," Turner wrote. As a result its federalism would "be found to lie in the relation of sections and nation, rather than in the relation of States and nation" (pp. 158–159, 20, 52, 115, 120, 321).[18]

In not dissimilar fashion, the size and resources of the frontier West had a striking influence on foreign and domestic politics. The acquisition of Louisiana, for example, was "decisive" in setting the United States "on an independent career as a world power, free from entangling alliances." Again, the same expansion, by overcoming Jefferson's strict constructionism and by "swamping the New England section and its Federalism," revolutionized our political system (pp. 189, 25).

Most important of all by far, of course, the frontier made us national and made us democratic. The nationalizing influence of the frontier could hardly, it seemed to Turner, be exaggerated. It enforced unity and encouraged patriotism in many obvious and tangible ways. The menace of the Indians and the French made the frontier a consolidating agent, suggested the Albany Congress of 1754, and led to the building of forts and the creation of a national army (pp. 15–16). Again, the frontier was geographically more unified than the seaboard. Thus, toward the end of the Colonial Period, the Piedmont frontier "stretched along the western border like a cord of union" (p. 15); while later the Mississippi Valley transfixed the barrier set up by the slavery dispute. In the third place, the mobility of population and the ease of interior communication prevented the development of provincialism (p. 29). In the fourth place, the empty frontier regions became the melting-pot of European stocks, and even the New Englander tended to lose "the acuteness of his sectionalism" on the way through New York and Pennsylvania to the West (pp. 23, 27–28). Again, "the economic and social characteristics of the frontier worked against sectionalism"; the middle-western frontier developed special needs; hostility to class and regional privilege fostered a cooperative point of view; and the abuses of the railroads and eastern monopolies led to appeals for protection to the national government. Inevitably the frontier regions were soon trying to realize their interests in legislation. "Loose construction advanced as the nation marched westward" (pp. 25, 170–171, 189–190).

By this last, Turner meant to suggest that the frontier was responsible for much nationalistic legislation by the federal government, particularly in the economic field. Furthermore, such enactments automatically increased the strength of the Union and its government for general purposes thereafter. To quote Turner's proposition again:

The legislation which most developed the powers of the national government, and played the largest part in its activity, was conditioned on the frontier. . . . The pioneer needed the goods of the coast, and so the grand series of internal improvement and railroad legislation began, with potent nationalizing effects. . . . The public domain has been a force of profound importance in the nationalization and development of the government. . . . Administratively the frontier called out some of the highest and most vitalizing activities of the general government (pp. 24–25).

Such repetition of thought, within a very few pages, can be duplicated elsewhere in the essays (e.g., pp. 168–173) and gives a fair idea of the emphasis and conviction with which Turner kept returning to this favorite idea of his about the nationalizing influence of the frontier. Yet this last example or proof of frontier influence presents such curious internal inconsistencies that the commentator cannot forbear to pause a moment.

What Turner was thinking of, and cited again and again, was the tariff, banking, and internal improvement legislation of the period of Henry Clay on the one hand—and on the other, the western protest movements, with their proposals for the control and reform of big business by national legislation, in the era after the Civil War.

As to the first, it is well known that Clay found supporters for his "American system" in the Ohio Valley, but is it necessary to infer that genuine frontiersmen supported the idea of the tariff or were in favor of the National Bank? The pioneers may have voted for Clay on other grounds, and in any case they appear to have voted at least as heavily for Andrew Jackson, whose opinions on the tariff were nebulous and whose views on the bank were almost unprintable. A similar fate overtakes the case for internal improvements, that is, for the theory that the frontier led the central government into the building of roads and canals. What Jackson did to the Maysville Bill is familiar to us all. And what had happened to J. Q. Adams's really national program is surely no secret. As a matter of fact, in another connection, but without realizing that he was destroying his own argument, Turner stated the case exactly. He quoted Adams as confessing "My own system of administration, which was to make the national domain the inexhaustible fund for progressive and unceasing internal improvement, has failed." Then Turner gave the reason. "The reason is obvious; a system of administration was not what the West demanded; it wanted land" (p. 26). That is to say, the West wanted land far more than it wanted the federal government to go into any grand series of internal improvements. How had Turner been led into his error? The answer seems to be: he had equated the West and the continent with "frontier"; and the more densely settled this area became, the more it, as frontier, would demand internal improvements. The futility of this equation for any purposes of exact thinking is perhaps beginning to be clear.

As for the Granger and Populist and Progressive crusades, which were in part pioneer western and which did have nationalistic implications, the difficulty is this: what had happened to the ineradicably self-reliant, *laissez-faire* individualism of the Kansas frontiersmen to make them throw up their hands? And whence came the inspiration and the very shape of the reforms they advocated?

It would seem that Turner's evidence in the matter of internal improvements, and the nationalizing effect of the frontier on economic legislation, needs further study.

But that "the most important effect of the frontier has been in the promotion of democracy here and in Europe," Turner was positive. He said so in his first great essay (p. 30) and he stuck to the point right through to the end. The argument ran approximately as follows: the forest, the dangers, the lonely helplessness of life in the American wilderness, made the frontiersmen individualistic and self-reliant. At the same time, the deliberate abandonment of European societies and the separation from the more densely settled communities of the seaboard, together with the difficulties of the journey and the confusion of races and types in the new settlements,[19] tended to destroy old social disciplines, old class arrangements, old privileges and superiorities. Finally, and most important of all, the extraordinary wealth of the continent, particularly the opportunity represented by the free land, gave everyone a chance to become as wealthy and self-respecting as his neighbor. Hence, the creation of a race of optimists and democrats. From democrats and from the frontier surroundings, of course, came democratic institutions.

To review Turner's presentation of this argument would require many pages,[20] but a few quotations may be useful in establishing the poetic and dogmatic flavor of his pronouncements as stated in these famous essays. "The frontier is productive of individualism," he announced (p. 30). "The frontier individualism has from the beginning promoted democracy" (p. 30). "Liberty and equality flourished in the frontier periods of the Middle West as perhaps never before in history" (pp. 153–154). "The Mississippi Valley has been the especial home of democracy" (pp. 190, 183). More particularly "American democracy came from the forest" (p. 154). In translation, the word "forest" could mean many things, but generally the ingredients seem to be one part hardship, three parts free land. "Most important of all has been the fact that an area of free land has continually lain on the western border" (p. 259). These free lands were the "gate of escape." They "promoted individualism, economic equality, freedom to rise, democracy." "In a word, then, free lands meant free opportunities. Their existence has differentiated the American democracy from the democracies which have preceded it" (pp. 259–260). Finally, in 1914, twenty-one years after his first optimistic rebellion against the germ theory of American development, Turner put his thoughts into their most challenging and controversial form (p. 293):

American democracy was born of no theorist's dream; it was not carried in the *Sarah Constant* to Virginia, nor in the *Mayflower* to Plymouth. It came out of the American forest, and it gained new strength each time it touched a new frontier. Not the constitution, but free land and an abundance of natural resources open to a fit people, made the democratic type of society in America for three centuries while it occupied its empire.

If this was so, what democratic institutions in particular did the American forest produce? Apparently most of those that had gained repute since 1775. First, of course, came the reforms of the Revolution and the Jeffersonian period: the abolition of entail and primogeniture, the disestablishment of the churches, the demands for public education and the abolition of slavery. "Jefferson was the first prophet of American democracy, and when we analyse the essential features of his gospel, it is clear that the Western influence was the dominant element" (pp. 250, 114).[21] From the Mississippi Valley in the thirties came manhood suffrage and all the reforms of Jacksonian democracy, including that for the elimination of imprisonment for debt (p. 192). In the forties and fifties came new state constitutions with provisions for an elective judiciary. Finally, after the Civil War, the Mississippi Valley and the Plains gave birth to the Granger and Greenback movements, and to the Populist crusade. Bryan Democracy and the Republicanism of Theodore Roosevelt "were Mississippi Valley ideals in action" (pp. 203–204).

The reader will recall that Benjamin F. Wright and a number of others have long since perceived and stated the surprising poverty of at least certain frontier areas in democracy and in political invention. Yet a few additional queries may legitimately be raised at this point. For instance, are we really prepared to ascribe the platform of the Populists and the reforms of Progressivism to the frontier? Does not the history of social legislation in England and on the Continent indicate a quite different explanation? Again, it would appear that the woman suffrage idea originated in Europe and found but slim support in the Ohio Valley. The direct dependence of our belated Civil Service legislation on the earlier English movement will be apparent to anyone who cares to investigate that subject. As for manhood suffrage, whatever may have been the contributions of the wilderness frontier, is it not hard to believe that the American democrat sprang, as it were, full-armed, ballot in hand, out of the western woods? Surely one cannot today dismiss the long evolution of Parliament, the history of Colonial Legislatures, the methods of the New England town meeting, the self-government of Congregational churches, and the voting habits of trading-company stockholders without a thought. This leads to another disconcerting observation. Turner nowhere seriously credits Anglo-American Protestantism (what Tocqueville so discerningly called our "republican religion") with democratic tendencies. One is left to infer that such equalitarian and humanitarian interests as American Christianity has displayed must have derived from the experience of conquering the West.

Thus, to conclude our exposition of the Turner hypothesis, the West's "steady influence toward democracy" was not without its influence on the East, and on Europe. It was not until the early nineteenth century, and then "largely by reason of the drainage of population to the West, and the stir in the air raised by the

Western winds of Jacksonian democracy, that most of the older States reconstructed their constitutions on a more democratic basis. From the Mississippi Valley . . . came the inspiration for this era of change" (p. 92). The possibility that their citizens might escape to practically free land "compelled the coastwise States to liberalize the franchise; and it prevented the formation of a dominant class, whether based on property or on custom" (pp. 274, 30, 172, 185). As for Europe, what it derived from the frontier is less clear. The frontier is asserted to have turned both pioneer and Easterner away from Europe, and to have been the goal of peasant and artisan, the mecca for Europe's idealists and social reformers, through three hundred years (pp. 261–262, 349).[22]

"The men of the Mississippi Valley compelled the men of the East to think in American terms instead of European." When cities and sections turned their energies to the interior, "a genuine American culture began" (pp. 185, 190).

General Criticism

Turner's theoretical system, with proof and illustration, has now been developed and quoted at sufficient length to enable us to proceed to the next step: an attempt at an overall criticism.

First, then, let me say emphatically that it would seem small-minded to forget or to depreciate the inspiration that these essays originally offered to historians. Nor does it seem that we have yet heard arguments that would warrant us in discarding the celebrated hypothesis entirely, out of hand. Too much of Turner's interpretation still seems reasonable and corresponding to fact. Even in so condensed an analysis as has just been offered, the poetic insights and the masterful grasp of an understanding mind are hardly to be disguised. No blanket repudiation is therefore here to be proposed.

On the other hand, Turner himself did make a number of flat-footed and dogmatic statements, did put forward some highly questionable interpretations, did on occasion guess and not verify, did exaggerate—and stick for more than twenty years to the exaggerations. Hence it would seem that, however badly the master may have been served by his students and continuers in other particulars, these followers have been made the scapegoats a little too hastily. For they have not alone been responsible for the palpable errors and exaggerations that many of the rising generation recognize in the frontier theory as it is stated and applied today. At least they did not invent the safety-valve theory that now looks so dubious; they didn't misquote when they attributed political invention, and most of the reforms and the reformers, to the frontier;[23] they weren't the first local and national patriots. In his work with his students, Turner seems to have been modest and tentative and open-minded to a degree; but in his essays he could be and was as inclusive and sweeping as any have been since.

What were the statements and attitudes which we regard as extreme or with which we would disagree? A number have just been alluded to, or were earlier marked and commented upon. But the treatment has been parenthetical and fragmentary. Let me conclude, therefore, with a brief organization of the most cogent reasons for regarding Turner's original doctrine on the frontier and American institutions as defective and in need of repair.

To begin with the details and proceed to the general, it seems first of all necessary to suggest that—whatever may later be decided about Turner's theory—his evidence and proofs leave much to be desired. I am not here referring to our difficulty in accepting Turner's reasons for believing that the frontier stimulated invention, liberal ideas, educational improvements, or humanitarian reforms—a difficulty that remains substantial enough in itself. Rather, it is the quantity of his evidence to which I would now call attention. How few were his concrete examples, and how often he would repeat them is really astonishing. For twenty-seven years he kept the same happy illustrations, in the same language often, and even perhaps without testing them by fresh investigation. In his first essay Turner invited such testing, and suggested the specific investigation of a number of different frontiers: "It would be a work worth the historian's labors to mark these various frontiers and in detail compare one with another" (p. 10). Yet, if one goes to the later frontier essays for demonstration, one finds it only in the most general and vague terms. Undoubtedly, Turner was more interested in discovering than in proving. Undoubtedly, also, he must on occasion have carried his

analysis of special areas and his search for positive proof somewhat deeper, particularly in his work with his graduate students
and in his study of the different sections. Unfortunately, there is
astonishingly little to show for that research in the later essays.

Did Turner, perhaps, on the other hand, put his effort into theory and philosophy, into developing and revising his first grand
vision and interpretation? Once again, curiously, our examination
indicates that he did not. For not only did he republish his first
essay without substantial alteration, but his later essays show little
if any advance beyond the position taken in his first. Not only is
there small proof of fresh research; there is as little proof of fresh
thinking.[24] Elaboration, progress in application, repetition, certainly, but distressingly little in the way of genuine reconsidera-
tion or modification. If anything, the later essays are more general, sweeping, and blurred—as if the hypothesis had somewhere
already been proved. Yet when one turns back to the first statement one is startled to find in it reservations, moderation, and
doubt.

A critic is reduced, therefore, to finding the same theory
throughout, and is moved to protest at certain aspects of that theory. It is dangerous and ungenerous, I acknowledge, for a man
living in a later climate of opinion to disparage the attitude of an
earlier day. But since our problem concerns the *present applicability and future usefulness* of these frontier essays, certain assumptions and definitions cannot be allowed to pass without challenge.

As has been pointed out, first of all, the essays are in a high
degree unsatisfactory in clarity, or definition. Turner's Master
Force is defined and used as area, as population, as process. As if
such inharmonious and confusing interpretations were not sufficiently inclusive, this force is then made to cover soil and mineral
resources as well—and at times everything western, or pre-indus-
trial, or non-European! I think it fair to say that the word "frontier" has been, and will be found again, a Pandora's box of trouble
to historians, when opened to such wide interpretation.

Again, there seems to be haziness in the statement of *means*, and
real doubt as to many of the *results* claimed for the frontier. At
moments the wilderness, and even the flow of our population
westward, seem to have been destructive rather than constructive
experiences. And when the rebuilding is scrutinized, the propor-

tion of invention looks surprisingly small. In particular, the contribution of the frontier to our educational, economic, and political institutions needs cautious reappraisal.

Once again, the emotional attitudes or assumptions of the author—and of his generation?—color his essays unmistakably. It would have been strange had they not done so. No personal censure is therefore intended. On the other hand, for a contemporary interpretation of American history, the emphasis of 1893 may become a serious handicap; it may even obscure or distort the elements in the theory that are still most meaningful. To be specific, the frontier hypothesis seems—as has been indicated several times already—too optimistic, too romantic, too provincial,[25] and too nationalistic to be reliable in any survey of world history or study in comparative civilization. And it is too narrowly sectional and materialistic—in the sense of assigning deterministic forces to physical environment—to seem any longer a satisfactory gauge for internal cause-measurements. A thoughtful reading of the thirteen essays, or even of such materials as it has been possible to quote in this paper, ought to be conclusive on these defects. Yet perhaps a word more about one or two of them will not be out of place.

At an earlier point in the argument, the migration factor was isolated—as a sort of foreign substance—out of the frontier concept; and it was suggested that, at the least, a comparison with city-ward movements and with migrations the world around is in order. It now seems pertinent to suggest the extension of such comparisons from migration to the *whole story of settlement* or environmental adjustment in South America, Australia, and Africa. Did comparable situations always produce comparable results? Moreover, if we repeat such comparisons *within* the American experience, do we really find much similarity between the frontiers of Colonial Massachusetts, the Mississippi Delta, the Plains, and the mining country? If not, it would appear that the applicability of Turner's frontier hypothesis is far more limited than has been supposed.

Along another line of thought, I have suggested that Turner's views were deterministic. They were almost fatalistic.[26] Again and again one gets the impression that western man was in the grip of overpowering forces. "The people of the United States have taken their tone from the incessant expansion which has not only been open but has even been forced upon them" (pp. 37, 4, 211).

Now what makes this determinism particularly questionable is the fact that it is materialistic, yet in a high degree confused and cloudy in its statement of causes. Turner has been attacked by the economic determinists for not regarding commercialism, industrialism, and capitalism as more important than the continent—and the frontier essays certainly pay far too little attention to the commercial character of nineteenth-century American society, East *or* West. This school of critics is also quite correct in labeling Turner a geographer and a sociologist rather than a champion of the Marxian dialectic or interpretation.[27] Nevertheless Turner remains, in his own way, almost as convinced a materialist as the author of *Das Kapital* himself. Only Turner's mastering force is a multiple thing, a cluster of causes singularly disparate and inharmonious. Part of the time the essays cite the natural environment, the physical continent, the wilderness; at other moments the source of change is located in the state of society: the sparseness, mobility, or indiscipline of settlement. Admittedly, America represented both physical hardship and social opportunity. The West was rough (a geographic factor) and it was empty (a sociological force). Perhaps, then, Turner's greatest achievement was his successful marriage of these two dissimilar forces in the single phrase: *free land.* He did not invent the term or the ideas it contains. But he most certainly popularized them.

If this sounds like a defense of Turner, it is intended rather as a clearer definition of his special materialism, which remains objectionable. And it remains so—even disregarding the untenable variations in his definition of "frontier"—because too much is attributed both to the land and to the fact that it was easy to acquire. A number of Turner's ablest friends and admirers regard his "free land" doctrine as a contribution of extraordinary insight and importance, and unquestionably it does seem impressive. Yet the modern observer cannot but be disturbed by the failure of some non-English groups, and even of a tremendous number of native Americans, to heed this call. The open spaces do not seem to have acted as a solvent on the Pennsylvania Germans or the *habitants* of Lower Canada, and the migratory New England groups were only partially distintegrated, while an increasing number of farm boys gravitated to town and city (an even stronger solvent?) instead. It will bear repeating that Turner perhaps exaggerated the importance of "free land." [28]

On the other hand, I cannot but feel that too small a role is allowed to man's own character and ambitions, to his capacity for change, and to the traditions and momentum of the society which came to use this free land. Thus the continent masters, destroys, commands, and creates—while man is surprisingly passive. Where many of us are inclined to regard the physical environment as permissive, or limiting in its influence, Turner in his essays tends to make it mandatory. Vice versa, where sociologists are coming to recognize the factor of tradition and habit as very powerful, and where a man's ability to master circumstance is at times conceded to be extraordinary, the frontier hypothesis tends to ignore human origins and peculiarities, at least in the composition of American traits and American institutions. Thus first causes are made to lie in real estate, not state of mind. Hence, again, the first Colonial settlers are not examined with any care, but are treated as if they were *average* Europeans. And the later developments and changes in coastal society are handled as if they could have had only two sources: either a fresh migration or influence from Europe, or the powerful influence of an innovating frontier. Native invention in New England? Improvement in New York without the stimulus of the West? Apparently not.[29]

The Contradictions and Omissions

It remains to add two final comments. They concern contradiction and omission.

However optimistic, nationalistic, one-sided, repetitious, fatalistic, undocumented, or erroneous a number of Turner's proposals may appear, the curious fact seems to be that one of the most striking weaknesses of the essays as a whole is internal inconsistency. As has been hinted throughout this chapter, the frontier theory in its full development does not hang together. The nationalism of the frontier does violence to its sectional tendencies, innovations are derived from repetition, the improvement of civilization is achieved via the abandonment of civilization, and materialism gives birth to idealism. Such inconsistencies do not necessarily condemn the whole theory out of hand. But they do unsettle conviction; they make it hard to remain complacent; they invite the most careful, open-minded restudy.

To this should be added the thought of what Turner did not write. Making all due allowances for the fact that the master's essays were composed in the period 1893–1920, it remains true that in the single field of economics he slighted the industrial revolution, he didn't seem to understand the commercial revolution, and he said nothing at all about the agricultural revolution. Yet it might be asserted that the last alone will be found to have produced more changes in American farming in the nineteenth century than all the frontiers put together! Again, it must be clear from our restatement that the frontier essays entirely failed to check the hypothesis by setting American experience against world experience. Because Turner was primarily a *Western* explorer, his pupils and followers have tended to neglect the all-important comparative approach. When, then, we review the questions with which this chapter began, when we remember that the thirteen frontier essays treat the development of "American" and middle-western characteristics without reference to Romanticism, to Evangelism, to the eighteenth-century Enlightenment, to the scientific discoveries and the secularization of thought that in varying degrees have overtaken all Western peoples since the discovery of America, it may fairly be deduced that *for future purposes* these celebrated statements leave too much out.

Perhaps a conclusion may be stated in these terms:

In what it proposes, the frontier hypothesis needs painstaking revision. By what it fails to mention, the theory disqualifies itself as an adequate guide to American development.

Notes

1. At Union College, President Dixon Ryan Fox pointed out how the Turner doctrine has tended to encourage defeatism during the 1930's. Too many prophets have argued that the disappearance of free frontier land means the disappearance of opportunity. On the contrary, said President Fox, the word frontier ought to mean merely "the edge of the unused." In science, in business, in arts, challenge remains. "A failure now . . . would not be a failure of opportunity; it would be a failure of nerve."

I am indebted to President Fox for permission to quote from his address, and for some most pertinent suggestions; also, for criticism and encouragement to Charles A. Beard, to Professors Leonard W. Labaree and James G. Leyburn of Yale University, and to Professor Richard H. Shryock of the University of Pennsylvania.

2. The reference is to Turner's first great exposition of 1893, called "The Significance of the Frontier in American History," and to the twelve other essays or papers in this field, the whole collected and republished under the title *The Frontier in American History* (New York: 1920), hereinafter referred to as "Turner." Page citations in my analysis will be to this volume.

3. Attention in this chapter will be confined to *institutional* results because, in a preliminary study, "The Frontier and Frontiersmen of Turner's Essays," *The Pennsylvania Magazine of History and Biography*, LXIV, No. 4 (October 1940), 449–478 (hereinafter called "Pierson"), I have already subjected both Turner's definition of what the frontier *was*, and his interpretation of how it influenced the *persons* it touched, to scrutiny and challenge.

4. See Turner, pp. 4, 210, *et passim;* also Pierson, pp. 454–459 and 465–467.

5. I am indebted to Professor K. Asakawa of Yale University, and to Professor Owen Lattimore of the Johns Hopkins University, for stimulating comment on this point.

6. Pierson, pp. 462–465.

7. Pierson, pp. 468–476.

8. The echo of Rousseau is too strong here to be overlooked. Note also the old American theme of a corrupt and tyrannical Europe.

9. For contrast, see Dixon Ryan Fox's statement that for long years the student of civilization "as he went west, found himself going down stairs. . . ." "Refuse Ideas and Their Disposal," *Ideas in Motion* (New York: 1935), p. 125.

10. Pierson, pp. 464–465 and 476–478.

11. Had Turner devoted much thought to the arts, in relation to the environment, he would perhaps have given more attention to architecture.

12. That is to say, the pioneering state university should honor precisely those skills and those specialists the real pioneers cared least about.

The optimistic but unfortunate employment of a word in two different senses is by no means unusual in these essays. No doubt most such errors were as unintentional and unconscious as the case here underlined. Yet they reveal Professor Turner in rather cloudy thinking; and the worst of it is that for us such lapses in precision, such vagaries of definition, subtly and slowly convert what at first seemed a brilliant illumination into a golden but impenetrable mist.

13. Are the arts more encouraged by a rich than by a poor natural environment? May not hardship drive certain peoples to the solace of religion and the cult of beauty? Conversely, may not the materialism which sometimes results from economic success smother the artistic elements in a society? I cannot pretend to know. But sometimes it looks as if it were the drive, the will of a given population, that really mattered. Not all the hardships or poverty of history have apparently been able to squeeze out of the Jews their artistic cravings. Vice versa, Americans have sometimes given the impression of indifference, of lack of interest, rather than of any want of opportunity or time.

14. Notice the contradiction with Turner's optimism, and the agreement with the position of Dixon Ryan Fox, cited above.

15. The point cannot be argued at length here, but the reader will surely wish to look again at the essay "Pioneer Ideals and the State University." How little of what is new even our state universities owe to the environment of the frontier of the West, and how much to the inspiration of England, Germany, Switzerland, and France, one would never guess from these pages. "Other universities do the same thing," Turner admitted; "but the head springs and the main current of this great stream of tendency come from the land of the pioneers, the democratic states of the Middle West."

In 1918 the author modified his position to the extent of conceding that "the State Universities were for the most part the result of agitation and proposals of men of New England origin; but they became characteristic products of Middle Western society" (p. 354)! In 1920, nevertheless, the assertions of the earlier essay were reprinted without qualification.

16. Note also how nature "incites" man, how inert minerals are made to draw a whole society into new forms of economy. Professor Labaree remarks on the failure of cotton fields to produce cotton mills, at least in the older South. But perhaps this region "incited" Manchester and Liverpool instead?

Again, according to Turnerian logic, Wilberforce and the English anti-slavery movement ought to derive from the frontier—whereas in fact the free lands of the deep South and the Southwest seem to have prolonged the career of the peculiar institution, and to have made its asperities somewhat harsher. (See the reference to this point in Pierson, p. 471.)

The ancestry and naïveté of geographical determinism have been remarked by many scholars. For an excellent resumé by Louis Wirth, see *Critiques of Research in the Social Sciences*, III (New York: 1940), pp. 179–184.

17. For confirmation of this point of view, see the illuminating remarks of Isaiah Bowman in *The Pioneer Fringe* (American Geographical Society Special Publication No. 13, 1931), pp. 5, 41, 74, 81, *et passim*.

In his most suggestive book *The Golden Day* (New York: 1926), page 55, Lewis Mumford has stated this point as follows: "In America the return to Nature set in before there was any physical necessity for filling up the raw lands of the West. The movement across the Alleghenies began long before the East was fully occupied: . . . by the time the nineteenth century was under way, the conquest of the Continent had become the obsession of every progressive community."

The difference between the frontier, as actual opportunity, and this romantic European agrarianism needs clear definition.

18. Could the influence of the frontier be uniform and centralizing, yet at the same time lead to sectionalism? Perhaps, in the sense that all frontiers, however much they differed among themselves, might have certain limited characteristics in common. To get an *increased* nationalism and an *increased* sectionalism out of the same forest is clearly a little more difficult.

It may be argued that this part of the hypothesis should be corrected by a reading of what Turner later published on "Sections." Yet Turner himself failed to repudiate his earlier statements; and what such a repudiation would have done to the "nationalizing" influence of the frontier may be gathered from the exposition that follows.

19. Note again the incorporation of non-frontier factors within the symbol "frontier."

20. For example, it is not always clear what Turner meant by the word "democrats"; it is, as Beard warns, by no means certain that there ever was much "individualism" on the frontier; and one would hardly guess from

Turner's pages how inharmonious free opportunity and equalitarianism sometimes are (Pierson, pp. 468–472).

21. The student will note that T. P. Abernethy is also skeptical of the frontier explanation of Thomas Jefferson. See especially his "Author's Preface" to *Three Virginia Frontiers* (University of Louisiana: 1940), p. x.

22. That numerous idealists and reformers were drawn out of old Europe into the new West is certain, but it may be that the empty woods were more hospitable (i.e., less hostile) to Utopian experiments than were frontier populations.

23. In an 1899 version of his first great essay, Turner did grant that "the study of the evolution of western institutions shows how slight was the proportion of actual theoretical invention of institutions." But for some reason this reservation was thereafter omitted from his thesis. See *The Early Writings of Frederick Jackson Turner* (Madison, Wis.: 1938), p. 38.

24. Considerable awareness of the capture of the Middle West by industrialism appears, but this leads toward discouragement of exhortation rather than to a revision in frontier theory.

25. The hypothesis is "provincial" in two different ways; it ignores frontiers in other lands, and it slights one whole side of human culture in the United States.

26. This is shown, in a kind of inverted fashion, by the pessimism to which the disappearance of the safety-valve frontier has given rise. I do not suppose that Turner invented this "escape" concept. The pioneering legends, from which his hypothesis must itself have derived, have doubtless exercised their own share of influence, quite independently. Yet if today our leaders still hitch our star to a covered wagon, the frontier theory may share the responsibility.

27. This accusation would seem one to be borne quite cheerfully. To the present writer, the substitution of *economic man* for *frontier man* would constitute a most doubtful improvement.

28. Perhaps it is unreasonable to suggest that the North American Indians ought to have profited in the same fashion from so much free land. Yet what about the Spaniards, who had the run of the whole hemisphere? Did the Mississippi Valley make them democratic, prosperous, and numerous? In a word, do not the level of culture, and the "fitness" of a society for the wilderness, matter more than the wilderness? Employing again the comparative vista, were there no unoccupied forests in medieval France? And if today a new continent were to rise out of the Pacific Ocean, are we so sure that it would encourage small freeholds, not corporation or governmental monopolies? (For stimulus and clarification on this point I am indebted to the professors and students of history at the Johns Hopkins University.)

29. Turner did not write thirteen essays on the frontier without recognizing that the frontier area in which New Englanders settled turned out somehow different. Again he spoke of Germans in Wisconsin, of Scandinavian immigration, and the like. But by and large, it was the land these immigrants went to rather than the traits they came with that seemed to Turner *significant*.

❦ 4 ❦

Mody C. Boatright

THE MYTH OF
FRONTIER INDIVIDUALISM

There is no more persistent myth in American history than the myth that rugged individualism is or has been the way of American life. Many influences have entered into the creation of this myth, but the man who is chiefly responsible for its general acceptance is Frederick Jackson Turner, who, in 1893, when the western states were loud in their demands for national regulation of industry, said in his now famous Chicago address that the American frontier had promoted democracy—a democracy "strong in selfishness and individualism, intolerant of experience and education, and pressing individual liberty beyond its proper bounds." Its tendency, he said, was anti-social. "It produced antipathy to control, and particularly to any direct control." It permitted "lax business honor, inflated paper currency and wildcat banking." [1]

Later industrialists harassed by popular western agitation for social control of industry seized upon Turner's pronouncement as a justification of their Manchester economics. For had he not said that the frontier had been the dominant force in the shaping of American ideals and that the way of the frontier was uncontrolled individual initiative? E. H. Harriman, alarmed by governmental concern over the financing and operation of his railroads, issued a

Mody C. Boatright is Professor of English, University of Texas, and the author of *Folk Laughter on the American Frontier*, and editor of many works of American folklore.

Reprinted from *Southwestern Social Science Quarterly*, XXII (June 1941), 14–32, by permission of the author and the publisher.

statement calculated to convince the western agrarians that such regulation as was being attemped by the Interstate Commerce Commission was a violation of our early pioneer ideals. Herbert Hoover took up the cry in 1922 and has since continued to denounce "regimentation" and to proclaim his gospel of "rugged individualism" of which he finds the "American frontier the epic expression." [2] James Truslow Adams and others swell the chorus.

Although liberals and radicals, whose socioeconomic philosophy differs from that of the United States Chamber of Commerce and the National Manufacturers' Association, have pointed out that our national industrial policy has been one of paternalism rather than of individualism, they have for the most part accepted or questioned only timidly the Turner-Hoover interpretation of frontier democracy. Ernest Boyd's statement is typical: "Yesterday all the slogans and catchwords that beguile them [the apostles of rugged individualism] were true." [3] Parrington thought it odd that it was in the West that the spirit of social protest should "first express itself most adequately." [4] Charles Beard, who formerly announced that "Our fundamental philosophy of rugged individualism must be modified to meet the needs of a cooperative age," [5] has now expressed the opinion that Turner "overworked the 'individualism' of the frontier," [6] but his protest is tentative and overcautious. Henry Wallace speaks of "frontier freebooter democracy of the purely individualistic type." [7]

That there were freebooters on the frontier no one can deny; for the frontier attracted freebooters as a dead steer attracts buzzards. They came from the Atlantic seaboard, and they came also from England and Scotland and Germany. Some of them, though not as many as Turner implies, grew up in a frontier environment; but that they were products of frontier ideology can be demonstrated only when it can be demonstrated that all freebooters of whatever age, climate, or nationality are the products of a frontier ideology. If the liberals would read the documents of frontier history, and particularly the memoirs of frontiersmen, they would find many facts which have been ignored or underemphasized by the Turner school of historians, but which call for a modification of the dominant conception of the frontier environment. They would not find the frontier the Hobbesian state of nature our mythology has made it. They would no longer confuse

governmental policies determined by an eastern governing class
with the social philosophy of the western folk. They would learn
to distinguish between the conspicuous individuals who exploited
the frontier (and the frontiersmen) on a grand scale and the people who settled in the West seeking a fuller life than had been
their lot elsewhere.

One who examines the folkways of the settlers is impressed by
the numerous ways in which the principle of mutuality finds expression in frontier life.

First of all, it is manifest in the pattern of western settlement, a
pattern early established and repeated many times with variations.
The land policies of the colonies and later of the United States
were shaped by men to whose interest it was to keep wages low
and land values high. They did not wish to encourage emigration.
Rather, they were in constant fear that their labor supply would
be drained off by the West. Land acts, therefore, favored the in-
dustrialist, the seaboard farmer, and the land speculator. Even
after the Republican party had won the 1860 election by trading
homesteads for votes, the homesteads provided were throughout
the greater part of the West inadequate for the support of a family; no provision was made for getting the needy settler to the
land; and no paternalistic legislation protected his infant industry
when he got there. Hence it may be said, as the Beards have said,
that the people who went west went as individuals.[8] But this is not
to say that they went singly. Traders and trappers and hunters
might venture into the wilderness or onto the plains in parties of a
half-dozen or so; but those who went expecting to occupy the
Indians' land went in larger groups. In the absence of any governmental provision for group migration, they usually went under
the leadership of some promoter of a scheme of colonization. This
promoter might be a land speculator like Robertson or his agent
Boone; he might be a religious leader like Young; he might be a
philanthropist like Prince Carl Solms-Braunfels, who brought
hundreds of Germans to Texas; he might (under Spanish law) be
a legally constituted impresario like Austin. He was, in the later
phase of settlement, often the agent of a railroad.

When a sufficient number of families had been enlisted to give
some assurance of protection against the Indians as the place of
settlement, the migration began. If an overland journey was in-

volved, the travelers organized under strict discipline for mutual
protection. Upon arriving at their destination, they erected a
community blockhouse, or other fortification, where in times of
danger they could "fort up." From these earlier nuclei other communities branched out and other forts were erected. The duty of
informal military service devolved upon all able-bodied men.
Their common danger and their common poverty promoted a
strong corporate life.

Perhaps J. B. Finley had forgotten some of the local quarrels
when he wrote of the settlers in the Ohio Valley at the beginning
of the nineteenth century: "There was never a healthier, happier,
more hospitable or cheerful people. Their interests were one, and
their dependence upon each other was indispensable, and all
things were in common. Thus united, they lived as one family." [9]
But there is abundant evidence of the correctness of his essential
description. Noah Smithwick, Texas frontiersman, wrote:

Our common danger was a strong tie to bind us together. No matter
what our personal feelings were, when in response to the sound of
galloping hoofs, in the middle of the night, which we all knew heralded
a tale of blood, we started from our beds and were at the door in anticipation of the "hello" which prefaced a harrowing story of a neighbor slain and his family either sharing his fate, or worse still, carried
away into horrible captivity, we hastily saddled our horses, if the Indians had not been ahead of us, and left our wives and children, to
avenge the atrocious deed.[10]

After the danger of Indian raids was over, the pattern of settlement was not materially altered. Group migration was even more
conspicuous, partly because greater numbers of people were willing to migrate. Whole church congregations, sometimes virtually
whole communities where shifting economic conditions brought
hard times, came to the plains of Nebraska and Kansas and other
western states, not infrequently under the protection of some organization like the New England Emigrant Aid Society. They
came to found communities where they could enjoy a corporate
life, typically not with the aim of establishing communistic societies but of recreating on the frontier the simple agrarian and hand-
icraft economy that industrialism was soon to destroy.

They erected their homes, their schools, and their churches by cooperative labor. The log-rolling and the house-raising became characteristic frontier institutions. They helped each other plow and harvest. The cattle round-up began as a cooperative cowhunt in the mountains of the South; it maintained its cooperative character until the range was all fenced; and it is still cooperative among all but the largest ranchers. The reminiscences of the trail drivers of Texas stress mutual help, not individualism.

In 1863 [writes P. D. Butler] came the great drouth. The Nueces and San Antonio Rivers became mere trickling threads of water with here and there a small pool. The grass was soon gone and no cattle survived except those that had previously drifted across the Nueces River on to a range that was not so severely affected by the drouth. In 1864 rains came and plentiful grass, and a search for drifted cattle was organized. All the young, able-bodied men were in the army, so a party of forty-five boys and old men, headed by Uncle Billy Ricks, of Oakville, went to San Diego to the ranch of Benito Lopez, from which point they worked for a month rounding up cattle and cutting out those of their own brands. Every week a herd was taken across the river and headed for home, and in this way 500 head were put back on the ranges of Karnes County, where thousands had grazed before the drouth.[11]

If a widow had no men in her family, her cattle would be gathered and her calves branded with her own brand. If a neighbor were sick, his corn would be plowed for him. If his house burnt down, neighbors contributed food and labor and clothing. If a school or church was to be built, each contributed his share of materials and labor. Not all pioneers have put into their memoirs the piety of John Carr of Middle Tennessee, but the incident he relates is typical of hundreds:

We determined to build us a house to worship the God of our fathers in. We had a meeting, purchased a piece of ground on a beautiful eminence, convenient to a fine spring. We appointed a day to get timbers to build our house. When the day arrived, it was wonderful to behold the multitude of people that came out—wagons and teams, choppers and hewers. There could not have been less than forty or fifty men on the ground. By evening we had collected timber to build a large house; and in the evening we had laid the foundation; and it was proposed we should have prayer before we parted. . . . When we arose from our knees, I was requested to name the house. I saw such a spirit of brotherly love and union . . . I told them we would call it Union.[12]

Frontier hospitality, commented upon by practically every traveling writer who reached the frontier, was not due solely, as some of these travelers have egotistically imagined, to the settler's loneliness and hunger for news of the outside world. It grew rather out of the relationship of men engaged in a common struggle with distance and heat and drouth and blizzards and grasshoppers.

Such activities as these are evidence of a strong corporate feeling whereby the individual found deep satisfaction in identifying himself with the group. It would be a mistake, however, to infer that when the pioneer contributed to the recreational life of the community, donated a beef for the barbecue, shared his food with a traveler, helped his neighbor round up and brand his cattle, or plowed his sick neighbor's corn, he was indulging in mere philanthropy. His hospitality and his generous welcome to newcomers might have had some relation to land values. He helped his neighbor with his cattle because he needed his neighbor's help. He nursed his sick neighbor because he himself might need nursing. It wasn't that he expected immediate or specific repayment in kind. It was that he wanted the feeling of security that came from knowing that his fellows would bolster him so that stringent emergency need not mean permanent disaster. This sort of neighborly cooperation was the frontier's answer to the problem of social security.

Now cooperation involves some degree of social control, and Osgood and Turner and others who have made the pioneer impatient of control *per se* have misinterpreted him. He resented regimentation by the governing class in the East, but he did not hesitate to regiment himself, and, insofar as he was able, others whose interests conflicted with his.

This regimentation came about, in the first place, by the development of a set of folkways, a body of American common law, which no Blackstone has ever codified, and which was usually enforced only by public opinion, although frontier magistrates like David Crockett who were ignorant of the law books and who gave their decisions not on "law learning," but on "the principles of common justice and honesty between man and man and . . . natural born sense," [13] might proclaim it from the bench. On the plains "It was an unwritten law that upon the outbreak of a [prairie] fire every able-bodied man should come with fire-fighting equipment. . . . The man who slept while his neighbors fought fire all night was considered a traitor." [14]

There was an unwritten law, recognized by the good women of the towns as well as of the country, that whenever a party of cowhunters rode up and asked to have bread baked, it mattered not the time of day, the request was to be cheerfully complied with. Not from fear of insult in case of refusal, for each and every cowboy was the champion and defender of womanhood and would have scorned to have uttered a disrespectful word in her presence—but from an accommodating spirit and kindness which was universally characteristic in those frontier days. . . . The sack [of flour] was lifted from the pack horses and brought in, and in due time the bread wallets were once more filled with freshly cooked biscuits, and the cowboys rode away with grateful appreciation.[15]

It should be clear that if the "unwritten law" so often referred to in the memoirs of the frontiersmen seemed to give the individual wide liberty in the defense of his property and his life, it also put definite restrictions upon his use of his property. Acts that would have been regarded as trespass under the British common law and the statutory law of densely settled regions were made legal by the customs of the frontier. For instance, a bona fide traveler could kill game along his route of travel, and the indigenous common law, afterward enacted by the legislatures of some states, protected him from prosecution by the landowner. He could enter a house in the absence of the owner, and so long as he took only food required for his needs, no frontier court would convict him. He might use the kitchen, but he was expected to leave the dishes clean.

Characteristic of frontier culture were numerous mutual protective associations, many of them extra-legal in character. When the police power broke down, the settlers banded themselves together to establish, if not law, at least order.

At one stage of frontier history the settlers were menaced by well organized rings of horse thieves, operating by methods subsequently adopted by rings of automobile thieves. The settler's response was the organization of Anti-Horse-Thief Associations. Such an association was organized at Nemaha, Nebraska, in 1858.[16] Officers were elected, dues were fixed, and "riders" were employed to recover stolen horses and to apprehend thieves. Richard Garland belonged to a similar organization in Iowa. He nailed to his barn door a poster "which proclaimed in bold black letters a warning and a threat, signed by 'the Committee.' " This association employed an agent, Jim McCarty, and "its effectiveness," says Hamlin Garland, "was largely due to his swift and fearless action." [17] Garland does not say what happened to the thieves that McCarty apprehended. The usual frontier practice in more settled communities was to turn them over to the courts, but wherever orderly government was interrupted, as it was in Kansas and Nebraska during the fifties and throughout the Southwest during Reconstruction, action was more direct. A mass meeting would be called, a "jury" impaneled, and counsel appointed for the accused. If he was found guilty, he would probably be hanged the same day. Mass executions were not uncommon. A former member of the Oklahoma Anti-Horse-Thief Association remembers the simultaneous hanging of five men to the same tree. This deliberate and considered mass justice is not to be confused with mob violence. It is yet to be proved that it erred more frequently than the courts presided over by learned justices in robes.

The discovery of gold in California in 1848 created a situation unique in history. The miners found themselves in the presence of great wealth in the form of placer gold where there was no law to govern the acquisition of this wealth. Throughout the mining region the Argonauts, although for the most part interested only in getting rich quickly and returning home, exhibited a surprising degree of cooperation. The rights of the group were everywhere made superior to the rights of the individual. The gold, in fact belonging to the United States government and therefore legally subject to the disposal of Congress, was assumed to belong equally to all who could gain access to it. Rules were passed in each camp limiting the size of the claim a man might hold, making the holding of the claim contingent upon use, providing for the numbering and registration of claims, and prescribing the procedure by which a claim might be transferred from one man to another. Disputes were settled by the camps or by committees appointed for the purpose. When Captain Marryat felt that his claim of a hundred square feet was being encroached upon, he appealed to the camp. A committee was appointed which measured the claims and found for Marryat. The trespasser was told "to confine himself to his own territory, which he did." [18]

The miners' reminiscences are practically unanimous concerning the absence of disorder during the first stage of mining. Later, however, the presence of great quantities of portable and unidentifiable wealth attracted criminals from all parts of the United States as well as from Australia and Chile. These were at first summarily dealt with by miners' courts; when they became numerous enough to intimidate an entire camp, or where they seized the local government, as they did at one time in Virginia City, the vigilance committee was the miners' answer.

Another typical frontier development was the claim club, organized to accomplish what the politicians had refused to do: namely, to make the western lands available to needy settlers. These clubs were noted and commented upon by the British traveler Charles Wentworth Dilke, who came to the West in the late 1860's:

When a new State began to be "settled up"—that is, its lands entered upon by actual settlers, not land-sharks—the inhabitants often found themselves in the wilderness, far in advance of attorneys, courts, and judges. It was their custom when this occurred to divide the territory into districts of fifteen or twenty miles square, and form in each a "claim club" to protect the land-claims, or property of the members. Whenever a question of title arose, a judge and a jury were chosen from among the members to hear and determine the case. The occupancy title was invariably protected up to a certain number of acres, which was differently fixed by different clubs. . . . The United States "Homestead" and "Preemption" laws were founded on the practice of these clubs. The claim clubs interfered only for the protection of their members, but they never scrupled to hang willful offenders against their rules, whether members or outsiders.[19]

Judgments, says Dilke, were usually enforced by the local sheriff. In Kansas, for example, a certain man squatted on a piece of land and sold his preemption claim. He later returned and preempted it under the Homestead Act and attempted to eject the purchase. The club took action and directed the sheriff to "put the man away." He was never seen again. The attempted fraud was within the bounds of legality, but clubs did not hesitate to place equity above law. The territorial legislatures of Kansas and Nebraska passed acts allowing the settlers 320 acres of land in spite of the 160-acre limit of the federal statute, and the claim clubs attempted to enforce the territorial laws. In this they were only temporarily successful, as they were also in their efforts to maintain their claims against the railroads.

Many of the millions of acres granted by Congress to the railroads were occupied by "squatters"; that is, settlers who because of poverty or negligence had failed to file the papers necessary to give their claims legal validity. When the railroads or the purchasers from the railroads attempted to take possession of the land, they found themselves confronted by a group of organized settlers, who believed, as did the miners of the Sierras, the land titles should be contingent upon occupancy and use. In Kansas the Settlers' Protective Association collected annual dues, employed legal counsel, and kept the cases in litigation for several years. Of course, they eventually lost.[20]

Settlers in the prairie states also organized against the cattlemen. In Sherman County, Kansas, members of such an organization took the following oath: "I do solemnly swear not to tell anything that may lead owners of cattle which are running at large contrary to law and destroying settlers' crops to discover who has killed or crippled or in any way injured these same cattle. . . ."[21] In Montana a jury before deciding the fate of a man charged with killing cattle wished to know whether or not the accused had appropriated the carcasses. In the minds of these jurymen to kill stock for profit was a crime; to kill to protect a land claim was blameless.

These extra-legal organizations and their frequently illegal methods by no means prove that the frontier settlers were unfit to live in organized society. They reveal, rather, an attempt to organize a society in which human needs would be superior to special privilege. They reveal the inadequacy of the land laws passed by a Congress subservient to the interests of the industrialists and land speculators. They show how the settlers by collective action attempted to secure for the needy,—i.e., themselves, a meager share of the public domain which was being so generously handed over to the corporations.

The history of the range cattle industry in the United States exhibits many conflicts resulting from the inadequacy of national legislation; but at no stage of the industry did the cattlemen reveal an incapacity for collective action. In Texas, where the range industry originated, Spanish regulatory law and custom were accepted and modified from time to time as conditions changed. The constitution of the Republic of Texas, following Spanish precedent, declared that all grown unbranded cattle (of which there were thousands) grazing on the public domain were the property of the state. They were *ferae naturae*, ownership to which could be established by capture and branding with a legally registered brand. The ownership of calves was established by the brand of their mothers. Except on the Mexican border, where animosities growing out of the Revolution were strong and where international stealing went on intermittently until suppressed by the Texas Rangers in the 1870's, the development of the range industry was orderly and cooperative until the middle of the Civil War. Up to this time, said Charles Goodnight, it was "an unwritten law to mark and brand every calf in your range to its owner, if you knew him. If the mother cows were strays, or unknown, you branded the calves in the same brand that the cow wore." [22] When, however, practically the entire man power of the range was in the Confederate Army, "certain men scattered over the country," many of them deserters and draft evaders, began branding for themselves the neglected cattle of the men in service. A loose protective association was formed in Parker County, then on the frontier, but the elderly men and boys were unable to enforce the folkways of the range, and stealing was not suppressed until the restoration of orderly government at the close of the war.

During the late 1860's and early 1870's cattlemen not only in Texas but throughout the range country combined into close-knit associations. The local unit of the association was the round-up district, usually covering approximately 2000 square miles. Dates were set for the spring and fall round-ups, and where several brands were using the same range, owners were denied the right to gather their cattle at any other time. No general ever controlled the movements of an army more rigidly than the round-up committees controlled the movements of men and cattle during the round-up. Territorial and state associations undertook a variety of activities, including the employment of brand inspectors or detectives at the shipping centers and the maintaining of lobbies at the capitals.

In 1869 the range industry was still in the hands of the men who had pioneered it. By 1880 absentee and even alien ownership was a conspicuous feature of the cattle business. Eastern and British corporations became members of the associations by buying herds and range rights from the pioneers. In the Northwest they secured control of these organizations and used them to establish a monopoly of public grass by denying others membership in the associations. "Of course," wrote E. V. Smalley in 1885, "There is no legal power to keep out new men who may wish to bring in cattle, but such men would be boycotted by not being allowed to participate in the round-ups, by having their mavericks taken as the property of the association, and by being annoyed in many ways by the cowboys of the old occupants of the Territory." [23]

Through the control of the cattlemen's associations in Wyoming, the corporations secured control of the territorial government and passed various laws strengthening their monopoly. Wherever they dominated the associations, they introduced other practices of capitalistic industrialism, including the use of labor blacklists and the employment of private gunmen.[24] At the same time they tried to increase their own prestige by advertising the fact that the stockman was "no longer a semi-savage adventurer" but a practical man of business.

That it was the "practical man of business" rather than the "semi-savage adventurer" who was chiefly responsible for the conflict between the small cattlemen and the settlers on the one hand and the cattle corporations on the other is shown by the divergent histories of the range industries in Texas and the Northwest. British and eastern American corporations that had invested heavily in Texas sent their lawyers to represent them at the meetings of the Panhandle Stock Association, which had been organized under the leadership of Charles Goodnight in 1881. These servants of absentee capital proposed that the by-laws of the Association be

amended so as to grant "extra votes on the basis of cattle owned."
Although this amendment would have given him and his partner
the most powerful voting strength in the Association, Goodnight,
having grown up on the frontier, was too close to the pioneering
tradition to consent to such palpable subordination of human need
to wealth.

I knew nothing about oratory [he told his biographer, J. Evetts
Haley] but I got up and told them plainly that such a move would
defeat the purpose of the Association, which was to give the little man
equal rights with the big man, and before I'd see such a rule passed, I'd
disband the whole organization. But the rule did not pass.[25]

Not all the Texas organizations were as successful in preventing
theft as the Panhandle Association was, but they all resisted control by absentee capital, and the Texas and Southwestern Association, which resulted from the merger of the various smaller organizations, has until this day retained its democratic character.

This democratic policy, together with the fact that the land
and grazing acts passed by the Texas legislature were better
adapted to popular needs than those passed by Congress, minimized the conflict between cattlemen and settlers in Texas.

The absence of a strong labor movement on the frontier is not
to be attributed to individualism. The availability of land resulted
in scarcity of labor that kept wages relatively high. The wage
earner, until the invasion of the frontier by corporations, was in
close contact with his employer: the relationship was personal,
neighborly, and most often cordial; for where other employment
was available a man would not long remain in the employ of a
"boss" he did not like: he would "draw his time" and move on.
The laborer had equal access to arms with his employer. Before
there can be any serious oppression of labor there must be a well-
ordered community where the oppressor is supported by a subservient police and judiciary. A frontier ballad tells what happened to one entrepreneur who in the absence of these sanctions
attempted to introduce on the range a system of exploitation long
in use by whaling captains and eastern industrialists:

It happened in Jacksboro in the spring of seventy-three,
A man by the name of Crego came stepping up to me,

Saying, "How do you do, young fellow, and how would you like to go
And spend one summer pleasantly on the range of the buffalo?"

"It's me being out of employment," this to Crego I did say,
"This going on the buffalo range depends upon the pay.
But if you will pay good wages and transportation too,
I think, sir, I will go with you to the range of the buffalo."

"Yes, I will pay good wages, give transportation too,
Provided you will go with me and stay the summer through;
But if you should grow homesick, come back to Jacksboro,
I won't pay transportation from the range of the buffalo."

It's now our outfit was complete—seven able-bodied men,
With navy six and needle gun—our troubles did begin;
Our way it was a pleasant one, the route we had to go,
Until we crossed Pease River on the range of the buffalo.

It's now we've crossed Pease River, our troubles have begun.
The first damned tail I went to rip, Christ, how I cut my thumb!
While skinning the damned old stinkers our lives wasn't a show,
For the Indians watched to pick us off while skinning the buffalo.

He fed us on such sorry chuck I wished myself most dead,
It was old jerked beef, croton coffee, and sour bread.
Pease River's as salty as hell fire, the water I could never go—
O God! I wished I had never come to the range of the buffalo.

Our meat it was buffalo hump and iron wedge bread,
And all we had to sleep on was a buffalo robe for a bed;
The fleas and gray-backs worked on us, O boys, it was not slow,
I'll tell you there's no worse hell on earth than the range of the buffalo.

Our hearts were cased with buffalo hocks, our souls were cased with
    steel,
And the hardships of that summer would nearly make us reel.
While skinning the damned old stinkers our lives had no show,
For the Indians waited to pick us off on the hills of Mexico.

The season being near over, old Crego he did say
The crowd had been extravagant, was in debt to him that day—
We coaxed him and we begged him and still it was no go—
We left old Crego's bones to bleach on the range of the Buffalo.

No formal organization of buffalo hunters was needed for concerted action in an instance like this.

    That the cowboy was capable of working in harmony with his
fellows is shown not only by the highly cooperative nature of his
work, but also by a strike which occurred in the Texas Panhandle

in 1883. No representative of the Knights of Labor or other outside agitator had visited the region. Out of the casual talk of a
group that had met in a dugout came the decision to demand an
increase in pay from $30 to $50 a month. The demand was placed
in writing and submitted to the managers of five large ranches.
Provision was made for paying the board of any strikers without
funds. While there was newspaper talk of grass-burning and fence-
cutting, there was no disorder nor fear of disorder on the range;
no threat of violence was implied in the "ultimatum" drawn up
by the leaders of the movement. The members of the association
merely bound themselves not to work for less than $50 a month
and stated that "anyone violating the above obligations shall suffer
the consequences." After twelve days they won their demands.
According to the Bureau of Labor Statistics, 325 men were involved. Testimony from the range, however, indicates that the
number participating in the strike was much smaller and that the
cowboys regarded their action a good joke on the owners. Evidently they felt no deep grievances, for they made no attempt to
set up a permanent bargaining agency to maintain the wage scale
and regulate working conditions.[26]

When, however, progress with its attendant increase of corporate industry made it impossible for the laborer to meet his employer man to man—to secure redress of grievances by direct
conference and action, labor on the frontier was no more reluctant to organize and bargain collectively than labor elsewhere.

Contrast the experiences of Herman Melville and Mark Twain.
What Melville's earnings would have been if he had not deserted
his whaling ship, I do not know. If he had received the average
"lay" of men in the industry, and if the *Acushnet* had had average
success in taking whales, his pay would have been about nineteen
cents a day. Much of this would have been absorbed by debits.
For example, if he had required a reefing jacket from the ship's
commissary, he would have been charged $5 for a garment that
had cost the owners $2.50. If he had drawn $7.50 for shore leave,
his debit would have been $10.00. Moreover he witnessed the
flogging of men for the most trivial offenses, a form of brutality
which continued even after the prohibitory statute of 1850.[27]
When Samuel Clemens finished his apprenticeship, he could boast
that "a pilot, in those days, was the only unfettered and entirely

independent human being that lived on this earth." He was about
the only person who "failed to show, in some degree, embarrass-
ment in the presence of foreign princes." [28] And a pilot's salary
was commensurate with his dignity and importance. Clemens
began at $250 a month; before the river closed in 1861, this figure
had been doubled.

There was no whalers' union. But the steamboat pilots on the
edge of the frontier had organized what was "perhaps the com-
pactest, completest, and strongest commercial organization ever
formed among men." [29] Although the history of this organization
is told in Mark Twain's *Life on the Mississippi*, and should be
universally known, it has been generally ignored by writers on
frontier individualism. The pilots found that wages were falling as
a result of their having trained too many apprentices. They organized and agreed to control apprenticing through their association.
They demanded a wage of $250 a month, and provided
unemployment benefits of $25 a month for their members and a
like income for widows. The organizers were promptly
discharged, but the owners were eventually brought to terms,
partly by the intervention of the underwriters, who noted that
accidents were rare on boats piloted by union members, but common on boats not so piloted. A completely closed shop was established, and when the pilots announced that after September 1,
1861, wages would be advanced to $500 a month, the owners ac-
quiesced, and the captains took steps toward organizing an association of their own. The Civil War and railroad competition prevented the maturing of this movement.

It is significant that the first victory which labor won in its
struggle with the railroads was won in the Southwest, a region
which in 1885 was close to the frontier. Jay Gould, who had
crushed labor on the Erie and other systems under his control,
attempted to apply the same tactics to the unionized Missouri Pacific and Texas and Pacific. In the region traversed by these roads
he found public opinion strongly against him. True he was supported by the daily press, but the country weeklies, representing
more accurately the attitudes of the folk, were loud and all but
unanimous in their denunciation of the railroad management and
in their support of the Knights of Labor. Public officials were
unawed; the governors of Texas and Missouri refused to call out

the militia to suppress the strike, and Gould was forced to come to terms. The next year, however, through his receiver Brown, he repudiated his agreement of 1885. He had in the meantime secured the appointment of one of his henchmen, a lawyer on his payroll named Pardee, to a federal judgeship in the district where he precipitated a strike by causing the discharge of a shop foreman for attending a meeting of the Knights of Labor. Labor union officials and strike leaders were jailed by the score. Farmers passed resolutions of sympathy and sent food to hungry strikers, but the strike was lost in spite of public sympathy. The evidence is convincing that Gould could not have crushed labor in the Southwest without the aid of the federal judiciary.[30]

Historians have generally assumed that the agrarian movement of the late nineteenth century was a result of the closing of the frontier. The assumption has a superficial plausibility inasmuch as the movement reached its political climax in 1896, after the frontier was officially closed. Yet there had always been an agrarian movement on the frontier. The Granger cases reached the Supreme Court in 1876, when free land was still available. The frontiersman had always assumed that he could legislate for the common good. If he at times complained about the federal encroachment upon states' rights, it was because he distrusted the class in charge of the government in Washington. He caused his state legislatures to pass acts on all manner of subjects. In Nebraska all male residents between the ages of sixteen and twenty were subject to draft for fighting grasshoppers. The plainsman had no fear that the state in asserting this control over minors would encroach upon the prerogatives of parenthood.

The tendency toward minute regulation is manifest also in Texas cattle legislation of 1874. E. J. Davis, reconstruction governor, seeking to bolster his crumbling regime, appealed for support on the frontier by allowing the cattlemen to write their own legislative ticket. It should be remembered that the cattle corporations had not yet invaded the state and the industry was in the hands of the pioneers. The act, approved by Davis's successor, assigned a brand inspector to each western county. If an owner drove horses or cattle out of the state without road-branding them on "the left side of the back behind the shoulder," he could be fined $100 for each animal so driven. Possession, without a bill of sale, of any animal or hide bearing a brand other than that of the possessor entailed a fine of $100 for each animal or hide. A minor was prohibited from branding cattle except in the presence of his parent or guardian. Although a stockman might own several brands, if in the original branding he used more than one of them on the same animal, he could be fined $20. One who sold hides without having them inspected could be fined $5 for each hide sold.[31] It is true that these acts, originally passed at the instance of the cattlemen, were found unduly complex and restrictive and were later in part repealed and otherwise simplified, but the demand for simplification was based on expediency and not on any theory of individual liberty or upon any outcry against regimentation.

These acts show that the pioneer was not averse to regulating himself. The Texas railroad act of 1853, passed two years before the general railroad act of England, is an example of his attempt to regulate absentee-owned corporations. One group of provisions looked toward the public safety, and was concerned with such matters as grade crossings, drunkenness on the part of train crews, and the like. Other sections compelled cooperation among the different railroads, and others regulated rates. The second group of provisions is especially significant in view of the popular belief that early railroad regulation attempted to enforce competition. The Texas act required all roads to draw the cars of all other roads, and the amendment of 1860 allowed any road to draw its own cars over a road refusing to draw them. The power to fix rates was declared a function of the legislature, but there was to be no change for ten years. At the end of that time rates might be revised downward if profits exceeded twelve per cent. This figure suggests that railroad attorneys might have had a hand in the drafting of the act. Twelve per cent, however, did not seem an excessive profit to pioneers who were in need of railroad facilities and who were accustomed to pay two per cent a month and more on bank loans. Companies were required to maintain offices on their main lines, and their books were to be open at all times for inspection by the legislature. If a road became insolvent through the declaring of dividends, the directors were personally liable for the debts of the company. A clause, repealed in 1860, specified the terms upon which the state might purchase the railroads. An amendment of 1860 attempted to prohibit stock watering and other abuses of corporate finance by declaring that every officer or director should be personally liable for any stock illegally issued, and that no railroad company should issue stock "except at par value and to actual subscribers who pay, or become liable to pay, the par value thereof." [32]

In this act there is nothing to suggest that the frontiersman believed with Cornelius Vanderbilt that a man should be allowed to do as he pleased with a railroad merely because he owned it.

The pioneer regulated private enterprise when he thought it expedient to regulate private enterprise. He cooperated with his fellows under the same conditions necessary at all times for voluntary cooperation; that is, (1) when he thought his interests would be furthered by cooperation, and (2) when a technique was proposed that he thought had a reasonable chance for success. "Interests" here includes not only economic advantage, but whatever gives the individual his deepest satisfactions, including the association with and approval of his fellows. An Indian attack on one family was an obvious menace to all families. The technique was equally obvious. You armed and drove the Indians away. During a grasshopper plague you called out the available man power and fought the insects with whatever weapons were at hand; but in the meantime you agitated for a bureau of entomology. As the common menace became more complex, the technique became less obvious, and consequently cooperation became more difficult. As industry and transportation became national and destroyed the corporate life of the local community, frontier techniques of cooperation became less effective.

Early pioneer folkways suggest how people unconditioned by theoretical economics might react to an economy of abundance. There was on the frontier a scarcity of consumers' goods but an abundance of resources. Discoverers of placer deposits in the early days of Pacific mining rarely attempted to determine the extent of a deposit and claim the whole for themselves. Those who did attempt such monopoly did not succeed until statutory law had modified the folk law of the miners. Law and custom in Texas assumed that equal opportunity was to be given to all who might wish to capture wild cattle and mustangs. The pioneer's cry from the beginning was for equality of opportunity to acquire land. The Jeffersonian ideal of equal rights for all, special privileges for none, was only partially realized on the frontier; but it would have been more nearly realized if the pioneer had not been thwarted by Congress and the courts.

The pioneer believed in private property. Yet it is conceivable that he would have acquiesced in public ownership of land but for two potent reasons. Before universal male suffrage he could most easily acquire the status of citizen by becoming a freeholder. Then and later he had a well-merited distrust of Congress. He was eager to secure title to his land before it was given away. He did, however, socialize the mineral resources of Texas. In Texas, too, where several millions of acres of land yet belong to the state, pioneer cattle and sheepmen are content to occupy them by lease. Agitation for the sale of public land in Texas has come from the politicians who want to tax it, not from the people who occupy it.

If all this is true, why is the myth of frontier individualism so generally accepted? As I have implied, the myth springs in part from the social and economic predilections of historians. It springs in part also from the multiordinal nature of the word "individualism." The pioneer seems to have been less disposed than others to inquire into the private life of his associates, or to interfere in quarrels which he regarded as purely personal; he attached less importance to adventitious circumstances of birth and wealth; he was more tolerant of eccentricities of character; and he was more often called upon to exercise individual judgment and initiative. He was perhaps more self-reliant. But all this is not to say that he was individualistic in the sense that he eschewed collective action or advocated unrestricted individual opportunity to exploit the national resources or make money by other means.

Here is the typical non sequitur: The daughter of a frontiersman writes in her diary: "Father's saddle wore out, so he made a new one out of cypress and rawhide." Now the ability to make a usable saddle, however crude, is an evidence of resourcefulness. Resourcefulness means self-reliance, which implies scorn for collective action and exaltation of individual initiative. Or to express the argument more succinctly: the pioneer made his own saddle; therefore he believed in a laissez faire economy.

Notes

1. Frederick Jackson Turner, *The Significance of the Frontier in American History* (New York: 1920), pp. 30 ff.

2. Herbert Hoover, "American Individualism," *World's Work*, XLIII, 585.

3. Ernest Boyd, "Drugged Individualism," *American Mercury*, XXXIII, 308–314.

4. Vernon Louis Parrington, *Main Currents of American Thought* (New York: 1930), Vol. III, p. 319.

5. Charles A. Beard, "The Myth of Rugged Individualism," *Harper's Magazine*, CLXIV, 13–22.

6. *New Republic*, 97:359–362.

7. Henry A. Wallace, *New Frontiers* (New York: 1934), p. 277.

8. Charles A. Beard and Mary R. Beard, *The Rise of American Civilization* (New York, 1930), Vol. I, p. 509.

9. J. B. Finley, *Autobiography* (Cincinnati: 1853), pp. 70–71.

10. Noah Smithwick, *The Evolution of a State* (Austin, Tex.: 1910), pp. 239–240.

11. Marvin Hunter, ed., *Trail Drivers of Texas* (Nashville, Tenn.: 1925), p. 481.

12. John Carr, *Early Times in Middle Tennessee* (Nashville, Tenn.: 1867), pp. 154–155.

13. *The Autobiography of David Crockett* (New York: 1923), p. 90.

14. Everett Dick, *The Sod House Frontier* (New York: 1938), p. 219.

15. Hunter, *op. cit.*, pp. 196–197.

16. Dick, *op. cit.*, pp. 135–136.

17. Hamlin Garland, *A Son of the Middle Border* (New York: 1917), p. 146.

18. Charles Howard Shinn, *Mining Camps* (New York: 1885), p. 154. Shinn's work is especially valuable because of its copious quotation from primary sources.

19. Charles Wentworth Dilke, *Greater Britain* (London, 1869), Vol. I, pp. 201–202.

20. Dick, *op. cit.*, pp. 353–354.

21. *Ibid.*, pp. 150 ff. See also Ernest Staples Osgood, *The Day of the Cattleman* (Minneapolis, Minn.: 1927).

22. J. Evetts Haley, *Charles Goodnight* (Boston: 1936), pp. 100 ff.

23. *House Executive Documents*, 48th Congress, Second Session, 1884–1885, XXIX, No. 267, 77.

24. *Ibid.* See also *Senate Documents*, 1885–1886, I, No. 34, and Osgood, *op. cit.*

25. Haley, *op. cit.*, p. 365.

26. My own researches have been supplemented by those of Professor Ruth Allen of the University of Texas and her associate, Mr. Ben Owens, who have kindly allowed me access to their files.

27. Elmo Paul Hohman, *The American Whaleman* (New York: 1928).

28. Mark Twain, *Life on the Mississippi* (New York: n. d.), p. 119.

29. *Ibid.,* p. 127.

30. Here again I must acknowledge my obligation to Professor Allen and Mr. Owens.

31. Gammel, *Laws of Texas,* Fourteenth Session, VIII, 34.

32. Texas railway legislation is summarized by C. S. Potts in *Railway Transportation in Texas* (Austin, Tex.: 1909), University of Texas Bulletin No. 119.

☙ 5 ☙

Everett S. Lee

THE TURNER THESIS RE-EXAMINED

In a meeting at the Chicago World's Fair in 1893, Frederick Jackson Turner, then a young man of thirty-two, read a paper entitled "The Significance of the Frontier in American History," doubtless the most influential paper ever presented before a congress of historians. According to Riegel, "The rapid and almost complete acceptance of Turnerian ideas soon produced a flood of references by historians, sociologists, novelists, playwrights, and in fact by almost anyone sufficiently literate to put pen on paper. The historic Turner essay seemed to rate only slightly lower in the popular estimation than the Bible, the Constitution, and the Declaration of Independence." [1] Franklin Delano Roosevelt drew upon it to justify the ways of the New Deal. Said he: "Equality of opportunity as we have known it no longer exists. . . . Our last frontier has long since been reached, and there is practically no more free land. . . . There is no safety valve in the form of a Western prairie to which those thrown out of work by the Eastern economic machines can go for a new start. . . ." [2]

Part of the appeal of the Turner thesis was its boldness and simplicity. In his own words, "The existence of an area of free land, its continuous recession, and the advance of American settlement westward, explain American development." [3] It was the free lands of the West that constituted a safety valve for discontented eastern masses and furnished the nationalizing impulses

Everett S. Lee, Professor of Sociology at the University of Massachusetts, is a co-author of *Migration and Mental Disease.*

Reprinted from *American Quarterly*, XIII (Spring 1961), 77–83, by permission of the author and the publisher.

that bound the loose confederation of states into a strong central government. Even more important, it was "to the frontier the American intellect owes its striking characteristics. That coarseness and strength combined with acuteness and inquisitiveness; that practical, inventive turn of mind, quick to find expedients; that masterful grasp of material things, lacking in the artistic but powerful to effect great ends; that restless, nervous energy; that dominant individualism, working for good and for evil, and withal that buoyancy and exuberance which comes with freedom —these are traits of the frontier." [4] Regretfully Turner noted at the conclusion of his essay that "The frontier has gone, and with its going has closed the first period of American history." [5]

Most of us are now several generations removed from our pioneer forebears, if indeed we have any, and most of us have been rendered cautious by the reception accorded the monistic explanations of national character. It now seems obvious that the Turner thesis is too simple an explanation for such complexities as American democracy and American character, so after years of general and enthusiastic acceptance it is the fashion to attack Turner's propositions. It can fairly be said that the supporting evidence was meager and that the thesis was not so much proved as reiterated. Nevertheless, there is great intuitive appeal in this theory, and few are willing to abandon it entirely.

In part, the Turner thesis still commands credence because of the admittedly crucial importance of vast areas of free land during the formative period of American democracy, but another reason for its appeal is that Turner, in emphasizing the frontier, was developing a special case of a more general theory of migration. Most of the effects, desirable and undesirable, that were attributed by Turner to the frontier can, with equal or better logic, be attributed to migration, and in addition, the migration theory does not collapse or depend upon tradition for its maintenance after the frontier is gone. It is not meant by this to substitute one monistic explanation of American development for another. The point is that migration has been a force of greatest moment in American civilization, and that from the magnitude and character of migration within this country certain consequences logically follow. And yet these in turn reinforce the tendency to migrate, so that when we try to arrive at cause and effect we are caught in a never-ending circle in which the apparent effects viewed in a different way seem to have produced the very phenomena we first accounted as causes. It is therefore not maintained, paraphrasing Turner, that migration explains American civilization. It certainly does not, but that it was and is a major force in the development of American civilization and in the shaping of American character hardly anyone will deny. The magnitude and uniqueness of internal migration in the United States are, however, not generally realized, and research on migration differentials is only beginning to reveal the concomitants of continual movement from place to place.

In America we can say that migration is a part of our way of life. We are all but a few generations removed from our immigrant ancestors, whether they landed at Plymouth Rock or Ellis Island. Within our country, migration is of such scale as to astound foreign observers. In the late 1950's one in each five persons moved from one house to another in each twelve-month period, one in fourteen migrated from one county to another, and one in thirty from one state to another. These are crude figures for both sexes and all ages. At the age of maximum migration, 20–24, one in fourteen migrated from one county to another, and one in ten shifted state of residence. Over twenty per cent of the native population was living outside the state of birth, but again this figure is a weighted average for all ages and makes the incidence of interstate migration seem smaller than it is, since at ages 50 and thereafter nearly two out of five native Americans have set up residence outside the state of birth. Migration of this order has been the rule rather than the exception in American history, and calculations made independently by Henry S. Shyrock and myself indicate that this high level of interstate migration has existed since at least 1850.

Moreover the figures cited are underestimates. They all relate to net migrants, those persons who moved during a given period and who had not died nor returned to the county or state of birth. It is well known that net internal migration is generally but a small residue left from the interplay of much larger streams of in- and out-migration. Who has not known the migrant who returned from afar to his place of origin, or the person who is constantly moving from one place to another? Those of us who are not migrants have many contacts with such persons, some from distant states. There is probably no community of any size which is so isolated that it has not felt the impact of migration, either from the loss of its members, or from the entrance of persons from other communities, or almost invariably, from both. We are indeed a nation of migrants and we always have been.

Had our ancestors not been willing migrants and were we as a people not willing to pull up stakes to strike out for greener pastures, American economic development would have been seriously retarded and could not operate with its present efficiency. Modern capitalism demands the quick exploitation of new resources and the abandonment of those which no longer pay well. Here new resources, wherever located, can draw upon a large and almost instantaneous labor supply, and workers do not wait for local resources to be exhausted before moving elsewhere in desperation. The mushrooming mining towns of the West in the 1850's and 1860's have had their modern counterparts in the cities that were established around defense industries. The exodus of farmers from the rocky slopes of New England into western New York and Ohio has been exceeded in magnitude by the desertion of the dust bowl for California and the Northwest. Contrast this situation with that which is found in some other countries where a labor surplus may exist in a community ten miles from one in which there is a labor shortage, and yet the government finds it hard to persuade unemployed workers to make the short move toward ready employment.

In this connection, it should be pointed out that the true safety valve was not the frontier, even before its alleged disappearance about 1890: it was migration, sometimes to the frontier it is true, sometimes to better farming lands far behind the frontier, but more often it was from the farm to the city. Migration to the city has almost always exceeded the movement to the frontier, and in recent years the migration to Turner's West, however defined, has been to the city rather than to open country. The city has more often been an outlet for the underemployed of rural areas than the farm a haven for the unemployed workers in eastern industries.

We now know that migrants are not a cross section of the general population. Internal migration as well as external migration is selective, especially for young adults in the ages of greatest productivity and also of greatest reproductivity. The characteristics of migrants between states are somewhat similar to those of migrants from abroad in the days of peak immigration. Males predominate and they are concentrated at ages 20 to 30. Migrants are better educated than nonmigrants, and the highest migration rates are for those at the top of the occupational ladder. The fragmentary studies that exist even suggest that migrants are more intelligent than nonmigrants.

In addition to being young, migrants are likely to be single or in the early stages of family formation. As size of family increases, even when age of head is held constant, there is a decrease in migration. With migration recognized as a part of the way of life, an extra premium is placed upon family limitation and it may be suggested that students who are puzzled by the early fall in the birth rate in the United States, prior even to that in France, consider migration as a predisposing factor. More important, perhaps, than the stimulus to family limitation is the breakdown of the *grossfamilie* system with its encompassed generations and its extension of the privileges and obligations of kinship to cousins of remote degree. By migrating from his clan the individual removes himself from its control and from its protection. Were it not that a highly developed sense of individualism prompted his move in the first place, it would be necessary to acquire it. He and his family become a self-supporting and, to some degree, a self-sufficient little unit. Since he must fight his own battles and provide his own subsistence without the support of his clan he becomes impatient with the demands of distant relatives upon him.

In some persons individualism may manifest itself, as in Turner's frontiersman, in truculence and uncouthness, but most migrants find that a premium is placed upon the ability to adjust to new situations and new people. They learn the value of outward conformity and may come to place great value upon it. They make acquaintances easily—in short, they exhibit many of the characteristics of today's "organization man," and I wonder if the attributes of this gentleman are not largely those in which generations of Americans have been schooled. Incidentally, the "organization man" is likely to be exceptionally migratory because of the practice of large companies of regularly transferring officials from plant to plant or from branch to branch.

A highly mobile population is not one in which an hereditary elite is likely to develop. Migration diminishes the value of blood ties and the possession of a distinguished name may come to mean little. In Massachusetts and South Carolina Adams and Pinckney may be names to conjure with, but what do they mean in Brooklyn and Whisky Gulch? A different set of values distinguishes the mobile from the static society. Land ownership, for example, as a mark of status gives way to more transportable items, among which ability and money are prominent.

It is hardly necessary to note that in the long run nationalism is promoted by interstate migration. Turner, himself, remarked that "Nothing works for nationalism like intercourse within the nation" and that "mobility of population is death to localism.[6] The migrant from Alabama to Detroit is likely to waver in his devotion to state's rights, and the northern metropolis which acquires the product of a South Carolina public school for Negroes is led to wonder whether that state can be entrusted with so important a function as education. Not only does migration promote nationalism and lessen the attachment to a state or locality but it also serves to encourage the extension of the functions of national government into areas once reserved for the states.

With our set of values most of the things we have associated with migration seem desirable. Individualism and equalitarianism are usually associated with democracy, and the creation of a strong central government seems necessary for survival. But tendencies toward conformity and the extension of federal functions may be disturbing. Let us now consider some of the less desirable aspects of migration.

In studying one of our most migratory groups, young executives, researchers noted that though superficial friendships are made readily, there was reluctance to form deep attachments with emotional ties and mutual obligations, partly because they would be interrupted by migration. It would seem that an almost inevitable result of migration with its severing of friendships is the focusing of emotional relationships inward to the immediate family with perhaps too much expected of each member.

Such tensions, if they exist, are minor in comparison with those which result from unsuccessful efforts to adjust or conform, or from rebellion. It is now evident that rates of admission to mental hospitals are much higher for migrants than for nonmigrants and, while this may be true in part because of selection for disease-prone individuals as migrants, the struggle with the changing environment must also play a part.[7] Often the migrant does not understand the reasons for doing things in a particular way in a new community. For example, the detailed sanitary regulations of the northern city may be looked upon as restrictions of freedom by a migrant from the rural South. With rapidly shifting populations, custom cannot be depended upon for controls which are automatically effective in static societies and, since education is too slow and too costly, laws are proliferated.

Migration often breeds carelessness as to immediate surroundings. Few people hope to remain in the slums and not many young people expect to. If surroundings become too bad the quickest and easiest remedy is migration. Local reform movements are hampered and cities remain "corrupt and contented" partly because the natural leaders move to the suburbs. Newcomers are not always aware of the true nature of civic problems and may be tempted by the immediate favors of the political boss to vote against long-range improvements. And, when the newcomer realizes what the situation is, it is much easier to migrate than to attempt reform.

Migrants are likely to meet their numerous new situations with temporary expedients at the expense of long-run solutions. The most characteristic of American philosophies, pragmatism, which stresses continuous short-term adjustments in the conviction that whatever works is best, is a typically migrant philosophy. If, in the long run, we are not dead, we may at least be somewhere else. This carries over into a general emphasis on immediate practicality at the cost of interest in philosophical questions. Perhaps our national bias against basic science or "nonpaying" research is partly due to the spatial restlessness of the American people.

Also, the American penchant for change for change's sake may be associated with our geographic mobility. Migration has been phenomenally successful for Americans. The immigrants from abroad did find superior economic opportunities, and if they were fleeing oppression they found freedom. Within our country the major flows of migration have been from areas of lower to higher economic returns, or from areas in which the amenities were less well developed to those in which they were better developed. The natural interpretation by the migrant is that migration has been a good thing; having done it once he is willing to do it again if another area looks more attractive. This attitude he imparts to his children and to nonmigrants with whom he comes in contact. In itself, migration is one of the most drastic social changes; if this is so generally successful, why not other types of change?

In conclusion, it is again stated that no attempt is made to explain American democracy or American character. It is maintained, however, that from a psychological and sociological, as well as from an economic, point of view, migration is one of the most important factors in American civilization. There are few characteristics which are shared by so many Americans as migrant status and spatial movement has correlates which are both good and bad. They have not, however, been thoroughly studied. Turner's thesis set off a round of the most productive studies in American history. A case can be made that his frontier theory is a special case of an as yet undeveloped migration theory. The tools and the data are available for extensive research on the effects of migration, and it is hoped that historians and sociologists will begin to study migration in the larger context of its effect upon the development of the American people.

Notes

1. Robert E. Riegel, "American Frontier Theory," *Cahiers d'Histoire Mondiale*, III, No. 2 (1956), 367.

2. *Ibid.*

3. Frederick Jackson Turner, "The Significance of the Frontier in American History" in George Rogers Taylor, ed., *The Turner Thesis Concerning the Role of the Frontier in American History* (Boston: D. C. Heath & Co., 1949), p. 1.

4. *Ibid.*, p. 17.

5. *Ibid.*, p. 18.

6. *Ibid.*, p. 14.

7. See Benjamin Malzberg and Everett S. Lee, *Migration and Mental Disease* (New York: Social Science Research Council, 1956).

❦ 6 ❦

Allan G. Bogue

SOCIAL THEORY AND
THE PIONEER

"The West, at bottom," proclaimed Frederick Jackson Turner in 1896, "is a form of society, rather than an area." [1] Throughout the frontier essays runs the suggestion also that "a modification of the original stock occurred" in the frontier setting.[2] But never did Turner develop the implications of the first quotation in detail, nor concern himself greatly with the alchemic process implied in the second. This chapter is an exploratory and speculative one designed to investigate the possibility that the social structure of pioneer communities did influence the personalities of the residents. In treating such a subject the historian must look for aid in other disciplines. After a brief survey of Turner's social theory, I wish to discuss briefly the work of a number of behavioral scientists and, in the case of one pioneer region, illustrate the assistance that social science concepts may perhaps render in explaining how the westerner became a "new man." Let us assume for the time being that Turner and his followers were correct when they argued that the pioneer patterned his behavior in ways significantly different from those of the residents in older settlements. Three generations of the frontier school have unfortunately not proven this to be so beyond the shadow of a doubt.[3]

In describing the western personality, Turner varied his termi-

Allan G. Bogue is Professor of History, University of Wisconsin, and the author of *Money at Interest: The Farm Mortgage on the Middle Border*, and *From Prairie to Corn Belt: Farming on the Illinois and Iowa Prairies in the Nineteenth Century*.

Reprinted from *Agricultural History*, XXXIV (January 1960), 21–34, by permission of the author and the publisher.

nology somewhat. Perhaps the changes represented only the amplification and rewording of a literary stylist who offered his essays to a variety of audiences over a twenty-five-year span, but he did, on various occasions, ascribe patterns of thought and action to the West as a region and to western democracy, as well as describing the "intellectual traits" of the pioneer, frontier "ideals" and western "beliefs." In his later essays he pictured frontiersmen who acted in accord with ideals or beliefs rather than possessing intellectual traits; but if this represented a change in Turner's system of psychology, the end result—the westerner's behavior—was still the same. Because of variations in Turner's phrasing, one must be arbitrary in compiling a manageable list [4] of those social qualities which revealed to him the impact of the West on the individual. Even then internal contradictions seem to threaten the elegance of any grouping; the great frontiersman did not cut his buckskin patterns with a razor.

Let us consider the western type briefly. Most important as far as Turner was concerned, the hero of the frontier essays was democratic and equalitarian in his approach to social and political problems. At the same time he was individualistic and highly competitive, qualities that were softened by the breadth of opportunity offered by the "free lands." The fact that the pioneer was responsive to leadership and possessed the power of "spontaneous association" when necessary also modified his individualism.[5] He was nationalistic in outlook and expansive in attitude, but at the same time cherished strong sectional loyalties. His militancy showed in hatred of the Indians, his urge to slash down the forests, and his instinctive antipathy to the non-resident capitalists who might thwart him. In both politics and religion, the frontiersman displayed an emotionalism which was also expressed in a kind of mystic communion with the wilderness.[6] He was inventive in facing his problems, quick to judge and act, and a born explorer. Intrinsic to the western personality as well were materialism, optimism, energy, coarseness, strength, acuteness and wastefulness. Finally, the pioneer was mobile in both a horizontal and a vertical, or social, sense.[7] Restless, he moved from frontier to frontier, but at the same time he was eager and able to rise in station. Obviously, the items in this catalogue vary in significance and even in level of analysis.

Apparently, Turner believed that "the original stock was modified" mainly by the opportunity given its members to amass and manage a competence from the free lands on the one hand and the challenges of the physical environment faced by the pioneers on the other.[8] He did not explore to any extent the possibility that the attraction of the West was selective, drawing a particular type of individual, although the idea was incorporated in portions of his work. Turner's direct description of what we may call frontier social structure was brief indeed, limited for the most part to comments that it was "atomic," "not . . . complex, highly differentiated and organized. . . ," the frontier a region, where "almost every family was a self-sufficing unit."[9] Or again he might suggest that pioneer society was marked by lack of stratification.[10] But he did not elaborate upon the effects which such conditions might have on the individual, even though he did not disregard completely the possibility that being part of a new social fabric might alter the stuff woven into it originally.[11]

The social scientists have produced little work dealing specifically with frontier society. When dealing incidentally with the influence of the frontier, they have generally taken the work of historians at face value rather than trying to explain the frontier process in terms of their own theory. The early social ecologists saw Turner's migratory waves and successive stages of settlement as an illustration of the concept of succession which they had themselves borrowed from the natural sciences.[12] The analogy was faulty at best and told historians only that the personnel and economic organization of communities tended to change over time—facts which some of them at least already knew. But there are more rewarding studies as well. One anthropologist examined the frontier in an effort to derive social theory. During the last generation, sociologists, anthropologists, geographers, and agricultural economists have used their analytical tools in describing the development of new communities. If the historian is hardy enough, he may turn as well to the theories of society evolved and evolving in the areas and sub-areas in which sociologists and anthropologists pursue their work.

Some may well ask whether insights derived from the social behavior of the twentieth century can be safely applied to earlier eras. Certainly there is a point beyond which generalizations on social behavior that are valid in one situation cannot safely be applied in another. Critics may particularly challenge the broader use of conclusions derived from experience in some of the new communities discussed below because the residents were screened by supervisory agencies, whereas the origins and past standing of settlers on the Turnerian frontiers could be highly diverse. Perhaps, however, the social patterns which emerge in a group recruited from individuals of like origin differ only in degree rather than kind from the patterns found in groups of individuals with diverse backgrounds. I would not argue that any frontier historian will find magic formulas in the work of the social scientists. Their research may, however, help us to slip the leash of tradition and consider the old frontier sources in a new dimension.

In the introduction to *Frontier Folkways,* James G. Leyburn promised an answer to the question: "What happens to men's customs and social institutions when they go to a frontier?" [13] To Leyburn a frontier was "that region on the outer edge of settlement where pioneers are forced, for the sake of survival, to make new adjustments to a raw environment. It is a region, it is a process, it is even a state of mind." [14] His approach was to be a comparative one and on his pages appeared the French of the St. Lawrence Valley, the Portuguese, the Spanish, the Dutch, New Zealanders, Australians, and Boers, as well as the Puritans of Massachusetts Bay and the American frontiersmen of the nineteenth century. For the most part, his sources were historical monographs or articles; his anthropology stemmed mainly from W. G. Sumner and A. G. Keller. Leyburn shared Turner's assumption that study of the frontier could reveal much about the development of civilizations generally, and in the end his monograph proved to be less an explanation of the frontier process than an effort to induce general social laws from a series of brief historical descriptions of life on a variety of frontiers.

Explicitly Leyburn stated a primary assumption: "Adaptation to environment is the primary law of life." [15] The motivation of the pioneers was clear to him; they were self-seeking, "like all normal men." [16] Herein, he thought, lay the explanation of American democracy. He accepted Turner's contention that democracy was born on the frontier, but discarded the historian's favorite definition, contending, "American democracy was not in essence a rule of the people, by the people, and for the people." Democracy emerged only incidentally, he argued,

. . . coming about simply because it was the most obvious way for the pioneer to get what he wanted, because the population of the frontier was steadily increasing, and because the frontiersmen could make grim threats . . . In every frontier region of America . . . there was constant manipulation by land speculators, there was appeal to sordid gain, there was bickering among the pioneers. Yet democracy somehow flourished.[17]

Echoing Lewis Mumford, Leyburn challenged as myth the view that the Puritan settlers were "a band of brave adventurers, 'throwing off the bedraggled garments of Europe and starting life afresh in the wilderness!' " Rather, they "tried to keep them even when they were in rags. They threw off only what were definitely injurious to their quest for self-maintenance." [18] Frontier religious manifestations were of great interest to Leyburn and he attributed religious emotionalism to the fact that the pioneers lived "in isolated little groups, with a minimum of interesting companionship, doing strenuous physical work, having practically no mental stimulus in their ordinary workaday life." [19] But the multiplication of sects on the frontier could be explained, he believed, by changed economic conditions.[20]

One final aspect of Leyburn's work requires mention—"the temporary frontier." To him the

. . . hundred-day journey from the Mississippi Valley to the Far West constituted a frontier society in the truest sense of the words. On many of these treks, there were men, women, and children; an economic order was established . . . , religion practiced, marriages made. Each of the thousands of expeditions had its own variations, but in the main they followed a common pattern which gives distinct clues to the human mode of adjustment.[21]

Although he did not expand this idea, there is implicit in it a conception of frontier society as a complex of new groups evolving systems of social control within themselves.

In 1940, the rural sociologist, Charles Loomis, meticulously analyzed the development of social institutions on seven Farm Security Administration projects where the settlers were established on individual farms. He stated with approval the assumption that "man's nature requires participation in the life of an integrated group if he is to have a normal psychological existence. In such a group internal strife is at a minimum, a powerful 'we' feeling exists among its members, the morale is high, and all are loyal to common objectives entailing a spirit of self-sacrifice, if necessary." [22] Acquisition of such integration, Loomis implied, was a basic feature of community development. But on all of the resettlement projects, he found disintegrative as well as integrative processes at work. Problem families, migration from the projects, conflict between government administrators and settlers, cleavages between groups of different background or status: such were the disruptive influences.

A number of the findings of Loomis are suggestive for the student of the frontier process. The families that had been most mobile previous to settlement on the projects were found to be the most likely to leave. Families with children in school and with a record of participation in formal community activities in their former places of residence as well as in their new homes were most apt to stay. Movers tended to be somewhat less prosperous than those who stayed, but amount of education and the number of informal social contacts seemingly had little relation to the decision to move. But how and why did individuals decide to leave? A "common claim of disillusioned settlers was that their golden dreams . . . had not materialized." [23] Uncertainty stemming from changes in administrative policy stimulated rumors which ran speedily through the visiting groups on the projects. Movers, Loomis discovered, came to a much greater extent from the members of groups giving the rumors the most unfavorable interpretations. He concluded that the "decision . . . to move or not to move was made in a social setting rather than as a matter of cool, rational self-interest of individuals." [24]

A particularly broad social cleavage existed in one Farm Security Administration project, based on the regional origins and agricultural experience of the settlers. But in the face of mutual enemies and problems the members of the two groups tended over a period of time to break ranks and form new social groupings.

In general, settlers on the Farm Security Administration projects exchanged work and borrowed tools more frequently than did farmers in long established control communities. Such practice was related, no doubt, to the fact that the resources of the settlers were less adequate than those of farmers in longer-settled communities.

Loomis was interested in the way in which social groups developed in the new communities. He found that families tended to associate with families whose patterns of social behavior were similar, and that there was some tendency for families of similar economic status and levels of living to associate. But other sources fed the springs of friendship also; evidence showed that some individuals established strong ties with others whose personalities were complementary to theirs. Kinship was an important factor in visiting patterns and social relationships generally, but was less important in the new communities than in older ones. Loomis hypothesized "that one of the significant differences in community organization in the older established areas . . . may be traced to the more significant influence of kinship as a bond. . . ." [25] There was a greater tendency in the Farm Security Administration communities for social contacts to be more directly related to distance than elsewhere. Presumably scattered kin and interest group relationships had not had time to develop to the same extent in the new communities.

What were the backgrounds of the leaders who emerged on the resettlement projects? When the settlers looked among themselves for leaders, they tended, Loomis discovered, to choose individuals who had held positions of leadership before migration.

Where Loomis analyzed seven Farm Security Administration farming projects in a short government publication, Edward C. Banfield devoted a monograph to the description of one cooperative farm project of the same agency in Arizona.[26] He sought primarily to explain why the project failed, although at the time of failure serious economic problems had for the most part been solved and the community seemingly could look forward to a prosperous future under the management of the cooperators. Banfield set as his goal the task of understanding the sixty-odd families at Casa Grande and the government officials involved "as sensitive and perceptive people generally try to understand other people," rather than "in terms of culture, or psychoanalysis, or economic determinism, or behaviorism!" [27]

The history of Casa Grande was marked by ceaseless factionalism and criticism of government administrators and policy. The basic problem at the project Banfield believed was twofold. Federal officials committed a fundamental error in construing the causes of all behavior as rational and economic. On the other hand, the "settlers were unable to cooperate with each other and with the government because they were engaged in a ceaseless struggle for power." [28] Banfield described the complex of factors which produced such a situation:

Some of the settlers . . . felt that the resettlement project was a "come down" and evidence that they had failed in life, had strong feelings of guilt which they expressed in hostility toward fellow settlers and government officials who were placed over them. Some were aggressive personalities of a type not uncommon in American life. A few may have been neurotic. These settlers (and many of the others as well) felt, or from association with others of the group came to feel, an acute need to assert claims to status. The chief avenue to status in the project situation was power in the management of the farm. This power could be secured in one of two ways: it could be had by joining forces with the government and serving as a foreman, or, informally, as a supporter of the management or it could be had by leading or participating in an anti-government faction.[29]

Banfield further speculated that the settlers were afflicted by *anomie*, the term used by Durkheim to describe "the disturbed mental state of people who do not feel the restraint and discipline of socially-defined rules." [30] He admitted that there were things to be said both for and against applying this concept to the settlers at Casa Grande. Clearly, however, life on a cooperative farm required development of new patterns of social behavior by settlers who had been reared in the cotton culture of the Southwest. But they found it difficult, if not impossible, to develop within the group on the farm a new common system of conduct, belief, and expectation to replace that of a society which they believed unsympathetic to the kind of enterprise on which they were embarked.

In *Modern Homesteaders*, the social anthropologist, Evon Vogt, has studied a New Mexican community which was established in the early 1930's by settlers who left the main current of southwestern migration to California and sought to carve out homes for themselves on the Pueblo Plateau to the south of Gallup.[31] To a far greater extent than any other community discussed here, the circumstances under which "Homestead" was founded paralleled frontier conditions during the nineteenth century. The members of the group were not screened by any selection agency, nor had they known abject poverty in their former homes. They were on the move before the depression of the thirties blasted free the main tide of "dustbowlers" and "Okies."

Although he did not ignore the geographic, economic, and demographic bases of Homestead, Vogt's central concern was with the values, or more precisely the value orientations, of the residents. These last he defined as "patterned clusters of certain associated values around important foci in the life situation of a cultural group." [32] In the behavior of the homesteaders, "these revealed themselves as a strong stress upon *individualism* . . . ; an accent upon . . . *hopeful mastery over nature* . . . ; an emphasis upon the *future* . . . ; a patterned balance between *working and loafing* . . . ; and a very complex combination of *group-superiority* and *group-inferiority* orientations in their relationships to other cultural groups." [33] Persistence in these value orientations in 1955 Vogt believed was leading to the disintegration of the community, since continued adherence to them was producing a pattern of widely scattered small ranches in place of the original compact community. This interpretation, he argued, was a considerable modification of the usual explanation that cultural patterns and processes are determined primarily by the environmental situation, by considerations of biological and/or social survival, by basic economic realities, or by a combination of these. The contrasting cultures of nearby Mormon, Spanish-American, and Indian settlements provided material for comparative purposes. Vogt was not primarily interested in discovering and revealing those aspects of Homestead's social life which reflected the newness of the community, nor did he reveal any particular awareness that it may take time to develop cohesion in a new social system. Perhaps there never was a community at Homestead in the sense of many definitions of the word. There seems also implicit in Vogt's study the assumption that the group should have survived in its original form, rather than shifting in its patterns toward the ranching economy of the region. Granted that

value orientations were important in this transformation, the economic realities of the situation were probably more important
than Vogt was willing to admit. Had nineteenth-century pioneers
on the great plains been so dominated by their value orientations
as Vogt believed the settlers of Homestead to be, it is difficult to
understand how the region could ever have been settled.[34]

Two young historians, Stanley Elkins and Eric McKitrick, have
explored the theme of frontier democracy in two important articles
that owed much to a study of the psychology of housing directed
by Robert Merton.[35] Since they visualized the frontier basically
as a complex of new communities, it is appropriate to discuss
their work before moving on to other aspects of social science
thought. Turner, they wrote, had stated an "undeniable fact
—that an organic connection exists between American democracy and the American frontier." He provided no "conceptual
framework," however, in which it might be tested. This Elkins
and McKitrick proposed to do. To them democracy was "wide
participation in public affairs, a diffusion of leadership, a widespread sense of personal competence to make a difference," and
their specific hypothesis ran as follows: "Political democracy
evolves most quickly during the initial stages of setting up a new
community; it is seen most dramatically while the process of organization and the solving of basic problems are still crucial; it is
observed to best advantage when this flow of basic problems is
met by a homogeneous population." To them "homogeneity" involved "a similar level of social and economic status and aspirations among the people," but also the absence of "a traditional,
ready-made structure of leadership in the community." [36]

In one of the housing projects—Craftown—studied by the
Merton group, the failure of officials and agencies to provide adequate community services produced a spontaneous movement
among the new residents to create local associations and engage in
politics to remedy matters. On another project, Hilltown, where
an emergency of this sort did not occur, the occupants showed
little inclination to ape the agitated residents of Craftown. From
this contrast in behavior Elkins and McKitrick drew the inspiration for a "model" which involved "the establishment of new
communities. Its variables . . . a period of problem-solving and a
homogeneous population whose key factor . . . [was] the lack

of a structure of leadership." [37] The frontiers of the Northwest, the South, and Massachusetts Bay provided the data for testing the model. Elkins and McKitrick concluded that democracy reached its fullest expression where the pioneer population was homogeneous and the range of problems greatest, as in the Old Northwest.

The mechanics of proof applied by Elkins and McKitrick were less rigorous than the introduction of a theoretical model seemed to promise. Their comparisons between major frontier regions were too broad and their specific illustrations too incomplete and indiscriminate to be more than suggestive. In portraying communities reacting in unified fashion to common problems, these Neo-Turnerians may have paid too little attention to another element in social dynamics—the politics of conflict and community power structure.[38] Their stress on homogeneity of population may present difficulties also. Wisconsin research in action has shown that neighborhoods in which the residents were solidly of the same cultural background were often socially inactive.[39] On the other hand, some historians may question the proposition that the pioneers in the frontier communities of the Old Northwest were uniformly or even generally homogeneous. One wonders also whether the problems posed by the frontier period there were really of the same order as those that threatened to take the bemused residents of Craftown back to the era of the individual septic tank and the ambulatory school child. Despite such questioning, Elkins and McKitrick have produced exciting and imaginative history. Before leaving their work, however, it is well to stress that their theory of social behavior is basically the Turnerian one of simple response to the opportunities and challenges of the physical and economic environment.

In 1927, Pitirim Sorokin suggested that the individual in a society characterized by mobility tended to be more plastic, versatile, and individualistic, as well as less narrow minded. In such a society invention and discoveries were facilitated. At the same time, social intimacy diminished and the mobile individual faced psychological isolation and loneliness which might in turn stimulate emotional pursuit of friends or pleasures. Mental strain and mental disease increased among the mobile and the disintegration of morals was fostered.[40] Many of the social characteristics of Sorokin's mobile individual were similar to those attributed by Turner and his followers to the influence of the frontier.

In descriptions of new colonies of rural migrants from the southern uplands in urban centers during the last generation, one finds patterns of social behavior very similar to those attributed to the frontier. Before the American Historical Association in 1957, Everett S. Lee suggested that the major determinative force in shaping American development had been mobility of which the frontier movement illustrated one aspect.[41] Migration, he stressed, is selective and the frontier population could be expected, therefore, to vary in terms of age, sex composition, and other social characteristics from that of older settlements, and some differences in social behavior might be attributed to these circumstances.[42] Recurrently, of course, students have suggested that particular personality types are more prone to migrate than others.[43]

Among the reasons suggested recently by Harold D. Lasswell for the speedy acceptance of psychoanalytic thinking in the United States was the sexual tension in American life. This tension, he believed, was due in part to the process of western settlement which "introduced housewives and schoolmarms into the wide open spaces where men were men and women had been distant fantasies or immediate bargains." Important too, he believed, had been the uprooting of "country boys and girls or peasants from the ties of primary neighborhood."[44] Professor Lasswell's conception of the West may have stemmed from the projective techniques of the television industry rather than from more intensive research, but the implications of his argument are useful.

Viewing mobility as a major determinant in shaping the society of the frontier does indeed allow us to understand the frontier process more fully but perhaps it places the stress in the wrong place. Learning of opportunity in the West, journeying to it, seeking to exploit it while fitting himself into a new social *milieu* were all involved in the migration of a pioneer to the frontier. Movement from one location to another is a short-run matter. Is it not reasonable to attribute changes in social behavior of a continuing sort in part at least to the problems faced by the pioneer in fitting himself into the social groupings, the system of roles and status, the structure of influence and power, which made up the new community in the West? Such social structures no doubt might take as long as a generation to acquire the relative stability found in older communities while leaders jockeyed for position and followers wavered in their allegiances, while the disillusioned were replaced and the newcomers fitted into the locality and interest groups of the community. To explore some of the possibilities in these suggestions, let us turn to the pioneer era on the prairies.

In the following pages appear a number of characteristics of the population and environment which have held true in most new communities in that portion of the Middle West stretching from the central prairies of Illinois westward through Iowa and on into Kansas and Nebraska, a region settled for the most part between 1840 and 1900.[45] In no community, perhaps, did they all hold with equal force and some of the more important qualifications must be discussed. They are written largely in terms of the new settlers who chose to carve farms from the timbered bottoms and grassy uplands, but with little modification they can apply as well to those who sought their fortunes in the tiny service centers and larger county seat towns of the prairie frontier. Taken together, they constitute a kind of common denominator of conditions in middle western communities. If we can accept these generalizations as valid, we can go further and on the basis of certain assumptions about human behavior suggest patterns of social action that might be expected to appear in the new settlements of the Middle West.

Most settlers moved to the new lands in the expectation that they would improve their economic and social positions. The two are closely related and any considerable improvement in one is almost invariably accompanied by improvement in the other. Economic position is the most important determinant of social status in America today, and this was all the more the case on the frontier where no community tradition of deference to particular families existed to cloud the relationship.[46] Demographers have suggested that the individual who leaves his old surroundings is reacting to a combination of factors, which, in some cases, repel him from his old home and in others attract him elsewhere, the action being modified to some extent by the available transportation facilities. No doubt the attractive factors were most important in explaining our western movement. But the dream of the pioneer did not envision a society of new pattern, rather a more attractive place in the social fabric for himself and his family.

There were, of course, individuals who haunted the outskirts of the settlements and drifted on as population thickened. The frontier newspapers and country histories occasionally chronicle the wanderings of such men. These were the forelopers of Frederick Jackson Turner, who moved on evidently to maintain a way of life that was congenial to them. They had little desire to become part of a stable community. Despite the mobility of the population in the frontier settlements, it is doubtful if such adventurers formed any considerable percentage of the population. Our own age still has their counterparts. As Loomis discovered, those most apt to move on from the Farm Security Administration projects were those who had moved most often in the past.

By the act of migration the new settlers had broken those social relationships which had assisted them in patterning their lives in their former homes. Of course the severance was not necessarily absolute. The young bachelor making a start in life might journey to the West alone, but he might well be accompanied by friend or brother. If the migrant were married he was accompanied by his family or soon brought out the other members of his family circle to join him. A number of related families might well move together and old neighborhood friends might be discovered by accident or design in the new settlements. Colonization companies were organized in older communities occasionally for the purpose of migration. But unquestionably the move west shattered the social structure of which most pioneers had been a part and they had to fit themselves into a new one. The unity of the family and those other intimate social relations which are called primary relationships were broken, and much more completely shattered were the bonds of less intimate acquaintance which the resident of any locality builds up over time and which are sometimes called secondary relationships.

We must, of course, qualify our position to some extent. Although the practice was uncommon, a closely knit social group might move to the frontier in a body. The removal of the Ebenezer Society from western New York to the Amana settlements in eastern Iowa illustrated such migration.[47] At Amana the social structure was maintained and the members of the group faced only the task of re-establishing their means of livelihood in a new environment. The cohesion of such groups stemmed from the loyalty of the members to their peculiar social and religious beliefs. On the other hand, the community of interest shared by the members of a foreign language group might assist its members to build a new social structure but certainly did not eliminate the need to do so. Factionalism in the early history of the Sioux County Hollanders in Iowa, for instance, showed that the ethnic bond in itself was not enough to insure community peace.[48]

Frequently, the pioneers settled among neighbors who differed from them in cultural background. The foreign born, the Yankee stock and the members of the southern migration, which moved out of the southern border states in the years after 1800, constituted the major groups that participated in the settlement of the Middle West. But within these groups the social origins were varied. This was particularly so among the foreign born, but the settler of Yankee persuasion who was born and spent his early years in central New York differed somewhat in his standard of values and life training from one who had been born in New England or Ohio. Members of the major cultural groups tended to settle in the same areas, but there was usually some intermingling with other cultural groups, particularly in those regions where the dominance of one major group shaded into the dominance of another. Richard Lyle Power has described some aspects of the cultural mixing which occurred when Yankee and southern settlers intermingled north of the Ohio.[49]

But if the pioneer had neighbors, they were often distant at first. Isolation was the lot of the settler. Such isolation might be physical, it might be social, and often it was both. The frontier farmer could expect to go through a period when neighbors were few or scattered, and the tendency of the farm unit to increase in size as the frontier moved west through the prairies similarly worked to increase the isolation of the individual farm family. Socially, the pioneer was isolated until he could build up a net of primary and secondary relationships. Social isolation of this sort could be accentuated by language barriers or less striking, but still important, cultural differences. The "Nobscotter" members of New England settlements in Iowa might seem uncongenial neighbors indeed to nearby farmers of southern stock, and cultural schism of this sort retarded the formation of new group ties.

The members of most social groups do not participate on a basis of complete equality, but rather, informally or formally, ascribe varying degrees of leadership and status to each other. In a period when groups are being formed, competition exists among potential leaders to a considerable extent, creating a situation which is much more unstable than is ultimately the case when the group has shaken down and the members have come to know the virtues and deficiencies of their fellows more thoroughly. An important function of the leaders is to regulate the membership of the group. Acceptance of new members depends to a considerable extent upon the decisions of the leaders. The absence of a well-established leadership hierarchy duly recognized by a majority of the local residents was an important characteristic of frontier society. New residents, as a result, lacked authoritative guidance in fitting themselves into the social structure of the new communities.[50]

The new settlers faced a strange and untamed physical environment on the frontier. The farmer in the older settlements who moved to a new neighborhood also moved into a strange environment, but at least the resources upon which he expended his labor had yielded in large part to the ministrations of his predecessors. Although the pioneer might inherit a few improvements from a squatter or a previous owner, he still must face in some measure the rudimentary tasks of farm making—clearing, breaking, fencing, draining, and well digging in addition to the construction of farm buildings.

Settlers faced the challenge of the physical environment with differing degrees of preparation. The internal migration patterns of the nineteenth century show that the pioneers of American stock had themselves often been reared in frontier communities, and where such was the case they had a good understanding of the problems which they faced.[51] At the other extreme, of course, stood the European immigrant coming from communities where the agricultural resources had been in use for unremembered generations. But even the immigrants were usually rural in background and the agriculture of nineteenth-century America required few skills that were difficult for anyone reared in agriculture to acquire. The tendency of migrants to move along isothermal lines assisted them to some extent in acclimatization and removed the necessity of learning how to cultivate new plants. But the prairies and particularly the plains would present problems unknown on earlier American frontiers.

Migrants to the West seldom found themselves completely outside a formal institutional framework, although the wagon trains moving through the plains country constituted something of an exception. The land distribution agencies of the federal government served the pioneer and on occasion federal troops or officers assisted in maintenance of order. A system of territorial government provided laws for the settlers although settlement might be extremely scanty. Both in the territories and in the subsequent frontier states, local county government moved with the settler. The churches, the major private agencies of social control, were never far behind the settlers, the denominations to greater or lesser extent modifying their doctrines and organization to meet the special problems of the frontier.

But if a formal institutional framework did exist on the frontier of the agricultural settler and his town and village counterpart in the Middle West, it was often rudimentary or even sadly defective in its operation. The story of the agricultural frontier is interspersed with conflicts over land titles, and even the normal operation of the land laws in the Middle West operated in such a way that extralegal claim clubs developed or at best uncertainty over titles existed. In the early years of any agricultural community the revenues which could be raised by taxation might be inadequate to insure the satisfactory performance of community services by the local government or its agencies. Insofar as the churches were concerned, the means to support a full-time clergy could seldom be found within the community.

Finally, in generalizing upon the frontier community of the prairies, we can say that the economic foundations were infirm, for it was highly dependent upon a continued flow of new personnel and additional capital and thus extremely vulnerable to fluctuations in business conditions. The nineteenth-century pioneer farmer cannot be regarded as purely a subsistence farmer. Prior to the passage of the Homestead Act, and afterward to a considerable extent as well, he must meet the costs of his land as well as other expenses involved in the farm making process. Clarence Danhof has estimated that the farm maker of central Illinois during the 1850's was forced to meet cash costs of at least $1,000 in the first few years of his farming operations.[52] Such costs probably rose as the pioneer pushed farther westward into regions where lower rainfall put increased demands for capital upon him. The settler in the Middle West, therefore, had of necessity to think in terms of production for sale. Particularly if communications with the older settlements were poor, an important part of the settler's market was provided by incoming migrants who were forced to buy much of their own food as well as various services from the "old settlers" until their own acres came to bearing. Capital flowed into the frontier community in a variety of ways—as savings brought by the newcomers, in the form of loans made by residents of older areas, in the shape of goods sold to the frontier merchants on credit, and through the medium of speculative land purchases which were in turn sold to the pioneer settlers on credit or in some cases rented to them. Such movement was closely related to the business cycle throughout the nineteenth century. Both settlers and capital ceased to move to the frontier settlements in time of depression, leaving those who were dependent on the continued flow of settlers and capital in extremely hard circumstances, as they sought desperately to meet their current commitments and avoid making others.

At this point we can make explicit a number of assumptions about the social behavior of the individual, which may perhaps be relevant in explaining some characteristics of society on the prairie frontier.[53] In the first place, the individual finds primary and secondary relationships essential to satisfactory living. Few individuals are really content to be hermits. Taken from their accustomed web of social relationships they may suffer from what is termed *anomie* or normlessness.[54] The leading exponent of sociometry, J. L. Moreno, has carried this idea to the point of arguing that group relationships may actually serve as therapy for the maladjusted.[55] On such basis we can at least argue that most individuals who moved to the frontier were highly interested in re-establishing a satisfying system of social relations. We can safely assume as well that the skills and aptitudes of individuals in a particular social setting vary in the degree to which they are appropriate for solving the economic and social problems which confront them. Some individuals could, in other words, adapt themselves to frontier conditions more successfully than others.

Again, we can generalize that communication problems are an important source of conflict situations. If it was possible for individuals to explain their point of view perfectly there would be much less misunderstanding and argument. The greater the difference in the cultural backgrounds of individuals thrown into a common social setting the greater, it would seem, the danger of difficulties in communication. We can also suggest that the individual experiences deprivation when he fails to achieve a level of satisfaction which he considers minimal in the light of his experiences and future expectations. For the individual on the frontier undoubtedly the point at which deprivation set in was established, whether he realized it or not, prior to his movement to the new settlements—in that period of rosy dreams mentioned by one analyst of the resettlement projects. Finally, deprivation often prompts the individual to indulge in forms of substitute behavior. Failing to achieve adequate gratification by working in the recognized social channels, he goes beyond them, and resorts on the one hand, perhaps, to crime, or at the other extreme, retreats into fantasy.[56] Emotional religion is sometimes considered to be an illustration of substitute behavior and undoubtedly a greater degree of horizontal mobility than ordinary can be justly considered in the same light.[57]

On the basis of such postulates and the general characteristics of frontier communities we can draw certain generalizations or hypotheses. Since individuals on the frontier lacked both the well-established institutions and the social customs which had assisted them in patterning their behavior in the communities from which they came, since a heterogeneous population engendered difficulties in communication, and since the economic resources were temporarily inadequate or might become so in short order, they were involved in a greater number of conflict situations than before migration. Since the economic environment presented problems that the individual found impossible, or extremely difficult, to solve for himself, there was a greater amount of informal cooperation when conflict was absent on the frontier than in older communities. Conflict situations, the failure to re-establish satisfactory social relationships, the absence of clearly defined social norms, and the failure of the new environment to meet the expectations of betterment originally held by some migrants produced considerable deprivation. This was reflected in: high crime rates, resort to emotional religion, heavy incidence of mental disease, and continued mobility. Finally, there was a greater degree of political participation on the frontier than in older communities. This resulted from the efforts of individuals to gain status through leadership in a relatively unstructured society, from the effort to establish group ties, and from the greater relative significance of the economic rewards of politics in the frontier community.

If we wished to change the focus of our interest, other implications might be drawn from this prairie model. Rural sociologists, for instance, have given much attention to the way in which innovations in agricultural practices are adopted in rural communities.[58] Their findings, when viewed in the perspective of the mobility, the shifting channels of communication, and the unsettled influence and power structure of the pioneer community, may suggest rewarding lines of investigation to the historian interested in the two-fold transformation which occurred when the pioneers met the special challenge of the prairie environment and shared simultanteously in the mechanization of American agriculture.

Value orientations undoubtedly modified frontier social processes, holding the pioneers firm against environmental pressures at some points—predisposing them to yield at others. But each western settler was a unique individual and if many in a pioneer neighborhood reacted similarly and made similar decisions some did not. Knowing that this was so, we cannot be too rigorously deterministic in explaining the behavior of the pioneers.

Obviously, the ideas in this article are only prolegomena to appreciation of the frontier as a "form of society." Some may be able to suggest alternative social theories which are more meaningful than those discussed here. Such theories must be tested in such a way that we do not distort past realities. Several western historians have recently called for comparative studies of frontier societies. Comparison calls for more precise delineation of the social and economic structure of frontier communities and a greater appreciation of the complexities and significance of social relations than is found in the writing of most frontier historians. Comparison implies measurement also, although the word is one which rouses a good deal of suspicion in the minds of many disciples of Clio. Such meaurement demands the use of better measuring rods, or indices, of social, economic, and political characteristics than anyone has yet devised. There are challenges here. There is an additional challenge in the fact that history is a literary art and that many of those who generate social theory are hardly literary artists. The historian who consorts with behavioral theorists, who rides the wind of social theory, may indeed reap the whirlwind.

Notes

NOTE: This paper was read at the joint meeting of the Agricultural History Society and the Mississippi Valley Historical Association in Denver, Colorado, in April 1959. It grew out of study and research undertaken during 1955 and 1956 while I held a post-doctoral training fellowship awarded by the Social Science Research Council. I also wish to acknowledge the assistance and advice given during or after the fellowship period by Professor Carle C. Zimmerman, Harvard University, Professors Ray E. Wakeley and Robert Hamblin, Iowa State College, by Professor Richard Wilmeth, Professor Ray Ruppe, and Mr. Samuel McSeveney, State University of Iowa, by Dr. Mildred Throne of the Iowa State Historical Society, and by Dr. John Clifford, Southern Illinois University. Responsibility for errors of fact or interpretation is, of course, mine alone.

1. Frederick Jackson Turner, *The Frontier in American History* (New York: 1920 and 1947), p. 205. The quotation appears in "The Problem of the West," first published in the *Atlantic Monthly* in September 1896.

2. Turner, *op. cit.*, p. 139. The phrase "original stock" of course is one which no self-respecting social scientist would now use.

3. Only incidentally am I concerned in this article with the "Turner controversy." For those who wish to survey this blood-drenched field of debate I would suggest they begin with the bibliographical notes of Ray A. Billington, *Westward Expansion: A History of the American Frontier* (New York: 1949), pp. 760–763; and the same author's *The American Frontier* (American Historical Association, 1958), *passim.* The most recent extended summary is Gene M. Gressley, "The Turner Thesis—A Problem in Historiography," *Agricultural History*, XXXII (October 1958), 227–249. To me it seems much more important that America was a democracy than that Americans have enjoyed a unique kind of democracy.

4. In preparing my list I analyzed the thirteen essays included in *The Frontier in American History*, compiling a file of the qualities attributed to the pioneers by Turner and descriptions as well of the working of the frontier process. Generally accepted synonyms were grouped along with descriptive phrases or clauses that seemed to add up to the same thing. Readers

desiring a detailed and more critical analysis should turn to the articles of
Professor George W. Pierson, "The Frontier and Frontiersmen of Turner's
Essays," *The Pennsylvania Magazine of History and Biography*, LXIV (October 1940), 449–478; and "The Frontier and American Institutions: A
Criticism of the Turner Theory," *New England Quarterly*, XV (June 1942),
224–225, particularly the former. Here too will be found Mr. Pierson's summary of the way in which Turner saw the frontier altering the individual.
Like Pierson, I too find some of the western characteristics hard to reconcile
with each other. To be passionately egalitarian and "mobile, ascending" at
the same time was no mean trick. On the other hand it is difficult to con-
ciliate Pierson's seeming contention that Turner saw no contradiction between democracy and individualism ("The Frontier and Frontiersmen," p.
469), with Turner's passage, "They learned that between the ideal of individualism, unrestrained by society, and the ideal of democracy, was an innate
conflict" (*Frontier*, p. 203). Nor was it impossible, as Pierson suggests, for
the individual to become more nationalistic and more sectional at the same
time ("Frontier and Frontiersmen," p. 460, and "Frontier and American Institutions," fn. 19). A third loyalty, that to the state, was involved we must
remember. There is implicit in such criticism also the assumption that the
individual possesses a fixed quantity of any given emotion. Professor Jack H.
Hexter facetiously dubbed this kind of "either or" approach "The Theory
of the Conservation of Historical Energy," in his paper "Factors in Modern
History," delivered at the State University of Iowa, April 11, 1958. Finally
in considering the frontier personality sketched by Turner we must remember that it is possible to pay fervent lip service to a value while ignoring it in
practice. Indeed such behavior may provide a convenient and almost unconscious way of avoiding social responsibilities. If Turner's frontier could have
withstood Pierson's dialectics it would have been a "never, never" land
where only "economic man" and similar logical monsters could have dwelt.

5. The quoted phrase appears in Turner, *Frontier*, p. 344.

6. For instance the pioneer felt a "yearning 'beyond the sky line, where
the strange roads go down,' " and the wilderness appealed to him as "a fair
blank page on which to write a new chapter in the story of man's struggle
for a higher type of society," Turner, *Frontier*, pp. 271 and 261.

7. James C. Malin, one of the more cogent critics of the Turner hypothesis, dealt particularly with the problem of frontier mobility in a classic article,
"The Turnover of Farm Population in Kansas," *Kansas Historical Quarterly*,
IV (November 1935), 339–372. His findings raised a number of interesting
questions about the frontier process, but other western historians have not
produced comparable studies.

8. We must remember that Turner appended a qualifying footnote to
the famous list of characteristics of the American intellect in the frontier
essay of 1893. Numbered 54 and keyed to "restless, nervous energy" it ran
as follows: "Colonial travelers agree in remarking on the phlegmatic characteristics of the colonists. It has frequently been asked how such a people
could have developed that strained nervous energy now characteristic of
them. Compare Sumner, 'Alexander Hamilton,' 98, and Adams, 'History of
the United States,' 1:60; 9:240 and 241. The transition appears to become
marked at the close of the War of 1812, a period when interest centered
upon the development of the West, and the West was noted for restless
energy. Grund, '*Americans*,' 2, ch. 1" (Turner, *Frontier*, p. 37).

9. *Ibid.*, pp. 212 and 153.

10. *Ibid.*, p. 197.

11. "Just because, perhaps, of the usual isolation of their lives, when they came together in associations whether of the camp meeting or of the political gathering, they felt the influence of a common emotion and enthusiasm" (*Ibid.*, p. 345).

12. R. D. McKenzie, "Ecological Succession in the Puget Sound Region," American Sociological Society *Publications*, XXIII (Chicago: 1929), 60–80. Robert Park, "Succession, An Ecological Concept," *American Sociological Review*, I (April 1936), 171–179.

13. James G. Leyburn, *Frontier Folkways* (New Haven: 1935), p. 1.

14. *Ibid.*

15. *Ibid.*

16. *Ibid.*, p. 189.

17. *Ibid.*, pp. 189 and 191.

18. *Ibid.*, p. 21.

19. *Ibid.*, p. 197.

20. *Ibid.*, p. 202.

21. *Ibid.*, p. 223.

22. Charles Loomis, *Social Relationships and Institutions in Seven New Rural Communities*, Farm Security Administration, *Social Research Reports*, *18* (Washington: 1940), p. 9. Much of the same ground was covered by the author in two articles: "The Development of Planned Rural Communities," *Rural Sociology*, III (December 1938), 383–409; and (with Dwight M. Davidson) "Sociometry and the Study of New Rural Communities," *Sociometry*, II (January 1939), 56–76. The student approaching the voluminous literature on the rural community for the first time would do well to read the comments of Walter Kollmorgen and Robert Harrison in "The Search for the Rural Community," *Agricultural History*, XX (January 1946), 1–8. These writers argued that many rural sociologists were impressed by the need for more secure relationships in an age of pronounced individualism and that this belief shaped their approach and colored their research findings.

23. Loomis, *Social Relationships*, p. 15.

24. *Ibid.*, p. 16.

25. *Ibid.*, p. 32.

26. Edward C. Banfield, *Government Project* (Glencoe, Ill.: 1951).

27. *Ibid.*, p. 17.

28. *Ibid.*, p. 231.

29. *Ibid.*, pp. 232–233.

30. *Ibid.*, p. 239. Robert Merton brought this concept up to date in 1938, ultimately allocating a chapter to it in *Social Theory and Social Structure* (Glencoe: 1957, rev. ed.), pp. 131–160.

31. Evon Z. Vogt, *Modern Homesteaders: The Life of a Twentieth Century Frontier Community* (Cambridge: 1955).

32. *Ibid.*, p. 7.

33. *Ibid.*, pp. 11–12.

34. A number of other community studies are rewarding. Russell Lord and Paul H. Johnstone, *A Place on Earth: A Critical Appraisal of Subsistence Homesteads* (Washington: Bureau of Agricultural Economics, 1942); Alan R. Beals and Thomas McCorkle, *Lost Lake: A Study of an Agricultural Community Established on Reclaimed Land*, Kroeber Anthropological Society *Papers*, III (Berkeley: 1950); George W. Hill, Walter Slocum, Ruth O. Hill, *Man Land Adjustment: A Study of Family and Inter-Family*

Aspects of Land Retirement in the Central Wisconsin Land Purchase Area,
Wisconsin Agricultural Experiment Station, *Research Bulletin 134* (Madison:
1938); and George W. Hill and Ronald A. Smith, *Man in the "Cut-Over":
A Study of Family-Farm Resources in Northern Wisconsin,* Wisconsin
Agricultural Experiment Station, *Research Bulletin 139* (Madison: 1941).
Studies of older communities exist in great numbers. The treatment of his-
torical factors in them usually makes the historian cringe, but some are more
perceptive. Edward Moe and Carl C. Taylor, *Culture of a Contemporary
Rural Community: Irwin, Iowa,* United States Department of Agriculture,
Rural Life Studies, 5 (Washington: 1942), is one of a justly-respected series.
Richard E. Du Wors, "Persistence and Change in Local Values of Two New
England Communities," *Rural Sociology,* XVII (September 1952), 207–217,
is thought provoking. Walter M. Kollmorgen, *The German-Swiss in Franklin County, Tennessee: A Study of the Significance of Cultural Considerations
in Farming Enterprises,* United States Department of Agriculture (Washington: 1940), is a challenging study of cultural differences. Dwight Sanderson,
"Criteria of Rural Community Formation," *Rural Sociology,* III (December
1938), 373–384, is a distillation of the thought of one of the great rural sociologists of the last generation. There are a number of studies of housing
projects, but such studies hardly offer as close a parallel to the frontier of
the nineteenth century as do studies of new rural communities.

35. Stanley Elkins and Eric McKitrick, "A Meaning for Turner's Fron-
tier" (Chapter 8). The working title cited by Elkins and McKitrick was
Patterns of Social Life: Explorations in the Sociology of Housing, by Robert
K. Merton, Patricia S. West, and Marie Jahoda.

36. The passages paraphrased or quoted in this paragraph appear in "A
Meaning for Turner's Frontier," pp. 325, 330.

37. *Ibid.,* p. 330.

38. This possibility was first suggested to me by Mr. Robert Dykstra who
found the community response formula of the local and county historians
to be highly misleading in the course of his research on the early histories
of Abilene and Ellsworth, Kansas. My own reading in the newspapers of a
number of middle western county seats supports this criticism.

39. John H. Kolb, *Emerging Rural Communities: Group Relations in
Rural Society, A Review of Wisconsin Research in Action* (Madison: 1959),
p. 17.

40. Pitirim Sorokin, *Social Mobility* (New York: 1927), pp. 493–546. In
this work "social mobility" embraced both vertical and horizontal mobility.

41. Everett S. Lee, "A Sociological Examination of the Turner Thesis"
delivered at the joint session of the American Historical Association and the
American Studies Association, New York, December 30, 1957. The adjustment problems of southern highlanders in two urban centers are described
in Grace F. Leybourne, "Urban Adjustments of Migrants from the Southern
Appalachian Plateaus," *Social Forces,* XVI (December 1937), 238–246; and
by Morris G. Caldwell, "The Adjustments of Mountain Families in an Urban Environment," *ibid.,* XVI (March 1938), 389–395. Other work includes
Howard Beers and Catherine Heflin, *Rural People in the City and Urban
Adjustments of Rural Migrants,* Kentucky Agricultural Experiment Station
Bulletin, 478 and 487 (Lexington: 1945 and 1946).

42. James C. Malin tackled the problem of age and sex composition among
frontier populations in a study of Kansas settlement and concluded that "the
men (farm operators) were conspicuously middle-aged." He summarized

his research in Chapter 16 of *The Grassland of North America, Prolegomena to Its History* (Lawrence: 1947). The quotation is to be found on page 289. Professor Malin's figures do seemingly reveal that the farm operators in more recently settled areas usually were slightly younger than those in the longer settled regions of Kansas, but the differences were never as striking as the speculations of some Turnerians seemed to promise. More research of the same sort is badly needed in other states. Anyone interested in such work should read "An Approach to a Theory of Differential Migration," in Donald J. Bogue and Margaret J. Hagood, *Subregional Migration in the United States, 1935–50,* Vol. 2. *Differential Migration in the Corn and Cotton Belts: A Pilot Study of the Selectivity of Interstate Migration to Cities from Non-metropolitan Areas,* Scripps Foundation Studies in Population Distribution, No. 6, pp. 124–127.

43. American purveyors of the Teutonic myth used this idea for instance, but it has never been removed from the realm of speculation.

44. Harold D. Lasswell, "Impact of Psychoanalytic Thinking on the Social Sciences," in Leonard D. White, ed., *The State of the Social Sciences* (Chicago: 1956), p. 86. Lasswell's reference to the breaking of primary group ties seems to be linked to industrialization, but obviously the description would have applied to many on the frontier.

45. I shall not document the historical foundations of these generalizations closely. They are impressions based on work in the land disposal records of railroads, states, and the federal government, in county records, in the newspapers of some dozen county seats, in agricultural periodicals of the region, in the manuscript population and agricultural census rolls, in the records and correspondence of eastern investors and middle western credit agencies, in several hundred county histories and in the standard secondary works.

46. An introduction to research in social stratification is provided by Reinhard Bendix and Seymour M. Lipset, eds., *Class Status and Power, A Reader in Social Stratification* (Glencoe: 1953); and John F. Cuber and William F. Kenkel, eds., *Social Stratification in the United States* (New York: 1954).

47. Bertha M. H. Shambaugh, *Amana, The Community of True Inspiration* (Iowa City: 1908).

48. Charles L. Dyke, *The Story of Sioux County* (Orange City: 1942), pp. 99–101.

49. Richard L. Power, *Planting Corn Belt Culture; the Impress of the Upland Southerner and Yankee in the Old Northwest* (Indianapolis: 1953). The work of Douglas G. Marshall and Peter Munch is stimulating as well as the Kollmorgen study cited above. See "Nationality and the Emerging Culture," *Rural Sociology,* XIII (March 1948), 40–47; and "Social Adjustment among Wisconsin Norwegians," *American Sociological Review,* XIV (December 1949), 780–787. In "Pioneer Farmers and Innovation," *Iowa Journal of History,* LVI (January 1958), 1–36, I attempted to relate differences in farming patterns to ethnic differences with less success than the work of the sociologists had led me to expect.

50. George Homans, *The Human Group* (New York: 1950), p. 188, ". . . the leader is the man people come to . . . his rank carries with it the implied right to assume control of the group. . . ." Obviously the power of the leader in this respect varies considerably from group to group.

51. The extent to which this was true has probably been exaggerated, however. In his research on Kansas population, Professor Malin discovered

that from 1875 through 1905 as many as three out of four new farm operators from out of state had migrated from non-contiguous states (*Grassland*,
p. 288). It is probable that the proportion was lower before the development
of the American railroad net.

52. Clarence H. Danhof, "Farm-Making Costs and the 'Safety Valve';
1850–1860," *Journal of Political Economy*, LXIX (June 1941), 317–359.

53. These assumptions or postulates are derived in large part from the
findings in the community studies discussed or noted above. Deprivation and
substitute behavior are terms which are used quite generally in current sociological theory, although not always in quite the same sense as I have used
them here. A helpful introduction to current thinking is to be found in
Gardner Lindzey, ed., *Handbook of Social Psychology* (Cambridge: 1954),
"Contemporary Systematic Positions," I (part 2), pp. 57–258, but see also the
relevant chapters in Joseph B. Gittler, *Review of Sociology: Analysis of a
Decade* (New York: 1957); Daniel Lerner and Harold D. Lasswell, eds., *The
Policy Sciences: Recent Developments in Scope and Method* (Stanford:
1951); and Robert K. Merton and Paul F. Lazarsfeld, eds., *Continuities in
Social Research; Studies in the Scope and Method of "The American Soldier"* (Glencoe: 1950). Among more specialized studies I found *Culture and
Personality* (New York: 1954), by John J. Honigmann, and Floyd Hunter,
Community Power Structure (Chapel Hill: 1953) to be very helpful. The
student who accepts the approach of this and the following paragraphs has
made at least two obvious commitments. He is willing to agree that the motivation of *some* behavior is not rational in the usually accepted sense of this
word, and that the personality of an individual is sufficiently plastic that
changes may occur due to social or other environmental pressures after
adolescence let alone the very early years.

54. W. I. Thomas and Florian Znaniecki, *The Polish Peasant in Europe
and America* (2d ed., New York: 1927), Vol. 2, pp. 1647–1822, is required
reading for anyone interested in the problem of adjustment faced by immigrants or migrants.

55. J. H. Kolb and Edmund de S. Brunner cite J. L. Moreno, *Who Shall
Survive* (Washington: 1934), to this effect in their standard survey, *A Study
of Rural Society* (3d. ed., New York: 1946), p. 323.

56. An introduction to some of the thinking on the relation of the social
situation to mental disorders is provided by Edwin M. Lemert, "An Exploratory Study of Mental Disorders in a Rural Problem Area," *Rural Sociology*, XIII (March 1948), 48–64, including comments by A. R. Mangus;
and Robert E. L. Faris, "Ecological Factors in Human Behavior," in Joseph
Mc. Hunt, ed., *Personality and the Behavior Disorders: A Handbook Based
on Experimental and Clinical Research* (New York: 1944), pp. 736–757.

57. I first encountered this approach to religious behavior in "The Place
of Religious Revivalism in the Formation of the Intercultural Community of
Klamath Reservation," by Philleo Nash in *Social Anthropology of North
American Tribes* (Chicago: 1937 and 1957). Obviously it does not provide
a complete explanation to frontier religious behavior. See Charles A. Johnson,
The Frontier Camp Meeting; Religion's Harvest Time (Dallas: 1955). Other
books and articles provide interesting clues as well. H. Richard Niebuhr,
The Social Sources of Denominationalism (New York: 1929); Liston Pope,
Millhands and Preachers: A Study of Gastonia (New Haven: 1942), Chaps.
6–7; Gerhard Lenski, "Social Correlates of Religious Interest," *American
Sociological Review*, XVIII (October 1953), 533–544; Russell R. Dynes, "To-

ward the Sociology of Religion," *Sociology and Social Research*, XXXVIII (March–April 1954), 227–232.

58. North Central Rural Sociology Committee, *Bibliography of Research on: Social Factors in the Adoption of Farm Practices* (Ames: 1956).

❦ 7 ❦

Paul W. Gates

FRONTIER ESTATE BUILDERS
AND FARM LABORERS

To the simple democratic society of the American frontier consisting mostly of small farmers, as Frederick Jackson Turner described it, should be added two types, the one common, the other small in numbers but profoundly important in shaping landownership patterns, political action, and the beginnings of a cultured society. The first of these types includes the farm laborers, some of whom became farm tenants. The other type is the capitalist estate builder who took with him a "seemingly endless appetite for power and for land," as Arthur Moore put it.[1] It was these capitalist estate builders, whether cattle barons, land speculators turned developers, or men who went west with the set purpose of creating great plantations operated by tenants or hired hands, who made possible the employment of thousands of laborers.

The capitalist developer, big and little, was first revealed indirectly in 1860 when the Bureau of the Census presented statistics showing the number of farm laborers—statistics as noteworthy in their way as those showing the extent of farm tenancy in 1880 or the statement of the superintendent of the census in 1890 that the frontier was gone. Notwithstanding America's much-boasted opportunities, its seemingly limitless supply of public lands, its ever-

Paul W. Gates is John Stambaugh Professor of American History at Cornell University. He has written *Agriculture and the Civil War, Frontier Landlords and Pioneer Tenants, Farmers' Age: Agriculture, 1815–1860, Fifty Million Acres,* and other books.

Reprinted from Walker O. Wyman and Clifton B. Kroeber, eds., *The Frontier in Perspective* (Madison: The University of Wisconsin Press, 1957), pp. 144–163, by permission of the author and the publisher.

expanding and newly opening frontier, the farm laborer, ordinarily a landless person whose economic status was less secure than that of the European peasant, was shown to exist in large numbers, not only in the older and well-developed communities, but in the new states and middle border territories.

Consider for a moment Iowa, only fourteen years a state, still but lightly touched by settlement, not able to boast two people to the square mile, with less than a third of its land in farms but the bulk of its public lands already in private ownership. Despite the slight development of this state, largely concentrated in the eastern counties, its obvious frontier status, its abundance of raw unimproved prairie, Iowa in 1860 reported 40,827 farm laborers—6 per cent of its population. More to the point, out of every hundred persons engaged in agriculture, twenty-three were farm laborers. Or look at Kansas, which had neither attained the dignity of statehood nor acquired anything but a thin veneer of settlement along its eastern border in the six years since it had become a territory. Census enumerators found here 10,400 farms and, surprisingly, 3,660 farm laborers. Nineteen out of every hundred persons engaged in agriculture were farm laborers. For the states of the Old Northwest the percentage of farm laborers among the total number of people engaged in agriculture ranged from 20 to 28.

Throughout the rest of the century, the number of farm laborers grew rapidly in the newer states of the Upper Mississippi Valley, while in the older states it fluctuated up and down and took a violent upward turn in the last decade. In proportion to the total number of persons engaged in agriculture, the number of farm laborers reached a high point in 1870. The census for that year shows that the percentage of farm laborers in the total number of persons engaged in agriculture was 30 in Minnesota, 32 in Nebraska, 33 in Wisconsin, 34 in Kansas, and 37 in Iowa. All these states had fairly stable and well-developed areas by 1870; but all except Iowa also had portions not yet out of the frontier stage. With so many farm laborers in new as well as old communities, no picture of the West can be considered complete without attention to their social and economic background, the reasons why they existed in such numbers. But western historians have not been concerned about them. The stereotype of the mortgaged farmer is familiar to all students of Western lore, but the farm laborer has not been the subject of rowdy ballads, he does not appear in the fiction of the frontier, nor is he to be found in the works of Turner, Paxson, Riegel, or Billington.

Statistics of farm labor for these years in new states and territories are so startling that it seems desirable to look into their compilation to determine just who in the opinion of the census enumerators fitted into this category. Analysis of the original census schedules shows that older boys of farm families who were over fifteen years of age and were living at home were not infrequently listed as farm laborers. Undoubtedly they performed heavy routine work on the farm, but I have not thought of them as laborers, since they rarely drew wages and since they could expect to inherit a share of the farm some time in the future. Offsetting this factor was the exclusion of migratory workers who were employed for the harvest season but were not at the time of enumeration living with the farmers who had previously engaged them or were thereafter to do so. Clearly, the timing of the census was important in the matter of enumerating farm laborers. The first of June, the date for which information was collected, was not the busiest time for farmers in the Corn Belt, because crops were already in, haying had not begun, and wheat was not yet ready for harvest. A month or six weeks later, enumerators would have found greater numbers of hired hands to list.[2]

By 1870 the census takers were collecting information respecting the value of compensation, including board paid hired hands the previous year. True, this information was not processed and published, but a sample study of Poweshiek County in central Iowa shows that of 1,634 farmers owning land, 932 paid out for labor the previous year sums ranging from $5 to $2,000, the average being over $150. In nine townships in this county, payments to farm laborers, including the value of their board, amounted to $234,000.[3]

The census schedules also furnish information on the emergence of farm tenancy, a midway step from laborer to farm owner, which is particularly valuable since we have no specific data on tenancy as such until 1880. In a colloquy on land speculation at a meeting of the American Historical Association, this writer ventured to suggest to Dr. Joseph Schafer, then superintendent of the State Historical Society of Wisconsin, that in his examination of the profits and losses in speculation, he may have underestimated the rents speculators collected; this suggestion was scoffed at for intimating that tenancy existed on the frontier or that rents could have been collected for land use.[4] Dr. Schafer was a tartar in argument, but the fact remains that tenancy did exist on the frontier, it was not uncommon in Wisconsin in the fifties, and it does have to be taken into account in any consideration of the frontier process. In the absence of detailed census compilations, we can learn much about tenancy from earlier census schedules, the county deed records, local newspaper advertisements, and correspondence of land dealers and landlords.[5]

The censuses of 1850, 1860, and 1870 show a sharp increase in the number of farms in excess of five hundred acres, the expanding volume of hired hands previously alluded to, and numerous "farmers" and farm laborers who owned no real or landed property but did have personal property such as horses, mules, oxen, milch or beef cattle, and hogs. Some of these "farmers" and farm laborers may have been attempting to buy farms they were operating, but whether they were or not, they were at the time tenants. Analysis of the 1870 census listings of farmers and farm laborers in two lightly developed western Iowa townships and one well-settled central Iowa township shows that of 184 persons (excluding children) listed as engaged in agriculture, ninety-six owned land and eighty-eight owned no real property, but fifty-seven of these latter owned personal property and were presumably tenants. Thirty-one "farmers" and farm laborers listed no property of any kind. Of the agricultural population of these three townships (Belvedere, Ashton, and Shiloh), 53 per cent owned farms and 47 per cent owned no land.

Farm land was being rented to tenants in Ohio, Indiana, and Illinois as early as the 1820's, but the practice did not become common for nearly a generation.[6] After the frenzy of land speculation in the thirties, many investors, caught with heavy obligations in a falling market, with interest and tax costs growing, offered to rent their land to squatters or newly arriving immigrants too poor to buy, partly to protect their property but also to get at least the taxes out of them.[7] As early as 1842, Solon Robinson, the well-known agricultural writer, in describing the

attractions of the flat lands of northwestern Indiana to immigrants, said: "No matter if you have no money, you can rent land
very low, and will soon be in a condition to let land instead of
hiring it." [8] By the middle of the century, tenancy was emerging
everywhere in the prairies of Indiana, Illinois, and eastern Iowa
and a little more slowly in Wisconsin. From northern and eastern Indiana, the Military Tract and the central prairie counties of
Illinois, and the eastern counties of Iowa came many reports of
persons renting land who lacked the means to buy. Renting was
so common in La Salle County, Illinois, that the local newspaper
in its price current listed farms as renting from $1.25 to $1.50 an
acre. In eastern Iowa, where improved land also was renting at the
same prices, a dealer in 1852 advertised thirteen farms for sale or
rent. Elsewhere newspapers discussed the growing practice of
share renting.[9]

In mid-century Indiana, a move to define the rights of landlords
and tenants developed into a major political battle. Bills to give
landlords a lien on crops raised by their tenants had the support of
legislators from the prairie counties, where landlordism flourished, but were opposed by the Democratic representatives from
the small-farm counties of southern Indiana. Opponents, perhaps
not aware of how far landlordism had already developed in the
richer counties of the north, said that any such measure would
stimulate landlords to enlarge their domain, "increase their subor-
dinate tenancies," and strike at "our true policy to encourage
every man to become a land owner." It was legislation "in favor
of capital, the rich, and against labor, the poor." Another Hoosier
opponent of the measure proposed an amendment to give landlords liens on the furniture, the wife, and the children of the tenant! Session after session of the legislature gave consideration to
the question from 1857 to 1881, but not until the latter year was
action completed.[10]

The growth of tenancy was stimulated by the granting of lands
to railroads to aid in their construction. Two early beneficiary
railroads—the Illinois Central and the Burlington and Missouri—
after making their selections of land, found squatters on them
who could not easily be dispossessed without creating ill feeling,
but who were not in a position to pay the price asked for their
claims. The Burlington officials found that the easiest policy to

follow in such cases was to rent the land to the squatters for one to three years at a nominal price of twenty cents an acre with the hope that such improvements as the squatters made would enable the land to bring a good price when the lease expired and legal action might be taken to evict, if necessary. In 1878, the Burlington was renting Nebraska land which had been farmed during the past year for $1 an acre and idle lands for fifty cents an acre; its land in Iowa was then being rented for as much as $1.25 to $2 an acre. Railroad land-grant policy, like the government policy of permitting—and, indeed, encouraging—extensive speculation in western lands, hastened the coming of tenancy to the West.[11]

The rapid alienation of public land and swiftly rising land values helped to accelerate the renting of land in the sixties and seventies. In 1880, when statistics of tenancy were compiled, the figures for the public-land states, particularly those which still contained land available for homestead, alarmed land reformers. In Illinois 31 per cent and in Iowa 23 per cent of all the farms were tenant operated. The counties of greater land values and higher productivity had tenancy rates ranging into the high 30's and 40's. More surprising was the swift emergence of tenancy in the border counties of Kansas and Nebraska, where the land had been in private ownership no more than twenty-three years, much of it less than fourteen years. Here the tenancy figures ranged from 25 to 40 per cent. In the states of the Upper Mississippi Valley, the percentage of people engaged in agriculture who were either tenants or farm laborers ranged from 32 in Minnesota to 53 in Illinois.[12]

The early appearance of tenancy and agricultural labor in the amount that has been shown in or close to frontier areas, together with their rapid increase, provides convincing evidence that government land policy was not producing the results its defenders claimed. In view of the oft-repeated objective of American land policy—to assure a nation of freeholders—how is it possible to account for the early appearance of farm laborers and tenants in frontier communities?

Paradoxically, the fact that cheap, and finally free, land was to be had in the American West has a direct bearing on the appearance of farm laborers and tenants in that section. Government land prices were progressively reduced from $2 an acre in 1800

($1.64 for cash) to $1.25 in 1820, to 60¢ to $1 by the use of military bounty land warrants of 1847–55, to as little as 12.5¢ in 1854, until finally, in 1862, free land could be obtained. European peasants and debt-ridden farmers in older sections of America were lured west by the vision of cheap or free farms that they confused with cheap or free raw land.

Nor was it sufficiently noted that the cost of farm making was increasing as settlers moved into the tough-sodded, poorly drained, and timberless prairies, where in competition with construction and railroad building they either had to pay high wages for custom work such as breaking, harvesting, and threshing or buy expensive labor-saving equipment. Custom plowmen, using the heavy breaking plow pulled by a number of yoke of oxen, charged $2 and $3 an acre for breaking prairie. Lumber for the house, fencing, and perhaps a barn could no longer be "hooked" from neighboring government- or absentee-owned tracts and had to be brought in at heavy expense from the Mississippi River mill towns or Chicago. A yoke of oxen, wagon, plow, stove, chains, ax, shovel, grindstone, scythe or cradle, together with seed, funds to maintain the family until the first crop came in, fees for filing land-office papers, or money to make the down payment on a railroad tract, brought the amount needed to start farming to $500 at the minimum; safer estimates were two or three times that much. Land agents and representatives of the land-grant railroads warned prospective emigrants in the East and in Europe that they should bring some capital with them to the West.[13]

Notwithstanding these well-meant warnings, immigrants continued to reach the outer edge of settlement destitute, unable to start farm making. We need not probe their disillusionment when their scant resources proved insufficient to enable them to take advantage of the government's free homestead policy. They could still cherish the dream of owning a farm while they worked for others.

Immigrants newly arriving in the West soon learned that unless they quickly established a claim to land, their chances of making good selections would be minimized, perhaps lost to other more foresighted settlers or to speculators. The settler and the speculator were catching up with the surveyor, especially in Iowa, Kansas, and Nebraska, and land when offered or opened to entry was quickly snatched up. Consequently, a first step toward farm ownership was to select a tract, establish a claim upon it, and hope that it could be held for two or three years without cost even though the claimant was not actually living upon it or abiding by the provision of the pre-emption or homestead acts. Frontiersmen moving early into newly opened communities found they could sell their claims with but slight improvements for $50 to $100 to later comers and then go a little farther west and make another selection. Claim making, a species of land speculation, was indulged in by many who gradually acquired a little livestock and equipment through sales of claims or through outside earnings and were ready in a few years for more permanent farm making. A combination of claim speculation and temporary work on railroad construction jobs or building projects in growing urban centers was common. That many immigrants also took agricultural jobs as hired hands in areas close to, if not right in, the frontier is not as well known.

Some students and readers of fiction relating to western pioneer life have entertained the notion that western farmers never really prospered but were in a more or less chronic state of depression that was aggravated by periods of unusually low prices and near crop failures with resulting acute distress. Perhaps more attention has been directed to the agrarian reaction to such distress and the causes thereof than to periods of favorable prices and bountiful crops that brought early prosperity to many. Certain it is that in no comparable period did such large numbers of immigrants to a new region gain ownership of the farms they were improving and live well upon those farms as in the fifty-year period from 1850 to 1900 in the Mississippi Valley. Boomer literature of the time tells of numerous cases of individuals in Illinois, Kansas, or Nebraska who made enough on one good crop to pay for their land and equipment. That there were such cases cannot be denied, but whether they were typical it is impossible to say. We do know that industrious, skillful farmers blessed by good fortune did succeed not only in subduing the usual 80- to 160-acre tract of wild land to grain production and livestock use, but in many instances in developing even larger farms. This was accomplished not alone by the head of the family and his children, but with the aid of hired men.

The census schedules of 1870 reveal thousands of instances of farmers with no more than 160 acres employing one or two laborers.[14] These farmers did not attract the attention of journalists or travelers of the time, and, consequently, it is more difficult to reconstruct their operations than those of the larger capitalist farmers, whose operations were on a much bigger scale and who individually employed numerous farm hands.

The American West proved attractive not only to poor immigrants but also to men of means interested in developing not single family farms but estates of thousands of acres worked by laborers and tenants. Large capitalistic enterprises in the pioneer West are not unknown to historians, but most attention has been centered on the bonanza wheat farms of the Red River Valley of Minnesota and Dakota and on cattle ranching in the Great Plains. Carried out on a grand scale and with a dramatic flourish, they drew the attention of journalists and other commentators of the time and consequently found their way into most histories of the West.[15] Their day was short, their long-range influence not great, and they deserve a mere footnote in history compared with the quieter, more pervasive, and longer-lasting investments by masterful and aggressive capitalists in the Corn Belt, who came not merely to speculate nor to develop a bonanza farm but to create rent-producing estates composed of numerous farms operated either by hired hands or by tenants.

These estate builders were to be found in practically every portion, one can almost say in every county, of the Corn Belt. Their homes, in highly stereotyped and stilted engravings, the number of acres they owned, and the moral qualities of the owners all are presented in the numerous county atlases and biographical volumes that were the rage in the Gilded Age. Their investments ranged from a few thousand to hundreds of thousands of dollars and, for a score or more, to one or two millions.[16] That is not to say that they brought capital in this amount with them when they first ventured into the West. Much of their capital was made in the West.

The cattle ranchers and drovers who flourished in Indiana and Illinois in the forties, fifties, and sixties and in Iowa and Missouri a little later dominated great areas of the prairies for a time. They built upon their first investments by shrewdly buying the surplus stock of neighbors, fattening them on the prairie bluestem with the addition of a little grain, and then driving them to Chicago, Indianapolis, or the East, wherever they could get favorable prices. Later they brought in cattle from Missouri and Texas. Their profits were invested in land when it could be bought "dirt-cheap" to assure an abundance of grass and grain for their operations. Slowly, they turned to grain feeding and grain production and improved livestock, using meantime an increasing number of hands. By mid-century the operations of the successful cattle kings were being conducted on a huge scale, with herds of cattle numbering in the thousands, fields of corn covering thousands of acres, and scores of hands to carry on the business. Their holdings in land increased to 5,000, 10,000, 20,000, even 40,000 acres.[17] For every giant farm of this size there were a score or more of smaller operators with holdings ranging from one to four thousand acres.[18]

These bonanza farms, located as they were in Corn Belt counties with high land values, soon became as outmoded as the sickle and cradle. Farm workers proved irresponsible when hired at low wages. They were careless with tools, they slighted their tasks, overworked or abused the draft animals, drank heavily, and often engaged in fisticuffs. On slight provocation they quit their jobs, knowing that equally good opportunities were available elsewhere, and they demanded high wages when the peak of employment was reached in the harvest season. Old Isaac Funk, who accumulated a fortune of two million dollars in his land and cattle business in McLean County, Illinois, said in 1861 that no one could afford to hire men to grow and market grain at prices then prevailing. Their wages were too high and they worked too little, thought Funk. Another Illinois landlord, in deploring the wage of two dollars a day being paid to harvest hands in 1862, held that "cheap farm laborers" were essential for the winning of the Civil War.[19] The best agricultural laborers wanted to become tenants or owners and would remain in employment only as long as was necessary for them to accumulate the resources for starting on their own.

Continuing immigration into the prairies with its resulting pressure upon the supply of land, skyrocketing values, taxes, and assessments forced more intensive land use. Ranches with grain as a side issue could no longer be economically justified, and for a time the bonanza farms became grain farms with cattle as a side issue. Before long, central administration of the land was abandoned. The big farms were divided into small holdings and assigned to tenants. Though the workers might prove poor farm hands, it was seen that, given a share in the returns of farming, they were more responsible, more willing to exert themselves, more careful with their tools, horses, and oxen, and with their housing accommodations. In the transition to full tenancy the landlord might provide everything but maintenance for the operator and pay him eight or ten cents a bushel for the corn he produced. In 1870, a tenant who furnished his own team was paid fifteen cents for each bushel of corn, fifty cents for each bushel of wheat, and twenty-five cents for each bushel of oats he produced. A more common practice was for the tenant to pay the landlord one third to one half of the crops or a cash rent for each acre of cultivable land.[20]

The day of the Corn Belt cattle kings was short, as was their career as bonanza farmers. As entrepreneurs developing their estates they made jobs available for many workers who later were permitted, if not encouraged, to become tenants. In the tenant stage of land development some of the landlords continued to expend their surplus from rents in additional improvements, so that their constructive period lasted throughout the first generation and, indeed, well into the second. In the process of change, some land was sold; more, through inheritance diffusion, passed to a larger number of landlords. Analysis of the assessment records or the current platbooks of Corn Belt counties reveals a century later how tenaciously third- and fourth-generation descendants of the old cattle kings have clung to their possessions.

Side by side with these modern holdings are other equally large estates which sprang from another type of investment on the frontier, that of the capitalists who came west to create permanent estates like that of the Wadsworth family in the Genesee country of New York by buying and developing extensive areas. Some of these capitalists concentrated their attention entirely upon farm making, while others bought and sold real estate, acted as agents for eastern capitalists wishing to invest in the growing West, or perhaps ran a bank and made loans to squatters. Profits and fees they invested in land improvements. A number took construction contracts on railroads, receiving land instead of cash in payment. They were careful to keep their titles clear, to pay the taxes before liens were issued, and to protect their timber against the prevalent custom of "hooking." With all these side issues, they kept before them the goal of land development.

Extensive improvement of their holdings required these estate builders to seek out workers to break the prairie, fence, erect tenant houses for the families of workers and barracklike constructions for single men, to seed, cultivate, harvest, shuck, thrash, and haul the grain to market. To assure themselves an adequate labor supply, and subsequently to attract tenants, these entrepreneurs had at times to advertise, distribute handbills in eastern communities, and in a number of instances publish pamphlets describing the opportunities their lands provided to immigrants.[21] Workers could not save much from the low wages paid them, but many pioneers did make their start by accumulating small funds from such earnings and investing them, perhaps while still holding the farm job, in near-by land on which they might at the same time make some improvements.

For the western immigrant who was anxious to have a farm of his own but who lacked the means to acquire it, it was distinctly better to be a tenant than a farm laborer. He could, when he attained this status, feel he was moving toward his goal. Now he shared with the capitalist proprietor the profits from farming, but he also shared the losses. Furthermore, he was usually required by his lease to make capital improvements upon the rented land, and the cost would be deducted from the rent. Every improvement he made raised the value of the land and pushed farther away the possibility of his buying it. If he paid cash rent, continued improvement of the land was certain to be followed by a higher rent charge; if he paid share rent, the landlord might—and in the eighties did—exact a larger portion of the grain. Tenancy was no happy choice to the immigrant looking for the free or cheap land about which he had heard so much, but unless he was willing to go far beyond the railroad into areas lacking social facilities and market opportunities, there was no other alternative.

Some landlords were willing to pay for much of the cost of breaking and fencing, to provide machines and even credit to carry their tenants through harvest. Others insisted on the ten-

ants' making all the improvements, which they then might own or
at least have the right to sell to other tenants, subject to the approval of the landlord. Advertisements for tenants were increasingly common in the prairie newspapers, but more ominous from
the point of view of the tenant were advertisements of renters
looking for land.[22] Eviction for sloth, failure to make required improvements, poor farming, and cheating the landlord increased as
hordes of new immigrants looking for land to rent came in from
central Europe. The pressure for places to rent made it possible
for the landlord to exact more and to allow the tenant less. Farmers of older American stock found the role of tenant increasingly
unbearable. Disillusioned by their meager returns and unwilling
to compete with the new wave of European immigrants, they
abandoned their rented places in Illinois and Iowa by the thousands in the seventies and eighties for a new try at ownership in
western Kansas or Nebraska, or perchance in the Dakota country.
It was this emigration of older American tenants from the Corn
Belt that was responsible for the increasingly conservative character of agrarian politics in Illinois and Iowa. These disillusioned
and frequently angry tenants who emigrated farther west carried
their resentment with them and made the area in which they settled fertile ground for the Populist agitator.[23]

Meantime, the capitalist estate builders, having divided their
holdings into small tenant farms, were emerging as farm managers. Where they had erected tenant homes, set out fences, and
established orchards they needed to protect their investment by
making certain that proper care and maintenance were provided.
They naturally wanted for their tenancies good farmers who
would keep the weeds down, get their crops in and harvested at
the right time, protect the timber if any, and pay their cash rent
promptly or turn in a fair landlord's share of the grain. Good
tenants assured better yields and hence more share rent. Both
landlords and tenants were driven to exploit the land by their
need for high returns to meet costs of farm improvements, new
implements, and perhaps livestock. Rotation, the use of alfalfa or
clover, prevention of erosion were all subordinated to the production of grain, with declining fertility the natural—though not immediately apparent—result. Much the same thing can be said of
farm owners who were struggling to raise funds out of their crops

to purchase new equipment, to fence additional land, to drain the low places, or to enlarge their original two- or three-room houses to accommodate growing families. Economic circumstances were largely responsible for a pattern of land use that disregarded the lessons of the past in older states, was exploitative and destructive of values. In defense of the capitalist estate builders, it should be added that some of them early showed concern for proper land management by insisting upon rotation of crops; the use of alfalfa, clover, and lime; the elimination of weeds; and careful use of pastures.

Elsewhere the operations of capitalist estate builders, whose individual and family holdings ran as high as 60,000 acres and in one case to 200,000 acres, have been described. Few of these "feudal lords," as George Ade called them, would sell unless faced with disaster.[24] They instilled in their children a deep respect for the land they had improved and sought by every possible legal device to restrict the right of alienation. Because of their great success in retaining ownership of their many farms, the names of Scully, Moore, Davis, Vandeveer, Ennis, Funk, Fowler, Wearin, Rankin, and Lawrence-Lowrie are as familiar today to the residents of the prairie states as were the names of the great planters of South Carolina and Georgia to the ante-bellum residents of those states.

With all the plethora of information the Bureau of the Census had gathered, the problem of multiple ownership of tenant farms received no attention until 1900. Something of the concentration of ownership of tenant farms, the heritage of the capitalist estate builder in the nineteenth century, may be seen in the census data of that year (Table 7-1). The figures are not complete and are made less useful by the fact that they are compiled on the basis of residence of owner; but in the absence of anything better we must use them. For the states of the Upper Mississippi Valley, 3,800 landlords appear as owning 32,646 farms. Five hundred and fifty-one of these landlords had an average of 12.8 farms each, and 122 owners had an average of 35.5 farms each. In Illinois 34 landlords are shown owning 1,115 farms, or an average of 32 each.[25] Since one landlord owned 322 farms in Illinois and an additional 845 farms in Missouri, Kansas, and Nebraska but had his residence in the District of Columbia, it is easy to see how deceptive, how inadequate, the census data are.

TABLE 7–1

Ownership of Tenant Farms by Owners Living in
Upper Mississippi Valley, 1900

	NUMBER OF OWNERS	NUMBER OF FARMS OWNED
Owned one farm	419,900	419,900
Owned two farms	39,124	78,248
Owned three to five farms	12,070	39,831
Owned five to ten farms	3,127	21,263
Owned ten to twenty farms	551	7,052
Owned twenty or more farms	122	4,331
Total (plural ownership)	54,994	150,725

The estate builder brought much-needed funds to the West, developed substantial areas, and provided early employment and housing facilities for many newly arrived immigrants who lacked means to begin on their own. He aided others in getting started by lending them funds to commence farming as a tenant or owner; by furnishing them the necessary farming implements, seed, and food until harvest; and by providing livestock on a partnership basis. Much of the risk in these operations was his. Frequently, he undertook such investments with borrowed capital on which he paid 10 to 15 per cent interest. Taxes bore heavily on him, as the residents of his community seeking better schools and roads raised his assessments on tangibles that could not be hidden. Poor crops or low prices or, worse still, a combination of both might so reduce his income as to make it impossible for him to meet his obligations. One bad year he could take, perhaps two, but a larger combination of bad years was disastrous. The late seventies marked the final defeat of a number of large farm operators, and this was the result of poor prices, unfavorable weather, high interest rates, and perhaps poor management.

This chapter may have indicated that society on the frontier and in areas a generation beyond the frontier stage was more complex, had a wider range of economic well-being, than Frederick Jackson Turner thought. The early appearance of farm laborers and tenants, many of whom were never to rise to farm-ownership status, and of great landed estates, whose owners brought wealth

with them and added much to it, did not make for a "fundamental
unity in its [frontier's] social structure and its democratic ideals.
. . ." Concepts of the homogeneity of frontier society, similarity of frontier outlook, common addiction to democratic principles, may well be questioned.

Ante-bellum Democratic senators of the Upper Mississippi Valley appeared to be more concerned with their own land speculation schemes or the welfare of fur, lumber, mining, and railroad
companies than with the fortunes of their farmer constituents;
and they did little to loosen the reactionary control southern slave
owners had over their party. The land-owning aristocracy early
moved into politics via the Whig and Republican parties and
fought as vigorously for privilege as did eastern conservatives. It
was a combination of prairie landlords—Isaac Funk, Jesse Fell,
Asahel Gridley, and David Davis—who had an important share in
bringing the Republican nomination to Lincoln in 1860. Their activities contributed to fasten protection, the gold standard, land
subsidies to railroads, and an incongruous land system upon the
country. When the Democratic party in the Middle West recov-
ered from its debacle, it was in the hands of Bourbons no more
liberal in their outlook than the Republican officeholders they
sought to displace.

The appearance of the Greenback and Populist parties seemed
for a time to offer promise of effective agrarian leadership, but a
combination of upper-class landowning families that directed the
Greenback and Granger parties and a will-of-the-wisp search for
a magic commodity price formula by the Populist party offered
no aid to the farm laborer searching for a route to ownership or
to tenants struggling to retain their step on the ownership ladder.
While western newspapers were bewailing the fate of Irish tenants, they gave no heed to the emergence of the tenant class at
home whose rights were less secure, whose plight as serious. The
landlords and successful farmers were in the saddle politically,
and though they might erupt in condemnation of financial lords
of the East, railroad magnates, or tariff-minded manufacturers,
they did nothing to assure fixity of tenure, fair rent and compensation for improvements to tenants; in Illinois they joined together to beat down levels of wages paid to farm workers.[26]

At the close of the nineteenth century the agricultural laborers

and tenants outnumbered full owner-operators of farms in five of
the states we have studied, and in all the Upper Mississippi Valley
the numbers of farm laborers and tenants were fast growing.
Agrarian reform movements offered nothing to improve their lot.
It was not until the twentieth century that the status of the tenant
was substantially bettered with his gradual accumulation of livestock, equipment, and investment in improvements, which has
made him a substantial farmer with an equity worth thousands of
dollars.

Notes

1. Arthur Moore, *The Farmer and Rest of Us* (Boston: 1945), p. 131.
2. Information on the use of migratory laborers is meager, but the *Daven-port Gazette* (Iowa), published in an important river port, is helpful in its
issue of July 13 to 18, 1868. Daily mention is made of the demand for farm
hands, for which as much as $3 and $4 per day was being paid. A stampede
of city workers was reported which so depleted the community that construction projects could not be carried on. On the 18th, the steamer Dubuque
was reported as bringing in 75 field hands, who within thirty minutes after
arrival were engaged at $3.50 to $3.75 a day. Later reports of the movement
north of wheat harvesters indicate that migratory labor was a major feature
of agriculture in Illinois, Iowa, Wisconsin, and Minnesota.
3. The original census schedules of Iowa and Wisconsin are in the Iowa
Historical and Art Department, Des Moines, and the State Historical Society
of Wisconsin, Madison, where they were used for this chapter.
4. For his study of the land speculation of Charles Augustus Murray, who
bought 20,000 acres in Grant and LaFayette counties, Wisconsin, in 1836,
Dr. Schafer used the conveyance records at the county seats to determine
when the various parcels of land were sold and at what prices. He concluded
that Murray had not done as well as if the money had been invested in gilt-
edge securities. Since leases ordinarily were not recorded, he had no way of
knowing whether any of the land had been rented or what income might
have come from rents. In regard to farm tenancy in 1880, these two counties
ranked close to the top among Wisconsin counties. The state figure for 1880
is 9 per cent; figures for Grant and LaFayette are 14 and 18 per cent. For
Schafer's treatment see his *The Wisconsin Lead Region* (Madison: 1932),
pp. 148–154.
5. Notices of Wisconsin farms for rent in the fifties were found in the
Janesville Gazette, the Janesville *Democratic Standard*, the Baraboo *Sauk
County Standard*, and the *Eau Claire Free Press*. The papers of Catlin and
Williamson, Cyrus Woodman, and J. Richardson & Co. in the Wisconsin
State Historical Society and of Allen Hamilton and George W. Ewing in
the Indiana State Library are useful.
6. Solon J. Buck, *Pioneer Letters of Gershom Flagg* (Springfield, Ill.:
1912), pp. 22–46; *Indiana Oracle and Dearborn Gazette* (Lawrence, Ind.),

October 4, 1823. Nicholas Longworth had 27 tenants on his farms near Cincinnati in 1850. Ophia D. Smith, *The Life and Times of Giles Richards, 1820–1860*, "Ohio Historical Collections," Vol. VI (Columbus: 1936), p. 45.

7. Paul W. Gates, *Frontier Landlords and Pioneer Tenants* (Ithaca: 1945), p. 3.

8. Herbert A. Kellar, ed., *Solon Robinson, Pioneer and Agriculturist*, "Indiana Historical Collections," Vol. XXI (Indianapolis; 1936), I, p. 351.

9. Letter of J. W. Schreyer, June 22, 1946, in *Indiana Magazine of History*, XL (September 1944), 294; Anon., *A True Picture of Emigration: Of Fourteen Years in the Interior of North America* (London: 1838), p. 60; Florence E. Janson, *The Background of Swedish Immigration, 1840–1930* (Chicago, 1931), pp. 141–142; Harvey L. Carter, "Rural Indiana in Transition, 1850–1860," *Agricultural History*, XX (April 1946), p. 114; La Salle, Illinois, *Independent*, March 4, 1854; G. C. Beman, Croton, Lee Co., Iowa, January 12, 1853, to D. Kilbourne (Kilbourne Mss. in the Iowa Historical and Art Department); *Davenport Gazette* (Iowa), January 29, November 25, 1852; October 6, 1853; March 26, May 5, 1858; *Sioux City Register* (Iowa), March 17, 1860, and March 15, 1862.

10. *Brevier Legislative Reports*, 1852, 1857, 1859, 1861, 1865, 1881; *Laws of Indiana General Assembly*, 1881, p. 565; *Indianapolis State Sentinel*, January 14 and 23, 1857; *Monticello Herald*, April 1, 1875.

11. Peter Daggy, Land Department, Illinois Central Railroad, November 30, 1865, to C. E. Perkins; J. M. King, Clarinda, Iowa, June 21, 1865, to Perkins; J. D. McFarland, Lincoln, Nebraska, November 25, 1868, to A. E. Touzalin; W. W. Baldwin, Land Commissioner, Burlington and Missouri, August 23, 1879, to R. A. Crippen, Burlington Archives, Newberry Library. The correspondence of Edward Hayes of Oak, T. S. Goddard of Hastings, R. A. Crippen of Corning, Iowa, land agents of the B & M, contains allusions to numerous instances of the railroad's leasing to tenants on a cash or share-rent basis.

12. To arrive at these percentages I added the number of tenant farms (presumably farmed each by one tenant) to the number of farm laborers and computed what percentage that total was of the number of people engaged in agriculture. The figures are from the *Tenth Census, Agriculture* (Washington: 1883), *passim*.

13. *Guide to the Lands of the Northern Pacific Railroad in Minnesota* (New York: 1872), p. 22; Arthur F. Bentley, *The Condition of the Western Farmer as Illustrated by the Economic History of a Nebraska Township*, "Johns Hopkins University Studies in Historical and Political Science," Eleventh Series, No. 7 (July 1893), 28; Clarence H. Danhof, "Farm Making Costs and the 'Safety Valve': 1850–1860," *Journal of Political Economy*, XLVI (June 1941), 317ff.; Paul W. Gates, *Fifty Million Acres: Conflicts Over Kansas Land Policy, 1854–1890* (Ithaca: 1954), p. 223.

14. Paul S. Taylor, "The American Hired Man: His Rise and Decline," *Land Policy Review*, VI (Spring 1943), 3–17; LaWanda F. Cox, "The American Agricultural Wage Earner, 1865–1900: The Emergence of a Modern Labor Problem," *Agricultural History*, XXII (April 1949), 94–114.

15. Harold E. Briggs, *Frontiers of the Northwest* (New York: 1940), p. 509–522; and Fred A. Shannon, *The Farmer's Last Frontier, Agriculture, 1860–1897*, in David, Faulkner, Hacker *et al.*, eds., *The Economic History of the United States*, Vol. V (New York: 1945), pp. 154–161.

16. In Illinois alone a compiler found in 1892 the following "millionaires"

whose wealth was largely made in farm lands: Matthew T. Scott, Orlando Powers, L. B. Casner, Estate of John Shaw Hayward, John C. Proctor, George Pasfield, Horatio M. Vandeveer, William H. Ennis, W. H. Bradley. In Missouri the outstanding millionaire landowners were David Rankin and five heirs of Milton Tootle; in Nebraska, Stephen Miles; in Minnesota, J. A. Willard and A. H. Wilder; in Indiana, William H. English and the Estate of Moses Fowler. Other identifiable millionaires in these states added materially to their wealth through farming operations and land improvement.. *American Millionaires. The Tribune's List of Persons Reputed to be Worth a Million or More* (June 1892), reprinted in Sidney Ratner, *New Light on the History of Great American Fortunes. American Millionaires of 1892 and 1902* (New York: 1953).

17. Gates, *Frontier Landlords and Pioneer Tenants, passim.;* "Hoosier Cattle Kings in the Prairies," *Indiana Magazine of History*, XLIV (March 1948), 1–24; "Cattle Kings in the Prairies," *Mississippi Valley Historical Review*, XXXV (December 1948), 379–412.

18. The Census of 1880 shows 2,916 farms in excess of a thousand acres in the ten states of the Upper Mississippi Valley.

19. *New York Tribune*, July 30, 1861, and August 11, 1861; C. H. Moore to Dr. John Warner, July 21, 1862, Moore-Warner Mss., Clinton, Ill.; *Country Gentleman*, March 10 and May 5, 1864; July 1865.

20. *Columbus State Journal* (Ohio) in *Davenport Gazette* (Iowa), August 12, 1855; 1 Miscellaneous Record, p. 434, Logan County Recorder's Office, Lincoln, Ill.; James MacDonald, *Food from the Far West* (London: 1878), pp. 142–148; Appendix, "Agricultural Interests Commission, Reports of the Assistant Commissioner" (London: 1880), *Parliamentary Papers*, 1880, XVIII, 18, 38–39; *Bloomington Bulletin* (Illinois), March 4, 1887. On the Fowler lands in Indiana, in return for breaking land and putting it in corn, tenants were paid 25¢ a bushel for the corn they raised in the first five crop years (*Benton Review*, June 11, 1885).

21. *Sioux City Register*, January 12, 1861; Margaret Ruth Beattie, "Matthew Scott, Pioneer Landlord–Gentleman Farmer, 1855–1891" (Thesis, Cornell University Library, 1947), pp. 58ff.; Jacob Van Der Zee, *The British in Iowa* (Iowa City: 1922), pp. 57ff.

22. The *Champaign Gazette* (Illinois), clipped in the *Bloomington Pantagraph* (Illinois), January 23, 1879, reported "The demand for farms to rent far exceeds the supply, and men are compelled to seek other localities to get places." Monticello, Indiana, *Prairie Chieftain*, November 4, 1852; *Bloomington Pantagraph*, February 8, 1854, and November 5, 1856; Watseka, Illinois, *Iroquois County Times*, October 21, 1875; *Malvern Leader* (Iowa), February 8, 1883; February 26 and March 5, 1885.

23. Chester McArthur Destler, "Agricultural Readjustment and Agrarian Unrest in Illinois, 1880–1893," *Agricultural History*, XXI (April 1947), 104–116; Gates, *Fifty Million Acres*, pp. 244ff.

24. George Ade, "Prairie Kings of Yesterday," *Saturday Evening Post*, July 4, 1931, p. 14.

25. *Census of 1900, Agriculture*, Part I, p. lxxxviii; Howard A. Turner, *The Ownership of Tenant Farms in the North Central States*, United States Department of Agriculture *Bulletin*, No. 1433 (September 1926), 10.

26. A Farmers' Union meeting in Mason County, Illinois, in 1885 resolved "not to exceed fifteen dollars per month, by the year, for the best farm labor, . . . that for the limit of six months, the limit of wages be eighteen dollars

per month . . . that we pay no more than $1.50 per day for driving header wagon in harvest; $1.50 per day for labor in haying, and from 50¢ to $1.00 for common labor, to be regulated by time and circumstances" (*Mason County Democrat*, January 16 and February 6 and 20, 1885).

Stanley Elkins and Eric McKitrick

A MEANING FOR TURNER'S FRONTIER: DEMOCRACY IN THE OLD NORTHWEST

I

It would be difficult today to revive the sense of intellectual ardor with which Frederick Jackson Turner's paper on the American frontier was greeted so soon after its first inauspicious reading.[1] So full of promise did the remarkable theory then appear, so charged with import, that its present status as an academic curiosity seems to symbolize some profound intervening disillusionment. A crucial motif of American spiritual experience seemed at one time to have found its fittest expression in Turner's inspired essay, and with his ceremonial "closing" of our frontier in 1893 a generation of publicists began finding the terms, products of convictions already deeply felt, whereby great stretches of American history might at last be given meaning. Persistent echoes of these convictions are heard even today.[2] And yet by now nearly every attempt to impose conceptual structure upon the lyricism of Turner and his followers has been abandoned. Intuition and cool reason appear to have succeeded in baffling each other.

It needs little prompting to recall the "frontier thesis," with its message that the presence of cheap land and an ever-receding frontier "explain" American development; its arguments, indeed, could be assorted under three rough headings. Turner's first claim

Stanley Elkins is Professor of History at Smith College and the author of *Slavery: A Problem in American Institutional and Intellectual Life*. Eric McKitrick is Professor of History at Columbia University and the author of *Andrew Johnson and Reconstruction*. The authors have collaborated on a series of interpretive articles on major phases of American history.
Reprinted from *Political Science Quarterly*, LXIX, No. 3 (September 1954), 321–353, by permission of the authors and the publishers.

for American culture was one of "uniqueness"; in mutiny against the Johns Hopkins "germ theorists" of the 1880's and their genealogical accounts of American political institutions traced back to England, back even to the gloomy forests of central Europe, Turner felt that these institutions and their character were to be accounted for most plausibly in terms purely American. Next, he produced a metaphor: the open frontier with its easily available land was a "safety valve" for underprivileged easterners, its promise serving as a minimizer of urban unrest. The third claim, an extension of the first, was a report, again metaphoric, of the origins of true democracy. As settlers pushed out beyond the mountains, ties with the East and with Europe were steadily weakened, ancestral memories grew dim, and a "shearing-off" process took place: "layers" of civilization were removed until the pioneer stood in native worth, self-reliant, individualistic, a democrat of Jacksonian model. "American democracy was born of no theorist's dream; it was not carried in the *Susan Constant* to Virginia nor in the *Mayflower* to Plymouth. It came out of the American forest, and it gained new strength each time it touched a new frontier." [3]

A new phalanx of critics has now demolished the Turner conception. His vagueness, his abstraction, his hopeless imprecision, his poverty of concrete example, have each been held up to the scientific eye. Turner, in all but ignoring the English origins of our institutions, gains nothing but misunderstanding by his "ungracious exclusion of Locke and Milton." [4] The "safety valve," moveover, is at best a misleading poetic figure. How could the eastern worker, poverty-stricken and ignorant of agriculture, think seriously of so staggering a project as removing to the West? The new western farmer was most typically a recent eastern farmer who had emigrated with at least a little money in his pocket, and the cities themselves, ironically indeed, eventually came to serve as safety valves for all farmers embittered with the agrarian life. But the deadliest criticisms of all are reserved for the Turneresque vision of the frontier's role in the birth of American democracy. Turner's state of nature, his shearing-off of civilized corruption, hints at a pastoral anarchy neither realized nor remotely desired by the bands of settlers in their wilderness outposts. The first efforts of these pioneers were to set up and to stabilize those very political institutions, parallel in as many ways as might be, which they had left behind them in the East. A kind of primitive geopolitics is brusquely challenged by a riddle which Turner could not have answered: why the *American* forest— why didn't democracy come out of other "forests"—why not the Siberian frontier? [5] The few remaining defenders of Frederick Jackson Turner have been able to produce very little in the way of rejoinder.

And yet, though conviction now burns so low, it remains to be noted that even the unkindest of Turner's critics have conceded, with a kind of bedeviled monotony, that *some* relation most likely does exist between our history and our frontier. The fact thus stands that, in this direction at least, no advance has yet been made beyond Turner's own dazzling abstraction. The problem is still there, its vitality unextinguished. It is no further resolved than ever.

If we examine with suspicion the body of critical work, we discover an interesting paradox. Turner and his teachings have been approached with deadly seriousness on their own terms—no other—and handled with what turns out to be *textual* criticism: a method which is illuminating but whose value for the analysis and correction of theoretical material is acutely limited.[6] The result has been to demonstrate the absurdities of Turner's internal logic —which is an undoubted contribution to perspective. Yet it should still be recognized that no concrete attempt to restate Turner's idea has ever actually been undertaken. Now might there not, after all, be a way of rescuing Turner? Is it possible to ask the great question itself in a form permitting a concrete answer?

Turner's critics may be allowed the most sweeping of concessions. Nearly everything[7] could be sacrificed—everything, that is, except the one thing that matters: the development of political democracy as a habit and the American as a unique political creature. This was the supreme fact which overwhelmed Tocqueville in the 1830's; every American still knows in his heart that the frontier had something to do with it. "What?" is, of course, the crucial question. It has always been difficult to ask it, if only because it has never seemed very important to discover a working, functional definition of "political democracy." "Democracy" is alluded to, invoked, celebrated, its collapse predicted daily. Democracy, in our traditions, has rich connections with the yeoman farmer (involving, as it were, "grass roots" and freedom from the urban banker); it is at once individualistic and co-operative, equalitarian and fraternal; hand in hand with stout self-reliance goes the civic exercise of universal suffrage. For most of our daily purposes democracy is a synonym for all that is virtuous in our social traditions and on the public scene.

Yet it still appears that we need a *working* definition of political democracy. It should in some way account for concepts central to most traditional notions, but it should also be functional, in the sense that its terms may be tested. Its focus should undoubtedly be upon participation—participation by large numbers of people in decisions which affect their lives. But it should be real, not ceremonial, participation. The extent of the suffrage would not be its most dependable measure, any more than the casting of one man's vote is the quickest way of influencing a political decision. Awareness of the community's affairs should have something to do with it, but only to the extent that individuals themselves feel capable of interfering in those affairs. Would this be to the community's best interest? Often, but not always; yet here we are not required to think of democracy as a community virtue. Some have, indeed, called it a national vice.

Suppose that political democracy be regarded as a manipulative attitude toward government, shared by large numbers of people. Let it be thought of as a wide participation in public affairs, a diffusion of leadership, a widespread sense of personal competence to make a difference. Under what conditions have such things typically occurred? When have the energies of the people been most engaged? What pushes a man into public activity? It appears that nothing accomplishes this more quickly than the formation of a settlement.

Our national experience, indeed, furnishes us much material for a hypothesis. Political democracy evolves most quickly during the initial stages of setting up a new community; it is seen most dramatically while the process of organization and the solving of basic problems are still crucial; it is observed to best advantage when this flow of basic problems is met by a homogeneous population. Now "homogeneity" should here involve two parallel sorts of facts: not only a similar level of social and economic status and

aspirations among the people, but most particularly a lack of, or
failure of, a traditional, ready-made structure of leadership in the
community. A simple test of the effectiveness of structured leadership is its ability to command acceptance and respect.[8]

With a heavy flow of community problems, in short, and without such a structure of natural leadership, democracy presents itself much less as a bright possibility than as a brutal necessity. The
very incomprehensibility of alternatives has always made it most
unlikely that an American should see this. But Tocqueville saw it
instantly. "In aristocratic societies," he wrote, "men do not need
to combine in order to act, because they are strongly held together."

. . . Among democratic nations, on the contrary, all the citizens are
independent and feeble; they can hardly do anything by themselves
and none of them can oblige his fellow men to lend him their assistance. They all, therefore, fall into a state of incapacity, if they do not
learn voluntarily to help each other.[9]

Before turning to history for a trial of this so simple yet interesting idea, let us set it in yet another dimension by examining a
series of extremely important findings in contemporary sociology. Robert K. Merton has conducted a study of social behavior
in public housing communities.[10] A theory of political democracy
which would meet all our criteria may be derived from Mr. Merton's work; there is little that we shall say from a historical view-
point which has not already, in a present-day setting, been thoroughly documented by him.

He and his associates have observed two public housing projects, one being designated as "Craftown" and the other as "Hilltown." Craftown, located in southern New Jersey, administered
by the Federal Public Housing Authority, and set up originally to
house warworkers, was much the more active and interesting of
the two. The key to the activity there was a "time of troubles" in
the initial stages of the community's existence. The people who
settled in Craftown ("homogeneous" in the sense that a majority
were employed in near-by shipyards and defense plants) were immediately faced by a staggering series of problems of a fundamental sort, affecting the entire community. These bore on law and
order, government, public health, housing, education, religion,

municipal services, transportation, and markets. Slovenly construction had resulted in leaky roofs, flooded cellars, and warped floors. There were no schools, no churches, no electricity, no community hall, no grocery stores. Bus service was irregular and the nearest depot was a mile away. There were no hard-surfaced roads or sidewalks and much of the area was flooded during the rainy season. There was a wave of vandalism and no organization for its suppression. There was an epidemic of poliomyelitis. There were no municipal services of any kind; the environing township did not want to assume the cost of such services and by legislative action Craftown was gerrymandered into an independent township—which meant that it had to set up its own institutions for government and for the maintenance of law and order.

Craftown did have a ready-made structure, as it were, of leadership; its affairs were under the administration of a federal bureau, the Federal Public Housing Authority, and handled by a resident manager and staff. Under stable conditions such a structure would have been adequate for most of the community's basic concerns. Yet the problems in Craftown were so overwhelming, so immediate, so pressing, that the residents could not afford to wait upon the government for action. They were therefore forced to behave in that same pattern which so fascinated Tocqueville: they were driven to "the forming of associations." Mass meetings, committees and subcommittees were organized, a township board was set up, officials of great variety were elected; a volunteer police force, fire department, and local court were established, with residents serving as constables, firemen, and judges. A co-operative store soon came into existence. An ambulance squad, a nursery and child care center, and a great variety of organizations devoted to community needs made their appearance during this critical period. Pressures brought upon the bus company and the government agencies resulted in the improvement of transportation, the paving of streets, repair of houses, drainage of swamps, and the erection of buildings for education, worship, and other functions of the community.

This experience resulted in an extraordinary level of public participation by people who for the most part had never had previous political experience; and it produced a political life charged with the utmost energy. Many jobs were created by the crisis—

by the flow of problems—and they had to be handled by someone; many roles were created, someone had to fill them. The key was necessity. Persons who had previously never needed to be concerned with politics[11] now found themselves developing a familiarity with institutions, acquiring a sense of personal competence to manipulate them, to make things happen, to make a difference. Thus the coin of necessity had its other side: there were compensations for the individual. With many offices to be filled, large numbers of people found themselves contending for them; the prestige connected with officeholding, the sense of energy and power involved in decision-making, became for the first time a possibility, a reality, an exploitable form of self-expression.[12]

Now Hilltown, in contrast to Craftown, may be regarded as something of a control case. Many factors present in Craftown were present here—but a crucial one was missing. Hilltown, like Craftown, was a public housing project in an industrial area; it too was managed by the Federal Public Housing Authority; its population was likewise characterized by "homogeneity"—insofar as that involved a similar level of social and economic status among the residents. What Hilltown did not experience was a "time of troubles." Unlike Craftown, it was well planned and operated; it was not faced with a failure of municipal services; it was not confronted by lack of transportation, stores, electricity, or facilities for education and religion. The residents, to be sure, had their individual problems—occasional badly fitting doors and the like—but they were not of a community nature, not of a sort that made community organization seem indispensable. Widespread public participation in community affairs was never needed there, and it never took place. Sporadic efforts toward the establishment of a council, the election of officers, and the setting up of community activities aroused little interest and met with failure. The original structure of leadership—the federal agency and its local office—proved quite adequate for the handling of Hilltown's concerns, it was never seriously challenged, and it required no supplementation by resident activity.[13] "Democracy," in short, was unnecessary there.

One more reference to the Craftown episode should be made, in order to note two interesting subsidiary consequences of this problem-solving experience, this wide participation, this sense of individual competence spread among such great numbers. One was a close supervision of the officialdom which the Craftowners themselves had created—and a lesser degree of respect for it[14] than had apparently been the case in their previous communities. The other was a body of shared "traditions," with a common vocabulary, rich with meaning, whereby the experience might be relived and reshared. Although the level of activity was never as high in later times as it was in the beginning—the problems by then had been solved—the intensity of the "time of troubles" served to link the "pioneers" and the later-comers together by a kind of verbal bond. Talking about it was important: once this experience had been undergone, it was not lost. In such a usable fund of tradition, resources for meeting a new crisis, should one appear, would remain always available.[15]

How might such a model square with the pioneer frontier? No sorcery of forest or prairie could materialize the democrat, yet it should be safe to guess that the periods of wholesale migration to the West forced a setting in which such an experience as that just outlined had to be enacted a thousand times over: an experience crucial in the careers of millions of Americans. Frederick Jackson Turner has stated the undeniable fact—that an organic connection exists between American democracy and the American frontier. The insight is his. But Turner never offered a conceptual framework by which it might be tested. We are proposing such a model; it involves the establishment of new communities. Its variables are a period of problem-solving and a homogeneous population whose key factor is the lack of a structure of leadership. We shall test these terms in various ways by the examination of three frontiers, each of which should illustrate a special dimension of the argument. They are the Old Northwest, the Southwest frontier of Alabama and Mississippi, and the Puritan frontier of Massachusetts Bay.

II

"The frontier," to Turner and his followers, as well as to most others, seemed almost automatically to mean the Old Northwest

—the "valley of democracy"—whose settlement took place during the first third of the nineteenth century. To discover why the
connection should be made so naturally, let us select this region,
with its key states Ohio, Indiana, and Illinois, as the first frontier
to be observed.

The chronicles of these states abound with reminiscences of the
pioneer; close upon them in the county histories came haphazard
statistics which proudly mark progress from howling wilderness
to fat countryside and prosperous burgs. Between these points
come many a crisis, many a relished success. We should consider
not the solitary drifters, the Daniel Boones, but the thousand isolated communities each of which in its own way must have
undergone its "time of troubles." There, the basic problems of
organization were intimately connected with matters of life and
death. They were problems to be met only by the united forces
of the community. Think of the basic question of housing itself,
and how its solution was elevated by necessity, throughout the
Old Northwest, to the status of institution and legend: the cabin-
raising.[16] The clearing of the forest and the manner in which this
was accomplished gave an idiom to our politics: the logrolling.[17]
Defense against the Indians required that the experience of the
Marietta settlers, forced to raise their own militia in the 1790's, be
repeated elsewhere many times over at least until after the War of
1812.[18] And there was the question of law and order: the traveler
Elias Fordham, stopping one night in 1818 at a cabin near Paoli,
Indiana, found himself in the midst of preparations by the citizenry for apprehending a gang of brigands. How often must such
a scene—the formation of *ad hoc* constabularies, the administration of emergency justice—have been enacted in those days? [19]

Close behind such supreme needs came that of educating the
young, which claimed an early order of concern throughout the
Northwest. Traveling instructors were often employed to go
from house to house; later, when the children could pass through
the forest without danger, they might gather for a time at one of
the settlers' houses until community labor could be assembled to
put up a school.[20] The demand for religion was little less urgent;
first came the circuit rider to a house or barn designated for worship; denominational differences might then have to be submerged

in the erection of a common chapel until each sect could build its own meeting house.[21] Even problems of public health, with no hospitals and few doctors, had to be solved occasionally under heroic circumstances. When cholera struck Jacksonville, Illinois, in 1833, the cabinetmaker John Henry boarded thirteen persons at his house for three weeks, supervised a crew of assistants in the building of coffins for each of the fifty-five dead, personally visited each house of sickness, took fifty-three corpses to the burying ground, and, assisted by two farmers, a blacksmith, a shoemaker, a brickmaker and a carpenter, dug the graves and interred the dead—a series of functions quite above the line of normal business.[22]

Now as these communities toiled through the process of stabilizing their affairs, what effect must such an experience have had upon the individuals themselves, exposed as they were to the sudden necessity of making great numbers of basic and vital decisions, private and public? With thousands of ambitious men, predominantly young men[23] looking for careers, pouring into vast unsettled tracts, setting up new communities, and being met with all the complex hazards of such an adventure, the scope and variety of new political experience was surely tremendous. A staggering number of public roles was thrust forward during such an enterprise, far too many to wait upon the appearance of seasoned leaders. With the organization of each wilderness county and pioneer township, the roster of offices to be filled and operated was naturally a perfect blank (how long had it been since this was so in Philadelphia?); somebody, willing or unwilling, must be found to fill each one.

Whether farmers, lawyers, merchants, artisans, or even men of means, the "leading citizens" in county after county were typically men of no previous political experience.[24] For example, there was Morgan County, Illinois. Its first settler was Seymour Kellogg, who brought his wife and seven children from New York State, was made a commissioner at the first election, and shortly afterward became justice of the peace. Murray McConnel, who read law on his farm at odd hours and became Jacksonville's first lawyer, was forthwith sent to the legislature (though unwillingly) and later served the community in various other capacities.

Jacksonville's first cabinetmaker, the aforementioned John Henry (scarcely literate), was drawn into politics immediately, and before his career was over had been an assemblyman, state senator, and member of Congress, not to say superintendent of the local insane asylum and patron of learning to the Female Academy. The first printer there was Josiah Lucas, who had arrived from Maryland ("without friends") and established a paper with local support. Championing Henry Clay, he was shortly in a maelstrom of politics, and the experience thus gained netted him a postmastership to the House of Representatives and "many offices both civil and military," culminating in a minister's post in Europe.[25] Variations on this typical pattern are to be found in county after county in the Old Northwest.[26]

What we exhibit here are the elements of a simple syllogism; the first settlers anywhere, no matter who they were or how scanty their prior political experience, were the men who had to be the first officeholders. This meant that the pioneers, in the very process of establishing and organizing their settlements, were faced with a burden of decision-making disproportionate to that exacted of the later-comers. The political lore, the manipulative skills, which must have been acquired in that process should somehow be kept in the foreground when judging the ferocious vitality, the extravagant energy, of early political life in the Old Northwest.

Inasmuch as many new political roles were being created by the needs of this new society, both necessity and opportunities for political careers might more and more be seen reflected in the long lists of candidates and high level of participation. In Hamilton County, Ohio, there was an election of delegates to the constitutional convention of 1802, and for ten openings there were ninety-four candidates—twenty-six of them receiving from 121 to 1,635 votes apiece.[27] The personal canvass, the practice of hawking one's political appeal from door to door, not generally assumed to have entered American politics until the Jacksonian era, was familiar in the Northwest well before 1824. A cabin-dweller's effusion in the *Illinois Intelligencer* of July 1, 1818, describes how hosts of candidates, at the approach of an election, would descend upon him with whisky, trinkets for the children, compliments, and grand promises.

> But what most rarely does my good wife please,
> Is that the snot nos'd baby gets a buss! [28]

"And every body," wrote Baynard Rush Hall of Indiana's New Purchase, "expected at some time to be a candidate for something; or that his uncle would be; or his cousin, or his cousin's wife's cousin's friend would be; so that every body and every body's relations, and every body's relation's friends, were for ever electioneering." Even boys verging on manhood were "feared, petted, courted and cajoled." [29] Such arts of cajolery could be appropriate and necessary only to a society in which officials were watched far more closely and respected far less than was the magistrate of Boston or the justice of the peace in Fairfax County, Virginia. Hall, an easterner of refinement, reflected with deep distaste that if "eternal vigilance" were the price of liberty it was well paid in the New Purchase, the "sovereign people" there being "the most uncompromising task masters": "Our officers all, from Governor down to a deputy constable's deputy and fence-viewer's clerk's first assistant, were in the direct gift of the people. We even elected magistrates, clerks of court, and the judges presiding and associate!" [30]

Thus the extraordinary animation with which the people of Craftown flung themselves into political activity may be seen richly paralleled in the life of the Old Northwest. Every militia muster, every cabin-raising, scow-launching, shooting match, and logrolling was in itself a political assembly where leading figures of the neighborhood made speeches, read certificates, and contended for votes. Sometimes at logrollings rival candidates would take charge of opposing sections of workers, fitness for office having much to do with whose group disposed of its logs first. The enterprising farmer understood, it is said, that this political energy could be exploited at its height about a month before election time, and tried to schedule his logrolling accordingly.[31]

Our concept of political democracy, it may be remembered, involved a homogeneous population. Can it be asserted that these early Northwest communities were characterized by such a population? There is striking evidence that both attributes of "homogeneity"—a similar level of aspiration and status, and conditions rendering impossible a prior structure of leadership—were widely present here, just as they were in Craftown. A leading symptom of this may be found in the land arrangements. Beverly Bond has made calculations, based on lists of lands advertised for delinquent taxes, as to typical holdings in the Northwest about 1812, and concludes that the "average farm" at that time was probably less than 250 acres.[32] Though such tentative statistics are embarrassing in themselves, the limiting conditions which make them plausible are clear enough—uniform conditions not only permitting but forcing a reduced scale of holdings. Much has been made of large engrossments of land by speculators in the Northwest Territory, yet before the admission of Ohio in 1803, and many years before that of Indiana and Illinois, it was apparent to all that the day of the great land magnate was at an end. His operations were doomed by the very techniques of settlement and by the measures taken by the settlers themselves to thwart his designs.

Despite large quantities of government land on the market, much of which was bought by speculators, the attraction of choice locations led regularly to settlement in advance of purchase—squatting, in short—especially when sales were delayed, as they often were. Thousands of such petty *faits accomplis* all over the Northwest frontier could hardly be reversed,[33] no matter how powerful the petitioners, and the terms of sale, reflected in a series of land laws ever more generous,[34] were but one indication of such a state of things. An even more formidable token of doom to the great absentee holder was revealed in the tax rates levied on unimproved land by the early legislatures. While all these future states were still under one territorial assembly, that body at its first session passed a law taxing three grades of land—a law which was only the first of several, each more severe than its predecessor, consecrated to the mission of breaking up large unimproved tracts held by nonresidents. Increasing powers were given to local sheriffs presiding over the sales of delinquent holdings.[35] This meant that in practice the large speculator, forced as he was to pay cash for these tracts, must effect relatively quick turnovers in a buyer's market: there was really plenty of land to be had and the costs of holding it for a rise were becoming higher year by year.[36] For the rest, with labor costs uniformly high and with a population whose average resources, either in land or in liquid wealth, must initially be moderate, the great farm on the southern model could never be a widespread reality. What this particularly indicates is that a land-holding élite—with all the traditional functions, social and political, that such an élite would certainly exercise—was rendered quite out of the question. The leadership of *this* society would have to be recruited on manifestly different terms.

Who was it, then, that organized the pressure for these land acts; who goaded the federal Congress into passing them; who connived in the legislature; who wrote the tax laws? Who indeed but the frontier politician who kissed the "snot nos'd baby" in that lonely cabin? He well understood how his majorities depended upon the zeal with which he and his friends could manipulate the government on their constituents' behalf. Their problems were concrete; the guaranteeing of pre-emption rights was an urgency of the topmost order; this was the primary stimulus which forced the tax laws, the universal suffrage clauses in the state constitutions, and the Congressional land legislation. The "sovereign people" of the Old Northwest was a "most uncompromising task master" to its servants. Symbolic of the future was the case of William Henry Harrison, to whom fell the unhappy office of mediating, so to speak, between "the people" and the Northwest's greatest land speculator, John Cleves Symmes. Harrison, as territorial delegate to Congress, was successful in bringing about the Land Act of 1800 in the interests of the settlers but a dismal failure in his efforts to get justice for Symmes, his father-in-law, whose vast holdings in Ohio were crumbling away in an avalanche of claims and judgments. The unfortunate Symmes was no match for a thousand ruthless frontier manipulators.[37] The democracy of the Northwest would be that of the squatter, the frontier business man, and, no doubt, that of the *small* speculator.

Granted that a structure of *landed* political leadership was impossible, might not a different species of élite appear, say an élite of lawyers? It is true that admission to the bar in the early days was a virtual guarantee of political advancement. But the stability of any such structure must be certified by some recognized assurance of self-perpetuation. The very recruitment patterns, the conditions under which political preferment had to be gained and held in the Northwest, should make us think twice before considering the great majority of lawyers in politics there as constituting such a structure. Every lawyer was literally on his own. It was the desperate need for wits and talent on the frontier that gave him his chance, a chance renewed by the community as long as he continued to deliver. Here the roles of patron and client are reversed; it is difficult for a "ruling class" to establish and guarantee tenure under such conditions. Murray McConnel, the self-made lawyer of Jacksonville, was once warned that his politically ambitious young clerk—Stephen Douglas—was using him as a stepping-stone. "No matter," he replied, "his ambition will probably prove of more worth to the nation than all our modesty." [38] This was about the only kind of laying on of hands possible in the Northwest: the embodiment of success, of frontier virtue, was the self-made man.

What we have done so far is to discover a kind of "primitive" level of the frontier experience, a level at which a vast flow of problems forced a high degree of participation in the making of decisions, an acute pitch of political awareness among the settlers. The traditions of the pioneers remind us that this experience was not lost. An egalitarian tone was set, and ceremonial observances by which the experience was reinvoked and reshared made their way into the social habits of the people. Stephen Douglas, for one, understood its obligations, and by stopping at Geneva on one of his county canvasses to assist at a logrolling he was performing a symbolic act.[39]

Now another frontier was being developed at this same period in the Southwest, the frontier of Alabama and Mississippi, where scenes more or less similar were enacted. Yet we are unable to speak of "democracy" there with quite the same lack of ambiguity as we may with the Northwest. One reason for this is that throughout the Northwest the "problem-solving" experience did not generally stop with the taming of the savages and the establishment of law and order, but was continued, and indeed more or less perpetuated, on another level.

This second level of experience may be called that of town life. Let us remember that our focus has been fixed upon the *community* character of political democracy, involving a setting in which the people are close enough together to make common efforts possible, and a social texture thick enough to make it not only feasible but crucial to organize for a variety of objects. It is true enough that the basis of most such settlements was rural agriculture. But it is undoubtedly true as well that the ease with which the basic agrarian experience flowed into that of commercial small-urban enterprise was much greater and more natural in the Northwest than in the Southwest. The primitive, "agrarian" level of democracy is the one from which we have drawn democracy's folklore, a folklore still appropriate enough for our ceremonial. But it has been chronically difficult for our serious thought to go very far beyond it. The very vision of "grass roots democracy," with its herbivorous overtones, is itself a reproach to an urban culture to which it no longer seems to apply.[40]

Yet we should not feel that there is actually any paradox. Indeed, there are formidable reasons for concluding that the development of American small-town enterprise (and by extension, of urban capitalism) is most centrally—organically—connected with that of American political democracy.[41]

Watching the organization of the Old Northwest, county by county, we are struck by something which is not duplicated on our southern frontier: the appearance of teeming numbers of *small towns*. By this we mean, not the post-office hamlet with its fifty souls, but rather the market center which had two hundred or more people and was struggling to become bigger. It was a development quite automatic and logical in the Northwest. Cheap land and dear labor set fatal limits on wide-scale land engrossment for purposes other than speculation (and we have already seen the limits set on speculation), so that, for agriculture, subsistence and market farming, rather than extensive raising of staples, would largely be the rule in the thirties and forties. It was toward the town that an increasingly market-conscious population was orienting itself, not toward the plantation, nor to the cosmopolitan port city, nor yet to the crossroads courthouse. Large amounts of money, if and when made in the Northwest, had to come from commerce, from industrial activity, and from real estate whose value depended greatly on its nearness to or location in a town. It was unquestionably the town from which the tone of life in Ohio, Indiana, and Illinois came to be taken, rather than from the agriculture in which an undoubted majority of the population was engaged. It is no exaggeration to say that there were five to six times as many such towns per capita here as in Alabama or Mississippi.[42]

The town, becoming the natural focus of exchange for goods and services in the Northwest, must thus inexorably be the focus of politics as well; this fact on the very face of it would mean a faster tempo of political life than on the rural countryside. Things were less simple in the town; the organizational needs were more involved; there were more functions to perform, more offices to fill. But what was it that so energized the Northwest town, what sustained this tempo, what made its democracy *real?* It was the fact that every town was a promotion.

The bright young man of talent and enterprise in the Northwest—unlike his opposite number in Alabama—naturally gravitated to the town; it was there that his future lay; roles in politics or business were enacted from there rather than from rural strongholds. In the Northwest the typical success story of the young man with wits or money, or both, does not show him accumulating baronial acres for the cultivation of profitable staple crops. Instead, if it shows him buying up choice lands—and oftener than not it does—it is with quite different designs in view, designs centering on the development of town sites. It was estimated that during the boom years 1835, 1836, and 1837 over 500 new towns were laid out in Illinois alone.[43] The energetic Wesley Park, first settler at Auburn, Indiana, besides filling many local offices, besides using his cabin as hotel, jail, church, and courthouse, had as a matter of course personally platted the town. He had done so, as had all Northwest town planners, to increase the value of his real estate and future business prospects.[44] But there was an essential difference in type between this petty-urban speculator and the speculator who engrossed vast cotton lands and held them for a price rise. The distinction was between the monopolist and the promoter.[45]

It was the promotion which gave the tone to the entire life of the town, and most particularly to its politics, which meant that the placation and "cajolery" so displeasing to Baynard Rush Hall in the New Purchase would become, so to speak, universal in the town. Everyone understood that success must depend upon the town's prosperity, that it must be advertised, its virtues broadcast.

The town must grow—it was vital to get people there and keep them there. Capital must be attracted—it was of the essence to allure the man with money.

The result was, naturally, a torrent of problems centering in the advancement of business. It was important for the town to obtain for itself the location of the county seat. Here the promoter donated land and made large promises to the county commissioners; in Mississippi the commissioners typically had to *buy* the land for a courthouse site.[46] The population must be increased, for this meant automatic benefits, more customers; in the cotton country it might mean greater competition and a drop in cotton prices. Capital must be brought in; expansion of plant was easier and less risky in an Indiana town than it would be on an Alabama cotton plantation. The town must be made attractive; it must be a suitable place to live in; it must have stable government; lapses of law and order would be a reflection upon its peace. Schools and seminaries must be established. (No general public school system would exist in Alabama or Mississippi until after the Civil War. See Table 8–1 for a comparison of the two sections in 1840 with respect to primary and common schools.) Roads, bridges, canals,

TABLE 8–1 *

	ALA.	MISS.	OHIO	IND.	ILL.
Population	590,756	375,651	1,519,467	685,866	476,183
No. Primary & common schools	659	382	5,186	1,521	1,241
Scholars in common schools	16,243	8,236	218,609	48,189	34,876

* Abstracted from *Sixth Census*, U. S. Census Office (Washington, 1841).

and banks were crucial for the nourishment of the town's enterprise. Civic services, churches, facilities of every sort, were urgently demanded. And the keynote, the watchword, the trumpet call, must be Opportunity.

Without a ready-made structure of leadership, how would such a myriad of problems be met and who would meet them? "In no country in the world," wrote Tocqueville, "has the principle of association been more successfully used, or more unsparingly applied to a multitude of different objects, than in America." [47] How familiarly do the county chronicles dwell upon mass meetings for worthy objects, upon committees for the advancement of this or that; how appropriate that John Henry and Murray McConnel should trouble themselves for the Jacksonville Lunatic Asylum, for the College, for the Female Academy. Here was a society in which the setting up of institutions was a common experience; indeed, Tocqueville thought that the typical American addressed him "as if he were addressing a meeting," and would infallibly say, "Gentlemen." [48] Everything on the balance line between politics and civic consciousness was directly related to the prosperity of the town's citizens. There was an acute general awareness of this. For instance, the business prospects of a town were much enhanced by its becoming the county seat, and a perennial feature in the history of each Northwest state was the "county seat war" in which entire communities took part. The efforts of towns to make the legislature locate or relocate the seat in their favor typically occasioned great lengths of maneuvering and often actual violence. Scarcely a county in all of Indiana failed to see one or more such "wars." [49]

The very factor of success—an accelerating population—created new enterprises and new opportunities in the Northwest town: an index might be found in the sheer numbers of small businessmen there in contrast to those in the Southwest. (The story is best told by the census figures—see Table 8–2.) It also

TABLE 8–2 *

	ALA.	MISS.	OHIO	IND.	ILL.
Population	590,756	375,651	1,519,467	685,866	476,183
No. persons in commerce	2,212	1,303	9,201	3,076	2,506
No. persons in mfg. & trade	7,195	4,151	66,265	20,590	13,185

* Abstracted from *Sixth Census* (1840).

created new problems, all of which meant that talent was at the highest premium. Consider the variety of roles, commercial and political, to be filled. There would be a role for the man with money looking for a place to invest it, a role for the businessman with a heavy stake in the community (the natural organizer, the booster); there would be one for the early settler businessman who knew the scene and who knew everyone (he would be the mediator of interests, the grand master placator). And a role would exist for the bright young lawyer who could make connections, who could manipulate the legislature: he must get a charter for the bank, a charter for the academy; he must press for the county seat, the highway, the canal. Directly to his rear would be the entire town, pressing *him*. This dependence for success upon growth and development, this need for aggressive political representation, forced the community to seize upon whatever talent it could find and watch it closely. Those who rose in politics must continue to placate; the relation between economic welfare and politics was direct and continuing. Such a society would reward its adroitest politicians, not so much with awe and veneration[50] (their activities were too much a matter of general concern), but by re-electing them to office; they were too badly needed to be dispensed with. Responsibility, here, meant the art of returning home with whatever a politically sensitive electorate might demand.

There is no better illustration of this complexity of political life on the local level, this intimate connection between business and politics, this variety of demand, diffusion of power, and diffusion of pressure than in the promotion of the internal improvement system of the 1830's. Enthusiasm for improvements found expression all over the country, but the energy of the Northwest states was unmatched for subtle haggling, deep maneuvering, and grandiose objects. The "System" in each of them was like a tract of jungle, lush, overgrown, unplanned, extravagant, magnificent. In Ohio a public works program involving roads and canals at an estimated cost of $8,577,300 was coupled in 1837 with a general law for state aid in credit and subscriptions to private improvement schemes, an act variously known as the "Loan Law," the "General Improvement Law," and the "Plunder Law." The most relentless pressures from all counties lay behind the fashioning of the bill.[51] The Indiana system, even more spectacular, was in 1836 embodied in a mammoth law of forty-four sections which

provided for a network of roads, canals, and railroads, omitting
virtually no community in the state. It reflected the grand aggre-
gate of many local pressures; the entire movement was of local
rather than metropolitan origins,[52] and the interested assemblymen
were involved in endless deals and logrollings.[53] The growth of
the Illinois Internal Improvement Act of 1837, an imperial scheme
of canals and railroads, was the result of a monster bargain. It was
kindled by illuminations, bonfires, and conventions of the citizenry
everywhere, it was energized by the hopes of real estate speculators up and down the state, complicated by the rivalries of
Springfield, Alton, Vandalia, and Jacksonville over the location of
the capital, and compounded by prodigious scheming and haggling in the legislature. Two master Illinois politicians, Stephen
Douglas and Abraham Lincoln, were in the very midst of it.[54]

Nothing of any resemblance to this occurred in Alabama or
Mississippi, though they too were seized by the internal improvements enthusiasm of the 1830's. Allowing for the probability that
the river systems of these states to some extent relieved the need
for wide-scale transportation schemes, it is at the same time true
that political machinery there was not organized in such a way
that local pressures could be anticipated and reacted to with the
sensitivity so characteristic in the Northwest. Little or nothing
was done there.[55]

Now what was it in the Northwest that made these activities so
classically democratic? It was dependence on the favor of large
numbers of people in market communities where manipulation
was a daily habit, dependence on a favor which must be constantly renewed. This was the process by which the "equal
rights" attitude, so symbolic of the Jacksonian period, was developed: room for the aggressive young man on the make. This was
the setting in which intolerance of cultural and religious differences could not be permitted to interfere with the promotion: the
organizer must be free to boast of schools and churches for all.[56]
And this fundamental tolerance,[57] this built-in attitude of placation, had its other side. The booster would adjust to his neighbors
but would adjust to no one who tried to limit *his* activities; he
would instruct his representatives but would not tolerate their in-
structing *him*. The balance was a delicate one and easily upset by
the vicissitudes of business.

Under such conditions a prior structure of leadership, a self-perpetuating planter oligarchy, an aristocracy of money and birth, would simply have melted away. A burgeoning capitalism recognizes no prior structures, is impatient of élites, tolerates few restraints. Expressed in classical theory this is *laissez faire;* acted out on the Illinois frontier it meant unfettered opportunity for all, careers open to talent, and a gleeful willingness to manipulate the government, starting at the local level, in any and all ways that might advance business. The principle whereby a small-town culture such as this accomplished its political needs was typically not that of *noblesse oblige,* but of the bargain. The agents were numerous, the demands constant, the haggling intense. The parallel, then, cannot be that of an élite holding sway, but rather of tradesmen maintaining a clientele.[58]

It is possible to compress virtually everything we have said about political democracy in the Old Northwest into the experience of a single county in Ohio. Let Stark County, organized in 1809, furnish that profile. There, the "primitive" level of pioneer democracy, forcing upon the settlers the burden of organizing communities and fashioning institutions, was to be seen in every township. There, the lack of seasoned leadership in Sandy township did not absolve the Hewitts, the Downings, the Van Meters, from serving as constables, sheriffs, justices of the peace, or from organizing themselves against the Indians. Nor was it possible to be fastidious in Plain township, where the uncouth Henry Friday, a paroled Hessian soldier, was the only man available for constable. (Once during a plague of locusts he had a locust pie made, "which he ate.") Rudy Bair, whose wife once threw firebrands at the wolves to protect her baby, was the first settler in Paris township; he was the first justice of the peace, a delegate to Ohio's constitutional convention, and a member of the first legislature.[59] The very profusion of public roles during the first few years should give a key to the energy of the people who would shortly organize Canton, Massillon, Alliance, and Louisville. The very first election in Lawrence township involved the naming of two justices of the peace, a clerk, a school examiner, three trustees, two overseers of the poor, two fence viewers, two appraisers of property, three supervisors, two constables, and a lister of taxables. This, multiplied by the number of townships (there were fourteen in Stark County by 1816) and added to the county officers,[60] is in striking contrast to the relatively simple organization of the Mississippi county court.

Stark County did have one landed baron, Bezaleel Wells, who had all the attributes which would seem to make for influence, leadership, and power. Wells's career there, however, so similar in some respects to that of John Cleves Symmes, may typify the vulnerability of the great speculator to the aggressions of small operators in the early Northwest. Brought up in surroundings of refinement, Bezaleel Wells had become a staunch Federalist in the 1790's and had excellent political connections which included Arthur St. Clair and George Washington. His own public activity in Ohio included service as judge of probate, prothonotary to the Court of Common Pleas, clerk to the court of general quarter sessions of the peace of Jefferson Country, member of the Ohio constitutional convention, and state senator. Having realized substantial profits from purchases of over 15,000 acres in the Steubenville area, he shifted his activities in 1805 to the present Canton township, undoubtedly with foreknowledge of the Indian treaty of Fort Industry. Though the tax laws and the Harrison Land Act had meanwhile made large-scale operations less feasible than they had been at Steubenville, his holdings of 6,500 acres in Osnaburg, Plain, and Canton townships still put him in a class by himself.

Since competition had become greatly enlarged, with new towns being platted everywhere, it was clear to Wells that at Canton he must become a promoter. His inducements for attracting settlers were of the most royal sort: wide streets were laid out, whole blocks were donated for schools and churches, and special terms were offered for the purchase of town lots. He even sponsored a horse race at the south end of town to stimulate interest in sales. He made princely offers to the county commissioners to induce them to fix the county seat at Canton; sizable gifts of land and proceeds of sales were to be turned over to the county should Canton be chosen. The seat was, in fact, located there in 1808, but the artful commissioners—themselves small businessmen and petty speculators—seized upon the vague and contradictory wording of the proposals to exploit Wells in the most callous fashion. They accused him of fraud; by means of court action and merciless pressure they finally made him disgorge 150 unsold lots and a choice courthouse location. Meanwhile Wells, attempting to set up another town in Wayne County, was forced to liquidate the venture when his town failed to be chosen as county seat, and after the disastrous fray with the Stark commissioners his name virtually disappears from Canton history. By 1829 we see Bezaleel Wells—the only man in Stark County's early annals who might possibly have qualified, by virtue of wealth, experience, and extent of landholdings, for anything like a position of privilege—taking the pauper's oath in a debtors' prison. He had failed as a placator.[61]

What of the "secondary" level of democracy in Stark County, that of small-town enterprise? The county's first eleven permanent towns were established between 1805 and 1816—an average of one a year—which was different from the way it was in Alabama: there, even by 1850, only twenty-eight towns of over 200 inhabitants could be found in the whole state.[62] For the success of any of these eleven towns the factor of growth was crucial, and the promoter's art was at a premium. It involved the immediate setting up of services; schoolhouses were built before there were children enough to fill them. It called for toleration, since business always came before religious particularism; it called for placation, and, especially, for the instinct of manipulation; James Leeper's failure to donate lots for churches and schools cost Osnaburg the county seat.[63] The initial problems of settlement were thus carried over into those of promotion, and roles for the politician and manipulator went hand in hand with roles for the businessman and promoter.

That these roles, both commercial and political, were not only profuse but interchangeable is seen in the careers of Canton's earliest leading citizens. One result of Bezaleel Wells' disappearance from Canton's town life "was the growth of a democratic, self-reliant, enterprising group of town leaders, who took matters into their own hands." Among the foremost of these, as might be expected, was the chief man on the board of commissioners which had ravished Wells of his holdings, the tavernkeeper Samuel Coulter. Besides entertaining the public Coulter practiced law, speculated in land, was one of the first trustees of the Farmers' Bank, and served as Judge of the Court of Common Pleas. William Fogle, who kept a general store, was also a county commissioner and later became trustee, director, and cashier of the Farmers' Bank, from which he resigned in 1816 to accept the county treasurership. John Shorb, Canton's first storekeeper, became the bank's first president, was instrumental in founding the first Catholic church, and was highly active in public affairs at large. James Lathrop, a young Connecticut Yankee brimming with talent and ambition, having been admitted to the bar the year of his arrival, plunged instantly into public life, organizing Canton's first library, becoming its librarian, and leading the movement for an Academy. Lathrop was appointed receiver for the bank when it failed in 1818; he helped get the town incorporated in 1822 and became the first town president; he was elected county auditor the same year and went to the legislature two years later, serving several terms and heading the committee which wrote Ohio's first compulsory school tax law. His name is preserved in Canton legend. The hatter, George Stidger, arriving from Baltimore in 1807, organized and commanded his own company in the War of 1812 and rose to the rank of general. Upon his return, having accumulated considerable real estate before the war, he built a tin and copper shop, set up a tanyard, and ultimately amassed a veritable chain system of such enterprises. He served as Judge of the Court of Common Pleas.[64]

These were the men who headed Canton's "first families." They and their descendants became the only "aristocracy" that Canton could ever have.

Notes

1. "The Significance of the Frontier in American History," read at the annual meeting of the American Historical Association at Chicago in July 1893.

2. See Henry Nash Smith, *Virgin Land: The American West as Symbol and Myth* (Cambridge: 1950) for proof that on a poetic level the frontier idea still has its fascinations. See also Walter Prescott Webb's *The Great Frontier* (Boston: 1952).

3. *The Frontier in American History* (New York: 1920), p. 293.

4. Benjamin F. Wright, Jr., "Political Institutions and the Frontier," in D. R. Fox, ed., *Sources of Culture in the Middle West* (New York: 1934), p. 36.

5. An excellent symposium of these critical views, containing all the subtleties denied them here, may be found in *The Turner Thesis*, Number 2

of the Amherst *Problems in American Civilization,* George R. Taylor, ed. (Boston: 1949). The criticism is well summarized in Richard Hofstadter, "Turner and the Frontier Myth," *American Scholar,* XVIII (October 1949), 433–443.

6. The "textual" approach has been used with more success in the analysis of modern poetry and is the principal tool of the "New Criticism." There are indications, however, that even here the method's shortcomings may be felt. See "The New Criticism," a forum discussion by William Barrett, Kenneth Burke, Malcolm Cowley, Robert Gorham Davis, Allen Tate, and Hiram Haydn, *American Scholar,* XX (January–April 1951), 86–104, 218–231.

7. This would involve principally the claim for institutional "novelty" (which puts an extra burden on the theory) and the "safety valve" (which isn't necessary). For that matter, although the frontier assuredly had little to say to the "underprivileged," its *real* "safety valve" aspect is all too seldom stressed. To the part-time real estate operator, whether tobacco planter of the early Tidewater or wheat farmer of the pre-World War Middle Border, the frontier as a safety valve against agricultural bankruptcy has always made perfect sense.

8. "Not only is leadership limited objectively by given patterns of authority but the will to lead of the leader is vitiated if what he stands for cannot command a following. . . . [The leader's] effectiveness in no small measure derives from how much loyalty he can count upon." Jeremiah F. Wolpert, "Toward a Sociology of Authority," in Alvin W. Gouldner, ed., *Studies in Leadership* (New York: 1950), p. 681. This is the point made by Guglielmo Ferrero in his discussion of "legitimacy"; see *The Principles of Power,* trans. by Theodore Jaeckel (New York: 1942), p. 23.

9. *Democracy in America* (New York: Oxford Galaxy Ed., 1946), p. 320.

10. The study's working title is *Patterns of Social Life: Explorations in the Sociology of Housing,* by Robert K. Merton, Patricia S. West, and Marie Jahoda. We are greatly indebted to Mr. Merton for his generosity in allowing us to examine the material in manuscript.

11. Mr. Merton offers various graphs and tables to establish this. In one of them, 88 per cent of the early comers were found to be more highly active in Craftown organizations than in their former communities; only 8 per cent had had the same degree of participation in both communities.

12. Two other communities, each of which underwent a similar experience in similar circumstances, were Park Forest, Ill., and Shanks Village, New York, described in William H. Whyte, Jr., "The Future, c/o Park Forest," *Fortune* (June 1953), 126–131, 186–196; and Bernard Horn, "Collegetown: A Study of Transient Student Veteran Families in a Temporary Housing Community," (unpublished master's essay, Columbia University, 1948.

13. Thus "homogeneity"—in the total sense which we have given that concept—did not exist in Hilltown. There was a clear distinction—to extend the analogy—between "the rulers and the ruled."

14. These facts seem to go together. An illuminating Craftown anecdote concerns a woman who was fined $5 by one of the locally elected judges for letting her dog run loose. "Well, that's just like working men," she declared. "A rich man wouldn't be so interested in money. . . . I don't think any working man should mix in politics. I think a man that has money is better able to rule." It is at the same time quite possible to imagine the same woman making *this* statement (also recorded at Craftown): "I never voted in the

city for mayor or things like that. I just didn't have the interest. In the city they get in anyhow and there's nothing you can do about it. Here they're more connected with people."

15. Mr. Merton points out that this phenomenon was taken as a concrete cultural fact by Malinowski, who called it "phatic communion." "Each utterance is an act serving the direct aim of binding hearer to speaker by a tie of some social sentiment or other . . . language appears to us in this function not as an instrument of reflection but as a mode of action." Bronislaw Malinowski, in C. K. Ogden and I. A. Richards, *The Meaning of Meaning* (New York: 1923), pp. 478–479. The connection between this kind of thing and the folklore of democracy is seldom appreciated: consider, for example, the typical American reaction to disaster—the ease with which the traditions of the frontier are converted into spontaneous organizational techniques for coping with the emergency. The community response to the tornado which struck Flint, Michigan, in 1953 provides a perfect case in point; examples like it are numberless.

16. "When the time comes, and the forces collect together, a captain is appointed, and the men divide into proper sections, and [are] assigned to their several duties." Henry B. Curtis, "Pioneer Days in Central Ohio," *Ohio State Arch. and Hist. Pubs.*, I (1887), p. 245. Almost any state or county history or pioneer memoir will refer to or describe this familiar social function; see, e.g., William T. Utter, *The Frontier State* (Columbus: 1942), pp. 138, 139–141; W. C. Howells, *Recollections of Life in Ohio* (Cincinnati: 1895), pp. 144–151; etc., etc.

17. There is a vivid contemporary description of a combined logrolling and political rally in Baynard Rush Hall, *The New Purchase*, James A. Woodburn, ed. (Princeton: 1916), pp. 202–205. See also Logan Esarey, *History of Indiana* (Indianapolis: 1915), pp. 421, 425–426.

18. Beverly W. Bond, Jr., *The Civilization of the Old Northwest* (New York: 1934), pp. 249, 268, 351, 357. "The shrill whistle of the fife and the beat of the drum, calling to arms for the defense of their countrymen, was answered by many a gray-haired sire and many a youthful pioneer." H. W. Chadwick, comp., *Early History of Jackson County* (Brownstown, Ind.: 1943), p. 14. The War of 1812 in the Northwest, particularly in Ohio, had as much or more to do with hostile Indians as with the British, and defense was typically handled by the raising of local militia. See "Ohio and the War of 1812," ch. iv in Utter, *op. cit.*, pp. 88–119.

19. Elias P. Fordham, *Personal Narrative*, Frederic Ogg, ed. (Cleveland: 1906), pp. 154–155; Hall, *op. cit.*, p. 196; Charles Francis Ingals, "A Pioneer in Lee County, Illinois," Lydia Colby, ed., *Illinois State Historical Society Journal*, XXVI (October 1933), 281.

20. "As soon as conditions were favorable the pioneers of the neighborhood constructed a rude cabin schoolhouse. . . . There was no school revenue to be distributed, so each voter himself had to play the part of the builder. The neighbors divided themselves into choppers, hewers, carpenters, and masons. Those who found it impossible to report for duty might pay an equivalent in nails, boards, or other materials. The man who neither worked nor paid was fined thirty-seven and one-half cents a day." William F. Vogel, "Home Life in Early Indiana," *Indiana Magazine of History*, X (September 1914), p. 297.

21. The "interfaith chapel" was invariably the early solution to this problem (there was one in Craftown, also in Park Forest and Shanks Village).

"The first church . . . was free to all denominations, and here, for miles and miles, came the prioneer and family on the Sabbath day to worship God." Chadwick, *op. cit.,* p. 35. See also Vogel, *op. cit.,* p. 291; Morris Birkbeck, *Letters from Illinois* (London: 1818), p. 23; John D. Barnhardt, Jr., "The Rise of the Methodist Episcopal Church in Illinois from the Beginning to the Year 1832," *Illinois State Historical Society Journal,* XII (July 1919), 149–217.

22. C. H. Rammelkamp, ed., "The Memoirs of John Henry: A Pioneer of Morgan County," *Illinois State Historical Society Journal,* XVIII (April 1925), 55.

23. In a history of the town of Lancaster, Ohio, which was founded in 1800, there is a longish series of biographical sketches of its "leading pioneers." Twenty-seven of these sketches concern settlers who arrived within the first ten years of the town's existence and who held office, and of these 27, age data are given for 15. For what such a haphazard sample is worth, the average age of this group at the date of the town's founding was twenty-four. C. M. L. Wiseman, *Centennial History of Lancaster* (Lancaster: 1898).

24. The county histories make every effort to secure the immortality of their leading citizens by reciting as many of their accomplishments as are known. Thus if the biographical sketches make no mention of public office held elsewhere, it should be safe to assume that at least in most of the cases their civic careers began in the new settlement.

25. Frank S. Heinl, "The First Settlers in Morgan County," *Illinois State Historical Society Journal,* XVIII (April 1925), 76–87; Rammelkamp, *op. cit.,* pp. 39–40 and *passim;* George Murray McConnel, "Some Reminiscences of My Father, Murray McConnel," *Illinois State Historical Society Journal,* XVIII (April 1925), 89–100.

26. The seemingly fabulous Wesley Park—who was the first settler at Auburn, Indiana, and DeKalb County's first sheriff, road commissioner, road supervisor, jail commissioner, and clerk of the first county board—was actually a figure quite typical. We see blacksmith-judges and carpenter-sheriffs everywhere. See S. W. Widney, "Pioneer Sketches of DeKalb County," *Indiana Magazine of History,* XXV (June 1929), 116, 125–126, 128. "Few of the officials prior to 1850 [in Parke County, Indiana] were men of education. For years it was the custom to elect a coroner from among the stalwart blacksmiths. . . ." Maurice Murphy, "Some Features of the History of Parke County," *Indiana Magazine of History,* XII (June 1916), 151.

27. Bond, *op. cit.,* pp. 102, 124.

28. Quoted in Solon J. Buck, *Illinois in 1818* (Springfield: 1917), p. 260. Consider again the power of "phatic communion": in the 1952 presidential election the governor of that same great state of Illinois might have been seen blandly kissing babies.

29. Hall, *New Purchase,* p. 178.

30. *Ibid.,* pp. 200–201, 177.

31. Vogel, *op. cit.,* p. 309. "Our candidates certainly sweat for their expected honours," Hall remarks. ". . . Nay, a very few hundreds of rival and zealous candidates would, in a year or so, if judiciously driven under proper task masters, clear a considerable territory." *Op. cit.,* p. 205.

32. *Civilization of the Old Northwest,* pp. 331–332.

33. Buck, *op. cit.,* pp. 47, 54–55. "The situation was so serious that the matter was taken up with the secretary of state, and the president issued a proclamation directing that after a certain day in March 1816 all squatters

on the public lands should be removed. Against the execution of this proclamation, Benjamin Stephenson, the delegate from Illinois territory, protested vigorously. . . . The marshal of the Illinois territory actually made preparations to remove the intruders; but the secretary of the treasury wrote him on May 11, 1816, recommending 'a prudent and conciliatory course'; and nothing seems to have been accomplished." *Ibid.*, p. 54.

34. Notably the Congressional legislation of 1796, 1800, and 1804.

35. Bond, *op. cit.*, pp. 337–338.

36. A special situation in Illinois added to the difficulty of amassing large absentee holdings; actual sales of public land could not begin there until 1814 owing to the complexity of the French claims, and the result was a growing population of settlers and slim pickings for speculators. Buck, *op. cit.*, p. 44.

37. Symmes had sold, in advance, a number of tracts outside his 1792 patent, expecting to take them up at 66⅔ cents an acre. Subsequently the price rose to $2.00 on which Symmes could not possibly make good. An original contract for 1,000,000 acres had been partly paid for in Continental certificates, and the patent of 1792 gave him title to those lands for which he had paid. Neither his influence nor that of Harrison was ever able to guarantee the entire claim of 1,000,000 acres. Meanwhile the Scioto Company had completely collapsed, and the representations of the Illinois and Wabash companies met with even less success than did those of Symmes.

38. McConnel, *op. cit.*, p. 95.

39. Heinl, *op. cit.*, p. 84. See also *supra*, note 15.

40. Thurman Arnold in his *Folklore of Capitalism* (New Haven and London: 1937) makes a parallel point in suggesting that the "traditions" of American business have been derived from a primitive phase in its development; Richard Hofstadter, in a work on Populism and Progressivism, notes the same interesting fact with respect to our agriculture. These writers in each case stress the conceptual difficulties which the "myths" of an earlier stage impose upon the realities of a later, much-advanced one. Mr. Hofstadter metaphorically characterizes this polarity as "soft" and "hard." It might be added that a humane view of American culture would recognize a need, on the part of both the businessman and the farmer, for "folklore": the need of each for dramatizing to himself his own role, for maintaining his self-respect.

41. For years the late Professor Schumpeter maintained a theory of this sort. "History," he wrote, "clearly confirms this suggestion: historically, the modern democracy rose along with capitalism, and in actual connection with it. But the same holds true for democratic practice: democracy in the sense of our theory of competitive leadership presided over the process of political and institutional change by which the bourgeoisie reshaped, and from its own point of view rationalized, the social and political structure that preceded its ascendancy: the democratic method was the political tool of that reconstruction." Joseph Schumpeter, *Capitalism, Socialism, and Democracy* (New York: 1947), pp. 296–297.

42. The very gaps in available statistics are dramatic. We have no early figures for the Southwest, but by 1853 there were in Alabama only thirty towns with a population of over 200 and only twenty-nine in Mississippi. On the other hand, as early as 1833 Indiana, with less than one half Alabama's 1853 population, had seventy-seven such towns, and Illinois, with one fifth the 1853 population of Alabama, had thirty-four. By 1847, when Indiana's population had reached the 1853 level of Alabama, it had 156 towns whose

population exceeded 200. If complete figures were available for towns of over 500 population the difference would be even more striking: while towns of this size were quite common in the Northwest, they were, aside from the port cities and state capitals, very rare in Alabama and Mississippi. As early as 1821 Ohio, with a population of 581,434, had sixty-one towns with a population of over 200, twenty-nine of 500 or more, and *twenty-two* of over a thousand. J. D. B. DeBow, *Statistical View of the United States . . . being a Compendium of the Seventh Census . . .* (Washington: 1854); John Scott, *Indiana Gazetteer* (Indianapolis: 1833); J. M. Peck, *A Gazetteer of Illinois* (Jacksonville: 1834); E. Chamberlain, *Indiana Gazetteer* (Indianapolis: 1850); John Kilbourn, *Ohio Gazetteer* (Columbus: 1821).

43. William V. Pooley, *The Settlement of Illinois from 1830 to 1850* (Madison: 1908), p. 564.

44. In 1836, lots in Peoria sold as high as $100 per front foot while good neighboring farm land was still to be had at the standard price of $1.25 an acre. R. Carlyle Buley, *The Old Northwest: Pioneer Period* (Indianapolis: 1950), Vol. II, p. 116.

45. This is very clear from an illuminating survey made by James W. Silver of land operations in Tate and Tippah counties, Mississippi, between 1836 and 1861. Most impressive in his findings are (1) the huge amounts of land in which the successful speculator had to deal, and (2) the lengths of time that these men customarily held their land before selling it. In these two counties alone, 337,000 acres were held by single investors, eight of whom held between 3,000 and 4,000 acres, six holding from 4,000 to 5,000 acres, four from 5,000 to 6,000, and three between 6,000 and 7,000; one owned between 10,000 and 15,000 acres, two between 15,000 and 20,000, and one over 25,000. Averages were struck for thirty-one individual speculators owning a total of 197,376.5 acres at an investment of $267,382.19 with profits of $244,824.24. But the average length of time held was *18.6 years;* the profit must thus be figured in terms not of quick killings but of average annual return. For a majority this came to less than 5 per cent. James W. Silver, "Land Speculation Profits in the Chickasaw Cession," *Journal of Southern History,* X (February 1944), 92. This may be called "speculation," but it was speculation on an order quite different from that typically occurring in the Old Northwest.

46. Here are two typical cases: Wesley Park, who in 1836 laid out the town of Raeburn, Indiana, gave one third of the lots to the county, "receiving no compensation," as he piquantly admits, "but the assurance that it would be permanently the county seat." Widney, *op. cit.,* p. 128. In that very same year, Bolivar County, one of the rich counties of the Delta, was being organized in Mississippi. The proceedings of the Board of Police (a year later) "show the acceptance of the offer of William Vick to sell five acres of land, including the overseer's residence, for the Seat of Justice," at a price of $100 an acre and $300 for the improvements. Florence Warfield Sillers and others, *History of Bolivar County, Mississippi* (Jackson: 1948), p. 12.

47. *Democracy in America,* p. 109.

48. *Ibid.,* p. 152.

49. In Crawford County, when the seat was first relocated, tradition says that the citizens of Fredonia went in a body to Mount Sterling and forcibly removed the records. "If the records were carried away by force," notes a chronicler, "it was only the first time; they have been carried away from

each of the later county seats by force." What more excellent instance of democracy could be found than this ardent and universal participation in the concerns of the community? H. H. Pleasant, "Crawford County," *Indiana Magazine of History,* XVIII (June 1922), 146. See also Ernest V. Shockley, "County Seats and County Seat Wars in Indiana," *Indiana Magazine of History,* X (March 1914), 26.

50. Max Weber was much impressed by the later counterpart of the master placator, the American urban political boss. The boss was thoroughly responsible but not quite respectable. See *From Max Weber: Essays in Sociology,* trans. and ed. by H. H. Gerth and C. Wright Mills (New York: 1946), pp. 109–110.

51. The Board of Public Works advised in its report "that nothing short of the extension of the canal navigation to every considerable district in the state will satisfy that public will, which justly claims that benefits conferred shall be coextensive with the burthens imposed; and that, in those districts, where canals cannot be made, an approximation to equality should be obtained by aid in constructing roads." The warning, in short, was that there must be something for everyone. Ernest L. Bogart, *Internal Improvements and State Debt in Ohio* (New York: 1924), p. 55.

52. "The role of local government was typically not the planning of a great system of transportation. It was an attempt to gain a favorable competitive position for the particular community. . . ." Carter Goodrich, "Local Government Planning of Internal Improvements," *Political Science Quarterly,* LXVI (September 1951), 442.

53. Esarey, *History of Indiana,* pp. 352–373.

54. Theodore C. Pease, *The Frontier State, 1818–1848* (Springfield: 1918), pp. 194–219. Interesting unpublished material on the Illinois system exists: Alan Heimert, "The Internal Improvement Act of 1837: An Introduction to the Study of Illinois Politics in the 1830s" (M.A. thesis, Columbia University, 1950); and John Henry Krenkel, "Internal Improvements in Illinois, 1818–1848" (Ph.D. thesis, University of Illinois, 1937).

55. The state of Mississippi sought in vain to make a modest loan of $200,-000 for internal improvements, backed by its 3 per cent fund, future land grants, and the faith of the state. Dunbar Rowland, *History of Mississippi* (Chicago-Jackson: 1935), Vol. I, pp. 553–554. Alabama likewise did next to nothing, and when the Northwest's improvement systems collapsed with the panic of 1837, the governor even congratulated his state for having remained inactive. As late as 1851 Alabama's Committee on Internal Improvements noted bitterly that there had been "not one serious effort on the part of the Legislature to advance the great interests of agriculture, commerce, or manufactures. . . . Other states are rich because they are old, but our destiny seems to be to grow old and poor together." William E. Martin, "Internal Improvements in Alabama," *Johns Hopkins Studies in History and Political Science,* XX, No. 4 (1902), 40, 73.

56. Baynard Rush Hall, the first professor at Indiana University, was unpleasantly aware of this. "With our own eyes we saw Cash! handled it with our fingers: heard it jingle with our ears! and all at once 'high larning' became as popular as common schools. . . . Only show that a school, an academy, a college, or *a church,* will advance the value of town lots—bring in more customers—create a demand for beef, cloth, pepper and salt, powder and shot; then, from vulgar plebeian dealing in shoe leather, up to the

American *nobleman* dealing in shops, and who retails butter and eggs, we shall hear one spontaneous voice in favour!" *New Purchase,* p. 400.

57. This connection between *practical* tolerance and business (ceremonial "tolerance" comes later) can hardly be too much emphasized. In 1849 there was a remarkable act of cultural assimilation in Jacksonville, Illinois. In that year 130 Portuguese exiles from the island of Madeira were brought there, civic committees having undertaken to find accommodations and situations for them, and urged that in coming the exiles "would thus learn our manners, our habits (we hope our good ones only), and our way of doing business of all kinds—and become useful to themselves, and in time amalgamated with us." It was a transaction managed with great efficiency by local groups, including the ladies of Jacksonville, and was highly beneficial to all. George R. Poage, "The Coming of the Portuguese," *Illinois State Historical Society Journal,* XVIII (April 1925), 100–135.

58. Max Weber insisted that this was still true at a much later stage of development. "Industrial monopolies and trusts are institutions of limited duration; the conditions of production undergo changes, and the market does not know any everlasting valuation. Their power also lacks the authoritative character and the political mark of aristocracies. But monopolies of the land always create a political aristocracy." Gerth and Mills, eds., *From Max Weber,* p. 383.

59. Edward Thornton Heald, *The Stark County Story* (Canton: 1949), Vol. I, pp. 42–50, 52–55; John Danner, *Old Landmarks of Canton and Stark County* (Logansport: 1904), pp. 43, 470.

60. Heald, *op. cit.,* p. 66. County organization at that time called for three or more justices of the peace, tax commissioners, a sheriff, a coroner, a recorder, a treasurer, a license commissioner, and justices and clerks of the various courts. Ohio Historical Records Survey Project, Inventory of the County Archives of Ohio, No. 76, *Stark County* (Columbus: 1940), p. 23.

61. Edward T. Heald, *Bezaleel Wells, Founder of Canton and Steubenville, Ohio* (Canton: 1948).

62. "All of them except Tuscaloosa were situated in agricultural communities and Tuscaloosa was not really an exception, inasmuch as the mineral resources in the vicinity had not then been developed." Thomas H. Owen, *A History of Alabama and Dictionary of Alabama Biography* (Chicago: 1921), Vol. II, p. 265.

63. Heald, *Stark County Story,* pp. 12, 94–96, 217.

64. Heald, *Bezaleel Wells,* pp. 113–114, 118–119, 122, 126; Danner, *Old Landmarks,* p. 451; Heald, *Stark County Story,* pp. 6, 94–114, 119–123, 126–133, 135.

❦ 9 ❦

Marvin W. Mikesell

COMPARATIVE STUDIES IN FRONTIER HISTORY

The Frontier in Comparative View

The principal failing of Turner, his followers, and most of his critics has been a neglect of comparative research. Without the perspective afforded by knowledge of developments in foreign areas, it is not possible to interpret the significance of the American frontier. A persuasive argument for comparative study was presented by Herbert Heaton in an address to the Economic History Association some time ago.[1] P. F. Sharp has called attention to the advantages of viewing American frontier history against the background of comparable developments within the British Commonwealth.[2] An effective demonstration of the value of comparative study is found in Dietrich Gerhard's thoughtful re-examination of the Turner thesis based upon the different histories of the Canadian, Australian, South African, German, and Russian frontiers.[3] In still another essay, J. L. M. Gulley presents an elaborately documented study of the diffusion of Turnerian and neo-Turnerian ideas.[4]

In 1954 the University of Wisconsin sponsored a series of lectures under the title "Wisconsin Reconsiders the Frontier." Thirteen of these lectures have been published in a volume designed to place the frontier hypothesis in the perspective of time and

Marvin W. Mikesell is Professor of Geography, University of Chicago, and author of *Northern Morocco: A Cultural Geography*, and *Readings in Cultural Geography*.

Condensed from the *Annals of the Association of American Geographers*, L (March 1960), 64–74, by permission of the author and the publisher.

place.[5] The range of topics considered in the volume—from "Roman Colonization and the Frontier Hypothesis" to "Mark Twain as an Interpreter of the Far West"—is too broad to form a coherent pattern of thought. The most original and hence most stimulating essays are those devoted to foreign frontiers.[6] The collection also includes an essay by Webb on his conception of a "World Frontier," and several papers on frontier settlement in the United States. The final chapter, "Backwash on the Frontier" by A. I. Hallowell, is an analysis of Indian contributions to American culture.

The aim of comparative study is to build a foundation for generalization that extends beyond the particular conditions found in a given area at a given time. Where and when should comparison be sought? The editors of *The Frontier in Perspective* sought "to reconstruct the frontier in the perspective of world history, to lay the numerous frontiers against the Turner hypothesis, to test its validity, and to search for valid elements in the non-Turnerian history areas.[7] With this observation as an introduction, it is not surprising that the volume lacks coherence.

It goes without saying that the establishment of objective standards of comparability is a necessary prerequisite of any comparative study. When settlement takes place during the same period and in similar environments, the advantages of comparison are obvious. As Jan Broek points out, "the Great Plains and the prairies of North America, the Pampas of South America, the Siberian and Australian steppes, and the African Veld were all drawn into the sphere of western culture in the nineteenth century. One does not have to be a geographic determinist to believe that a comparative study of the settlement of these grasslands would greatly enlarge our perspective.[8]

Similarities should also be evident in the relative numerical strength of the immigrant and aboriginal peoples. For example, the great numerical superiority of the American pioneer over the Indian facilitated the establishment of settlement patterns that were not feasible on the frontier of Spanish colonization in northern Mexico. In addition to relative numerical strength, important differences may be discerned in the relationships of immigrant and aboriginal peoples. One may speak of frontiers of *inclusion* (more properly *assimilation*), illustrated by Roman, Arab, and

Spanish colonization, and frontiers of *exclusion,* illustrated by American, Canadian, Australian, and South African colonization.[9] Again, one may speak of *static* and *dynamic* frontiers, depending upon whether colonization is or is not checked by environmental, technological, or human barriers.[10] China, to cite a complex example, has had a relatively dynamic frontier of inclusion in the south and a relatively static frontier of alternating inclusion and exclusion in the north.[11]

In addition to these general considerations, there is much to gain from awareness of the social and economic conditions prevalent on a given frontier. It is difficult, for example, to see any clear parallel between the westward movement in the United States and the advance of colonization in Latin America. The first areas to be colonized by the Spaniards were inhabited by sedentary farmers, the "peaceful" or "sensible" Indians (*indios de razón*). When the Spaniards moved beyond the Aztec and Inca territories, they encountered primitive Indians, either hunters and collectors or part-time farmers, who were more mobile and more difficult to subdue. The advance of the conquistadores into the more difficult areas did not result from a sizable European immigration, nor from a desire to till new land; it was encouraged by gold, silver, and missionary zeal. In the more peaceful and culturally advanced areas a hybrid society was formed based upon the acculturation of Indians and Europeans. The presence of a large mestizo element in the population of most of the Latin American countries is a clear reflection of the inclusive character of the colonial frontiers.[12]

In the few areas of Latin America that have experienced a permanent expansion of settlement in post-colonial time, the dominant theme has been one of intensification of land use rather than movement to the edge of "free land." As Preston James remarks, many of the South American frontiers represent hollow waves of exploitation followed by abandonment and population decline.[13] According to James, there are four main areas of durable frontier expansion: the highlands of Costa Rica, the highlands of Antioquia in Colombia, the central valley of Chile, and the three southern states of Brazil. But the large holdings in most of these areas, the predominance of a few staples, and the relatively discontinuous pattern of settlement do not resemble the westward movement in the United States. For example, on the coffee frontier of São Paulo hasty advance and bonanza production discouraged occupation of all but the most productive land.[14] Perhaps the closest approximation of a Turnerian frontier is that of Antioquia, where rural society is composed of small landholders and homesteaders in sharp contrast to the more prevalent latifundia.[15]

Historians have long been intrigued by the similarities seemingly evident in the *Drangnach Osten* and the westward movement in the United States. One of America's leading medievalists suggested that "the line of the Elbe, Oder, and Vistula rivers as clearly demarked the eastward expansion of Germany as the 'fall line' of the Atlantic seaboard, the Alleghenies, and the Mississippi delimited the successive stages of American westward expansion." He also suggested that the "return to primitive conditions" on the American frontier was "just as true of the history of the German border [*sic*]," and that the stages of economic development had been identical on the two frontiers.[16]

Many of these ideas have withstood the tests of critical review, but the underlying assumption, that the German and American immigrants shared a common experience, is now generally discredited.[17] The German colonists were not frontiersmen in the American sense of the word. Wherever they went they were subject to the authority of the church and the nobility. A substantial number of the immigrants were skilled artisans, and not a few were Flemings and Hollanders invited into the East to reclaim marshland. Moreover, the form of settlement almost everywhere was the village or hamlet, not the individual farmstead idealized in American literature. Nor did the German colonists move into "free land." Needless to say, there is no basis for a comparison of German relationships with the Slavs and American relationships with the Indians.

The great drift of Russian immigrants into Siberia, as D. W. Treadgold demonstrates, more closely resembled the westward movement in the United States.[18] Both frontiers were dynamic and exclusive, and both moved ahead of roads and rails. There may even be some justification for describing the Siberian migration as a "safety valve." The demand for fur, silver, and other products of Siberia led to the supplying of the natives with arms and liquor, thus creating what Turner described as a "trading frontier"; but the transition from trading to farming was slower than in the United States. Like their American counterparts, the Russian pioneers had to learn to accept the hazards of dry farming. Like the Canadians they had to learn to accept the limitations of the boreal environment. The first routes of migration in both regions followed the rivers, but the Siberian immigrants did not have to cross mountain barriers.

In other respects the Russian and American experiences were profoundly different. Between absolute monarchy and a republican form of government and between serfdom, however modified, and homesteading there is a chasm that no amount of neo-Turnerian generalization can bridge. The demographic patterns were notably different, since Russia experienced no substantial immigration from abroad. The Russians spent six hundred years getting to the Urals, and a hundred more moving from there to the Pacific coast, a much longer period of conquest than the Americans required. The slow movement of the Russian frontier is especially noteworthy, for immigration proceeded almost wholly into areas that were already under Tsarist control. In contrast, the more rapid American migration involved annexation and settlement of new territory. Some of the native Siberian peoples, especially those of the taiga, were as primitive and numerically weak as the American Indians; others, particularly the Muslim pastoralists, were difficult to dislodge. Indeed, in the thirteenth century the pattern of expansion reversed itself, and a substantial part of European Russia fell prey to Turco-Mongolian horsemen. In comparing the Russian and American migrations, A. Lobanov-Rostovsky puts stress on the fact that the Russian frontier ran into the Chinese frontier.[19] This "collision" seems real enough in modern time, but it must be remembered that the historic role of China's northern frontier was defensive. As Lattimore remarks, "nothing could be more static in conception than the Great Wall."[20]

Since most research in frontier history has been based upon interpretations of American developments, the issues just considered can be rephrased in a general question. Given the special circumstances of settlement history in the United States, where should one look for fruitful comparison? The answer suggested by the preceding discussion is that one should look to Canada, Australia, and South Africa.

Canada

In Canada, as in the United States, application of the frontier hypothesis meant rejection, at least in part, of previous attempts to interpret national history in a colonial setting. The first "school of thought" in Canadian historiography has been described as the "Britannic or Blood Is Thicker Than Water School." [21] In time, it became evident that the Canadian communities could not be described as mere exclaves of England and France. The Canadians had shared in the experience of driving back the wilderness. Their "West" had also been a source of transforming energy, pulling along the conservative "East." In short, the westward movement was North American, not just American in the narrow sense of the word.

One of the strongest statements of this point of view was presented in 1928 by W. N. Sage.[22] He described the settlement of Nova Scotia as a northern extension of the New England frontier; the Ohio Valley as a zone of conflict between the Quebec fur-trading frontier and the American agricultural frontier; and the settlement of the Prairie Provinces as an enterprise involving pioneers of both countries.[23]

The vogue of Turnerian interpretation was relatively brief, for in a country which had maintained many transatlantic connections, there could not be a strong assertion of separate growth in isolation from the rest of the world. Moreover, the environment, even when seen as a determinant, was specifically Canadian and not American in the broad sense of the word.[24] The "Appalachian barrier" was circumvented at the beginning of Canadian history when Champlain sailed up the St. Lawrence and founded the first settlement at Quebec rock.[25] The "frontier" of the Maritime Provinces was on the Grand Bank, not in the forest environment idealized by Turner. The most important barrier encountered during the early period of settlement was the Laurentian Shield, and its effect was to disrupt the continuity of the settlement frontier. During the eighteenth and most of the nineteenth centuries, rural colonization was restricted to the Maritime Provinces, the St. Lawrence Valley, and southern Ontario. This restriction is clearly shown on the population distribution maps for 1851 and 1871 in the new *Atlas of Canada*.[26]

Effective settlement of the North American grassland was accomplished by the railroads. This generalization holds true on both sides of the boundary. However, the advance of the Canadian rails lagged behind the American lines. When the Union Pacific and Central Pacific were joined near Ogden, Utah, in 1869, Canadian surveyors were still searching for a route across the interior plains. The slow progress of the Canadian Pacific was of major importance, for the prior existence of an export economy discouraged colonists from moving ahead of transportation lines; nor did they outrun the machinery of parliamentary government. The Canadian West was never "wild" in the American sense of the word.[27]

Another point to be emphasized in any comparative study is that Canada suffered almost from the beginning of its history from the competition of its more richly endowed neighbor. As Heaton remarks, "Canada felt the effect of the United States in the attraction of immigrants to New York rather than to Montreal, in the emigration of her own native born, in the pull of the Erie Canal and then of the American railroads which wrecked her hopes of channeling the produce of the Middle West down the St. Lawrence, and in the competition that her infant industries had to face from rivals across the border." [28]

During the earliest period of North American colonization, French Canadians, above all the fur-traders, were the most adventurous frontiersmen. But the *coureurs de bois* were not representative citizens of New France. The great majority of the French Canadians were *habitants*, devoted to their narrow fields. Moreover, the patterns of land division and tenure were influenced by the seignorial system inherited from Old France.[29] The extent to which the Canadian system differed from that of France can be explained by two and perhaps only two facts: in Canada land was cheap and labor was dear. When overpopulation fostered restlessness, the prospects of pioneer life held little appeal; the French Canadians preferred to move to New England or to their own industrial towns. In a pointed refutation of the frontier thesis,. Mason Wade describes the unifying thread of French-Canadian history as an "intense provincialism." [30]

Much of the credit for the development of durable interpretations of Canadian economic history belongs to Harold A. Innis (1894–1952), who demonstrated in many books and articles that the economic development of Canada should be approached from the standpoint of trade with other countries, France in the beginning, later Great Britain and the United States, and finally the Orient and the world generally.[31] Recognition of the vital role of trade stimulated interest in the history of transportation. By the mid 1930's most historians belonged to what Careless describes as the "Laurentian School." [32] The main tenet of this "school" was that the St. Lawrence and its tributaries became the basis of an extensive communication system around which Canada itself took shape.

Since interest in transportation routes presupposes interest in their foci, the "Laurentian School" quickly evolved into a "Metropolitan School." The metropolitan orientation is most explicit in D. C. Masters' study of Toronto, in which he traces the rise of the city to a position of dominance over Ontario, and describes its competition with Montreal for control of a broader Canadian hinterland.[33] The emphasis on the economic power wielded by cities is especially appropriate in Canada, where the major routes converge on Montreal, the national metropolis, Vancouver, the capital of the Far West, and Toronto, the communications hub of wealthy southern Ontario.[34] The functioning of these cities may do more to explain the course of Canadian settlement than the frontier theme. For example, the best perspective of the fur trade is gained from the entrepôts of Quebec. The organizing functions of the metropolis are even more clearly evident on the lumbering and mining frontiers. The building of the Canadian Pacific railroad far ahead of settlement is another illustration of the influence of urban business interests. In time, if not at present, Edmonton's position with respect to the Canadian Northwest may be comparable to Seattle's role as the "regional capital of Alaska." [35] Metropolitanism figures prominently in the latest general treatise in Canadian economic history, in which the authors describe the central focus of their work as an attempt to determine "the part

which business organizations, big and small, working in cooperation with government, have played in creating a national economy." [36]

Australia

Students of Australian settlement were slow to accept the challenge of the frontier hypothesis, but when they did, the American
West seemed remarkably like their own "Outback." In 1940
W. K. Hancock described the advance of Australian settlement in
language strongly reminiscent of Turner:

> There is a famous gap in the range of the Blue Mountains, that wall of
> rock and scrub which for a quarter of a century hemmed in this colony
> of New South Wales within the coastal plain. Stand at this gap and
> watch the frontiers following each other westward—the squatters'
> frontier which filled the western plains with sheep and laid the founda-
> tions of Australia's economy, the miners' frontier which brought Aus-
> tralia population and made her a radical democracy, the farmers' fron-
> tier which gradually and painfully tested and proved the controls of
> Australia's soil and climate. Stand a few hundred miles further west on
> the Darling River, and see what these controls have done to the fron-
> tier. The farmers have dropped out of the westward-moving proces-
> sion, beaten by aridity. Only the pastoralists and prospectors pass on.
> In the west centre of the continent, aridity has beaten even the pas-
> toralists. On the fringe of a dynamic society there are left only a few
> straggling prospectors and curious anthropologists, infrequent invaders
> of the aboriginal reserves.[37]

Here is the essence of the Australian reaction to the frontier
theme. The basic ideas of the frontier hypothesis are endorsed,
but not without recognition of the particular influences of the
Australian environment. The history of Australian settlement has
been in the main the story of a people inhabiting relatively narrow coastal belts in the eastern and southeastern parts of the continent, and a less thickly populated strip in the southwest. The
dry heart of the continent can readily be compared with the
American Southwest, but the Australian pioneer enjoyed no
counterpart of the rich lands located between the Alleghenies and
the Great Plains. A character in one of Henry Lawson's short
stories describes Australia as "a big, thirsty, hungry wilderness,

with one or two cities for the convenience of foreign speculators." [38] This appraisal may seem unjust, but Griffith Taylor's distinction between "Economic Australia" and "Empty Australia"
still holds true.[39] The historical significance of the hundredth me-
ridian in the United States and Goyder's line of "safe settlement"
in southern Australia are remarkably similar.

The applicability of the frontier hypothesis in Australian history is subjected to rigorous tests in a study by H. C. Allen, who
describes his task as an attempt "to study the history of man in the
environment of two untamed lands of continental extent." [40] He
considers the temporal relationships of the two histories, compares
the two environments and the peoples environed, contrasts Australian and American patterns of pioneer settlement, and in a
stimulating final chapter reappraises the frontier thesis in the light
of the Australian experience.

As might be expected Allen's conclusions justify the essential
Turnerian doctrine: the vital modifying effect of the open frontier. He concludes, again not surprisingly, that the notion of absolute determinism is absurd, "for what men are and what they
bring with them, both consciously and unconsciously, when they
come to the frontier, have far too great an effect upon their development." [41] What kind of men came to the Australian frontier?
The first Outbackers were wealthy sheep-ranchers with a wage-
earning personnel largely formed of ex-convicts. The Australian
frontier thus started, as one author puts it, as a "big man's frontier," in contrast to the American "homesteader's frontier." [42]
Thanks to the cooperation of the bankers, the Australian pastoralists were able to occupy the best land and discourage settlement
by small farmers. The difficulties of would-be farmers were aggravated further by the fact that Australia did not have an effective executive or legislative authority until after the six colonies
were federated in 1901. Land reform, stimulated by the clamor of
a hundred thousand ex-miners, was not as encouraging as the
American Homestead Act, for in addition to the terms of residence and improvement, the Australian settler had to pay.

The persistence of the pastoral oligarchy can be traced to Australia's imperial ties, for British capitalists were more interested in
wool for the Yorkshire textile mills than in the successful settlement of small farmers. Moreover, a substantial part of Australia

was better suited to extensive grazing than to any known combination of crops. Vast open spaces and a meager supply of labor encouraged the shepherd rather than the yeoman farmer. The typical Australian frontiersman in the last century was a wageworker who did not, usually, expect to be anything else.

Until 1880 the American census reports referred to a frontier *line*. In Australia settlement fanned out from six points scattered far apart on the coast. Since coastal shipping could handle most of the interstate traffic, the progress of the railroads was slow. Isolation encouraged sectionalism;[43] and one of the results of sectionalism was the use of three widths of track, a problem that has defied plans for a unified railroad system. The meager development of roads and rails is especially significant in view of the absence of navigable rivers. As Allen remarks, "Old Man River is not a conceivable figure in Australian folklore." [44]

One of the points stressed by Turner was that the frontier was the most effective agent of Americanization. Was it the most effective agent of Australianization? Perhaps it was at first, at least until pastoral ascendancy was checked by the gold rush. But urbanization was already well advanced by this time, and as an ever larger proportion of Australian immigrants, as well as native born, came to reside in the great coastal cities, the importance of the Outback came to be more symbolic than real. Australian historians, like their Canadian colleagues, have gradually shifted from an agrarian to a metropolitan interpretation of national institutions. The metropolitan orientation is especially prominent in George Nadel's study of the political and social history of New South Wales.[45] Nevertheless, it seems to be true, as Allen remarks, that "what a people believe themselves to be is often as important in determining their actions as what they are." [46] In another new book, similar in scope to Nadel's work, Russel Ward argues that "a specifically Australian outlook grew up first and most clearly among the bush workers in the pastoral industry, and that this group has had an influence completely disproportionate to its numerical and economic strength on the attitudes of the whole Australian community." [47] It cannot be denied that frontier settlements and indeed a frontier spirit are still to be found in the tropical environment of northern Australia.

South Africa

The Great Trek of the Boers is usually described as a withdrawal from civilization, a concerted effort to reduce contacts with the outside world. The first migration began in 1835; it took the *Voortrekkers* out of the Cape Colony, one group going to Natal, one to the valley of the Vaal, and another as far as Delagoa Bay. The second movement began in 1843, the year of the British occupation of Natal. This occupation, followed by the annexation of Transorgania in 1848, led to movement over the Drakensberg and the Vaal into what was to become the South African Republic.

At least two motives contributed to the *Voortrekker* movement. The first was a desire to seek new employment away from the area controlled by the Cape Company. The Boers were producing large families, and in the Cape market itself supply had outstripped demand. The second motive was the passion for independence which led to Afrikaner nationalism. The events of the Trek, like those of most of the world's frontier movements, have passed into legend. The Trek came to be seen as the birth of a nation, as an Exodus, with Natal as the Promised Land and the Cape Colony as the Land of Pharaoh.

The beginnings of the *Voortrekker* movement can be traced to the Hottentot cattle trade. As the Hottentots grew shy and animals became scarce, expeditions went farther afield. As population pressure increased within the colony, pastoralists began to roam over unoccupied Crown Land and then over land that had not yet been claimed. In addition to the general fanning out of the Boer population, there were also seasonal migrations and unplanned flights in times of drought. Finally there were the organized treks, incorporating shepherds and farmers, and all the paraphernalia necessary to establish a relatively self-sufficient life.

There were no natural barriers to retard the migration, especially after it reached the veld; but in the middle of the eighteenth century the Boers ran up against another and numerically superior movement, the great southward drift of the Bantu. During the next three quarters of a century there were no fewer than eight

Kaffir wars, and these conflicts were only highlights of incessant strife. Moreover, the farther inland the Boers trekked, the greater the difficulty they experienced in marketing their goods.

With these essential facts in mind it is possible to draw some comparisons between the South African and American frontiers. Both were relatively continuous movements, and both ran ahead of roads and rails. The succession of livelihood was basically similar, although pastoral activity was more prominent and more enduring on the South African frontier. The data of comparative study suggest that the *Voortrekker* movement represented a lessening of contact with the outside world. In contrast, the Australian and Canadian frontiers were pushed forward by men eager to produce for a distant market.

Part of this interpretation is challenged in a publication of the Stanford Food Research Institute. In it, S. D. Neumark argues that the essential causes of the migration should be sought not only in the conditions prevalent on the frontier, but also in the economic development of South Africa as a whole.[48] He objects to the characterization of the Trek as a self-sufficient movement and refers instead to a frontier exchange economy based upon the barter or sale of livestock. According to Neumark, the *Voortrekkers* were never self-sufficient in the strict sense of the word. Even the most remote settlements were visited by itinerant traders. The demand for tea, sugar, and cloth kept the Boers at least marginally within the European consumer group. Moreover, the Boers were obliged to obtain firearms, powder, shot, wagons, and the other things that insured their military and technological predominance over the Bantu. In exchange they offered livestock, hides, horns, sheep-fat, tallow, and other products of the frontier. Neumark suggests that "even if the frontiersmen were 99 per cent self-sufficient, it was the 1 per cent that tipped the scale, for it constituted the minimum factor in the frontier economy." [49]

The validity of this interpretation, as W. K. Hancock points out in an extended review, depends upon the meaning that is assigned to "self-sufficiency." [50] According to Neumark's definition, the Hottentot and the Bantu might also be classified as members of a market-bound exchange economy. It would be unfortunate if the semantic aspects of this discussion were allowed to obscure important historical issues.

Some Conclusions

The results of recent comparative studies indicate that there is much to compare and also much to contrast on the world's frontiers. In the first place, basic historical differences have to be emphasized. The American, Canadian, Australian, and South African frontiers were formed during a period of accelerated economic and social evolution. This fact distinguishes them from the German and Russian migrations which were influenced by feudalism. The characteristics of the Latin American frontiers reflect the numerical weakness of the conquistadores, the process of acculturation encouraged by that weakness, and the fact that Spanish colonists were not interested primarily in the cultivation of new land.

The relationships between immigrant and aboriginal peoples vary from extensive assimilation in Latin America to absolute extermination in Tasmania and near extermination in the United States. The relatively unimpeded advance of the Australian frontier contrasts with the bitter conflicts experienced during the early stages of colonization in South Africa. The advances of the Anglo-American, Latin American, and Russian frontiers were characterized at various times by peaceful penetration and violent conflict. The drift of the Germans into the Slavic lands seems to have been relatively uneventful, except, of course, during the crusades of the Teutonic Knights.

Environmental differences influenced the direction and rate of movement of the several frontiers. The St. Lawrence River enabled the first Canadian colonists to move into the heart of the continent, but the continuation of that movement was blocked by the Pre-Cambrian Shield. The simultaneous advance of Australian settlement from widely separated points on the coast presents a picture quite unlike the advance of the American frontier. The *Voortrekkers* enjoyed more favorable circumstances for a continuous advance, but the absence of navigable rivers impeded their communication with the outside world. The great, north-flowing rivers of Siberia did not equal the opportunities which the Mississippi and its tributaries offered to the American pioneer.

One of the main points of the Turner thesis is the claim that frontier movement and economic development were coincident. In Australia and South Africa the indigenous peoples offered little for trade, whereas in Canada and Siberia the fur-traders were the first and most adventurous frontiersmen. The early conflicts between pastoralists and farmers in the American West reappear in Australia, New Zealand, and to a lesser extent in Canada. In each of these countries legislation favorable to homesteading was encouraged by the agitation of ex-miners. It is difficult to trace an economic succession on the German frontiers, for nobles, peasants, merchants, and craftsmen often moved in organized groups. The pattern of succession in Latin America is obscured by the fact that the first colonists were drawn by missionary zeal or lured by gold. In modern time most of the Latin American frontiers have been scenes of highly specialized production for international markets.

The most challenging feature of Turner's thesis was his assertion that the frontier was a major influence in the formation of national institutions. The evidence drawn from other parts of the world neither confirms nor denies this claim. Indeed, comparative study has made no major contribution to this aspect of the Turner controversy; nor could it, for in the study of "national character," a vague concept at best, the historian quickly becomes entangled in a maze of multiple causes and effects.

In addition to these general observations, some critical conclusions can be drawn from this extended review. It seems clear that little can be expected from comparative study unless research proceeds in a more systematic manner. To speak of an idealized Australian or South African frontier and then to compare it with the American frontier is to beg important questions. It would be more rewarding to compare resource appraisal and technology, or, if a more general framework is desired, to compare the environments of the three frontiers. Discussion of the frontier "experience" has little meaning when the economic and environmental conditions of that experience are only vaguely recognized. In this connection it must be remarked that only one of the comparative studies, Allen's *Bush and Backwoods*, deals with the frontier environment in reasonably explicit terms. A failing common to all but one of the comparative studies, Neumark's *South African Frontier*, is the absence of a functional classification of settlements.[51] Needless to say, there is little to be gained from a comparison of single-family farmsteads and mining camps; yet such "comparisons" are inevitable when different types of settlement and different modes of livelihood are subsumed under "frontier." It is not the lack of precise data as such that is deplored, but the impossibility of making a functional assessment of any custom without some knowledge of who, among whom and in what context, indulges in it. W. R. Mead's study of the settlement frontier in Finland, a Thünen-type analysis, sets admirable standards of precise definition and accurate delimitation.[52]

These critical remarks are not intended to detract from the considerable heuristic value of the several studies reviewed here. If the frontier fails to emerge as an objective phenomenon, then it may at least be described as a research theme. The work of the frontier historians impinges upon the traditional interests of the geographer, for in their research, as in his, the principal variables are man and land. The fact that historians have not dealt adequately with such topics as settlement morphology, crop ecology, and resource management should stimulate geographers to make further contributions to the frontier theme.

Notes

1. Herbert Heaton, "Other Wests than Ours," *Tasks of Economic History*, Supplement 6 (1946) to *Journal of Economic History*, pp. 50–62. Heaton does not refer to the "pioneer settlement" studies initiated by Isaiah Bowman, e.g., *The Pioneer Fringe* (New York: American Geographical Society, 1931), *Pioneer Settlement* (New York: American Geographical Society, 1932), and *Limits of Land Settlement* (New York: Council on Foreign Relations, 1937). Perhaps this is a conscious omission, for students of frontier history and pioneer settlement have had different aims. The rationale of the frontier historians has been an attempt to interpret the influence of past frontiers on national institutions. Bowman and his associates were concerned chiefly with the practical problems of pioneer settlement in modern times. For a clear statement of Bowman's interests, see his essay on "Settlement by the Modern Pioneer" in Griffith Taylor, ed., *Geography in the Twentieth Century* (2nd ed., New York: Philosophical Library, 1953), pp. 248–266.

2. Paul F. Sharp, "Three Frontiers: Some Comparative Studies of Canadian, American and Australian Settlement," *Pacific Historical Review,* XXIV (November 1955), 369–377.

3. Dietrich Gerhard, "The Frontier in Comparative View," *Comparative Studies in Society and History,* I (March 1959), 205–229.

4. J. L. M. Gulley, "The Turnerian Frontier: A Study in the Migration of Ideas," *Tijdschrift voor Economische en Sociale Geografie,* L (March–April and May 1959), 65–72, 81–91.

5. Walker D. Wyman and Clifton B. Kroeber, eds., *The Frontier in Perspective* (Madison: University of Wisconsin Press, 1957).

6. Silvio Zavala, "The Frontiers of Hispanic America" (pp. 35–58); A. L. Burt, "If Turner Had Looked at Canada, Australia, and New Zealand When He Wrote about the West" (pp. 59–77); A. Lobanov-Rostovsky, "Russian Expansion in the Far East in the Light of the Turner Hypothesis" (pp. 79–94); and Eugene P. Boardman, "Chinese Mandarins and Western Traders: The Effect of the Frontier in Chinese History" (pp. 95–110).

7. *Ibid.,* pp. xix–xx.

8. Jan O. M. Broek, "The Relations between History and Geography," *Pacific Historical Review,* X (September 1941), 321–325, ref. to 324. For an interesting example of the kind of study recommended by Broek, see Donald W. Meinig, "Colonization of Wheatlands: Some Australian and American Comparisons," *Australian Geographer,* VII (August 1959), 205–213.

9. A full discussion of exclusive relationships can be seen in Archibald Grenfell Price, *White Settlers and Native Peoples: An Historical Study of Racial Contacts between English-Speaking Whites and Aboriginal Peoples in the United States, Canada, Australia, and New Zealand* (Melbourne: Georgian House; Cambridge: Cambridge University Press, 1949).

10. For fuller discussion of this distinction see Lattimore (*op. cit.,* p. 177). Kristof (*op. cit.,* p. 272) speaks of frontiers "as manifestations of *centrifugal* forces," in contrast to boundaries which indicate the "range and vigor of *centripetal* forces"; he also refers (p. 273) to the contrasting functions of frontier *integration* and boundary *separation.*

11. For a detailed study of China's southern frontier, see Herold J. Wiens, *China's March toward the Tropics* (Hamden, Conn.: Shoestring Press, 1954). The northern frontier is described by Owen Lattimore, *Inner Asian Frontiers of China* (New York: American Geographical Society, 1940); and Wolfram Eberhard, *Conquerors and Rulers: Social Forces in Medieval China* (Leiden: E. J. Brill, 1952).

12. For discussion of these points see the essay of Silvio Zavala in *The Frontier in Perspective,* and Philip W. Powell, *Soldiers, Indians, and Silver: The Northward Advance of New Spain, 1550–1600* (Berkeley: University of California Press, 1952).

13. Preston E. James, *Latin America* (rev. ed., New York: Odyssey Press, 1950), p. 7.

14. See Robert S. Platt, "Coffee Plantations of Brazil: A Comparison of Occupance Patterns in Established and Frontier Areas," *Geographical Review,* XXV (April 1935), 231–239.

15. For a detailed study of this frontier see James Parsons, "Antioqueño Colonization in Western Colombia," *Ibero-Americana,* No. 32 (1949).

16. James Westfall Thompson, *Economic and Social History of the Middle Ages (300–1300),* (New York: Century Co., 1928), pp. 517–518.

17. Cf. Gerhard, *op. cit.*, pp. 218–223.

18. Donald W. Treadgold, *The Great Siberian Migration: Government and Peasants in Resettlement from Emancipation to the First World War* (Princeton: Princeton University Press, 1957). See also his preliminary statement in "Russian Expansion in the Light of Turner's Study of the American Frontier," *Agricultural History,* XXVI (October 1952), 147–152.

19. Lobanov-Rostovsky, *The Frontier in Perspective,* pp. 93–94.

20. Lattimore, "The Frontier in History," p. 117. See also his discussion of Russian and Chinese colonization in "The New Political Geography of Inner Asia," *Geographical Journal,* CXIX (March 1953), 17–30, in which he calls attention to a historical influence that Lobanov-Rostovsky overlooks, namely, the presence of Mongol and Turco-Mongol "buffer zones" between the Russian and Chinese frontiers.

21. J. M. S. Careless, "Frontierism, Metropolitanism, and Canadian History," *Canadian Historical Review,* XXXV (March 1954), 1–21, ref. to 2.

22. W. N. Sage, "Some Aspects of the Frontier in Canadian History," *Canadian Historical Association, Report of 1928,* pp. 62–72.

23. The mingling of Canadians and Americans in the Old Northwest and the Prairie Provinces has been the subject of much research. See especially M. L. Hansen and J. B. Brebner, *The Mingling of the Canadian and American Peoples* (Toronto: Ryerson Press; New Haven: Yale University Press, 1940), and Fred Landon, *Western Ontario and the American Frontier* (Toronto: Ryerson Press; New Haven: Yale University Press, 1941). A. L. Burt (*The Frontier in Perspective,* pp. 68–72) emphasizes the role of American Loyalists in the settlement of Upper Canada (i.e., Ontario) after the Revolutionary War.

24. For discussion of this point see Morris Zazlow, "The Frontier Hypothesis in Recent Canadian Historiography," *Canadian Historical Review,* XXIX (June 1948), 153–167.

25. Cf. Reginald G. Trotter, "The Appalachian Barrier in Canadian History," *Canadian Historical Association, Report of 1939,* pp. 5–21; and Stanley D. Dodge, "The Frontier of New England in the Seventeenth and Eighteenth Centuries and Its Significance in American History," *Papers of the Michigan Academy of Science, Arts and Letters,* XXVIII (1942), 435–439.

26. *Atlas of Canada* (Ottawa: Department of Mines and Technical Surveys, Geographical Branch, 1957), plate 46. In order to appreciate the significance of these maps, one must compare them with compilations for the same periods in the settlement history of the United States. For example, cf. Charles O. Paullin, *Atlas of the Historical Geography of the United States* (Washington, D. C.: Carnegie Institution, 1932), plates 76–79.

27. For a full account of the history of settlement in the interior plains, see Arthur S. Morton and Chester Martin, *History of Prairie Settlement and "Dominion Lands" Policy,* Vol. II of W. A. Mackintosh and W. L. G. Joerg, eds., *Canadian Frontiers of Settlement* (9 vols.; Toronto: Macmillan, 1934–1940).

28. Heaton, *op. cit.*, p. 58.

29. E. R. Adair, "The French Canadian Seigneury," *Canadian Historical Review,* XXXV (September 1954), 187–207.

30. Mason Wade, *The French Canadians, 1760–1945* (London and Toronto: Macmillan, 1955), p. vii.

31. See the posthumous edition of his most influential articles in H. A.

Innis, *Essays in Canadian Economic History* (Toronto: University of Toronto Press, 1956).

32. Careless, *op. cit.*, pp. 14–16. The basic ideas of the "Laurentian School" are set out in Donald G. Creighton, *The Commercial Empire of the St. Lawrence* (Toronto: Ryerson Press; New Haven: Yale University Press, 1937).

33. Donald C. Masters, *The Rise of Toronto, 1850–1890* (Toronto: University of Toronto Press, 1947).

34. In his development of this theme, Careless, *op. cit.*, p. 17, gives some attention to the concept of an urban hierarchy. "The metropolitan relationship," he notes, "is a chain, almost a feudal chain of vassalage, wherein one city may stand tributary to a bigger center and yet be a metropolis of a sizable region of its own."

35. William R. Siddall, "Seattle: Regional Capital of Alaska," *Annals*, Association of American Geographers, XLVII (September 1957), 277–284.

36. W. T. Easterbrook and Hugh G. J. Aitken, *Canadian Economic History* (Toronto: Macmillan, 1958). The third part of the book, Canada's "Transcontinental Economy," is most relevant to the theme of this review.

37. W. K. Hancock, *Problems of Economic Policy, 1918–1939*, Vol. 11, Part 1 of *Survey of British Commonwealth Affairs* (London: Oxford University Press, 1940), p. 5.

38. Lyle Blair, ed., *The Selected Works of Henry Lawson* (East Lansing: Michigan State University Press, 1957), p. 60.

39. Griffith Taylor, *Australia: A Study of Warm Environments and Their Effect on British Settlement* (5th ed., London: Methuen, 1949), pp. 4–7.

40. H. C. Allen, *Bush and Backwoods: A Comparison of the Frontier in Australia and the United States* (East Lansing: Michigan State University Press, 1959). See also the earlier discussion of Fred Alexander, *Moving Frontiers: An American Theme and Its Application to Australian History* (Melbourne: Melbourne University Press, 1947).

41. Allen, *op. cit.*, p. 114.

42. Brian Fitzpatrick, "The Big Man's Frontier and Australian Farming," *Agricultural History*, XXI (January 1947), 8–12. This generalization also applies to the early stages of settlement in New Zealand. See Peter J. Coleman, "The New Zealand Frontier and the Turner Thesis," *Pacific Historical Review*, XXVII (August 1958), 221–237.

43. See K. A. Mackirdy, "Conflict of Loyalties: The Problem of Assimilating the Far Wests into the Canadian and Australian Federations," *Canadian Historical Review*, XXXII (December 1951), 337–355.

44. Allen, *op. cit.*, p. 9.

45. George Nadel, *Australia's Colonial Culture: Ideas, Men and Institutions in Mid-Nineteenth Century Eastern Australia* (Melbourne: F. M. Cheshire; London: Angus and Robertson, 1957).

46. Allen, *op. cit.*, p. 56.

47. Russel Ward, *The Australian Legend* (Melbourne and London: Oxford University Press, 1958), ref. to p. v.

48. S. Daniel Neumark, *The South African Frontier: Economic Influences, 1652–1836* (Stanford, Calif.: Stanford University Press, 1957).

49. *Ibid.*, p. 4.

50. W. K. Hancock, *"Trek,"* Economic History Review, 2nd ser., X (April 1958), 331–339.

51. For interesting examples of such classifications see Sauer, *op. cit.*, pp.

283–289, and James G. Leyburn, *Frontier Folkways* (New Haven: Yale University Press, 1935), pp. 5–6 and *passim*.

52. W. R. Mead, "Frontier Themes in Finland," *Geography*, XLIV (July 1959), 145–156. See also his *Economic Geography of the Scandinavian States and Finland* (London: University of London Press, 1957).

🌳 10 🌳

Fred A. Shannon

A POST-MORTEM ON THE
LABOR-SAFETY-VALVE THEORY

Since 1935 there has been a growing suspicion among historians that the venerable theory of free land as a safety valve for industrial labor is dead. Out of respect for the departed one even the newer textbooks on American history have begun to maintain silence on the subject. For generations the hypothesis had such a remarkable vitality that a dwindling remnant of the old guard still profess that they observe some stirrings of life in the assumed cadaver. Consequently, it seems that the time has arrived for the reluctant pathologist to don his gas mask and, regardless of the memphitis, analyze the contents of the internal organs. Are the stirrings in the body an evidence of continued animation, or merely of gaseous and helminthic activity? Before the corpse is given a respectable burial this fact must be ascertained beyond any possible doubt.

There can be no question as to the venerable age of the decedent. Thomas Skidmore foretold him as early as 1829 in *The Rights of Man to Property!* George Henry Evans and his fellow agrarians of the 1840's labored often and long in eulogy of the virtues of the safety valve they were trying to bring into existence. The *Working Man's Advocate* of July 6, 1844, demanded the realization of "the right of the people to the soil" and said:

Fred A. Shannon (1893–1963) was Professor of History at the University of Illinois. He wrote, among other works, *The Farmer's Last Frontier: Agriculture, 1860–1897, The Organization and Administration of the Union Army,* and *Economic History of the People of the United States.*

Reprinted from *Agricultural History*, XIX (January 1945), 31–37, by permission of the publisher.

That once effected, let an outlet be formed that will carry off our superabundant labor to the salubrious and fertile West. In those regions thousands, and tens of thousands, who are now languishing in hopeless poverty, will find a certain and a speedy independence. The labor market will be thus eased of the present distressing competition; and those who remain, as well as those who emigrate, will have the opportunity of realizing a comfortable living.[1]

Long before Frederick Jackson Turner tacitly admitted the validity of the theory,[2] even the name "safety valve" had become a middle-class aphorism. The idea was so old and so generally held that it was commonly repeated without question. The Republican Party had so long made political capital of the Homestead Act and its feeble accomplishments that the benefit to the industrial laborer had become an axiom of American thought. Turner, himself, made only incidental use of the theory as a further illustration of his general philosophy concerning the West. Apparently he made no effort to examine the basis of the safety-valve assumption. Had he done so, no doubt the theory would have been declared dead at the turn of the century, and the present autopsy would have been made unnecessary. It was some of the followers of Turner who made a fetish of the assumption, but few if any have gone so far as to say that eastern laborers in large numbers actually succeeded as homesteaders.

The approach has been shifted. An early variation of the theme was that the West as a whole, if not free land alone, provided the safety valve.[3] This, as will be seen, was no more valid than the original theory. Another idea, sometimes expressed but apparently not yet reduced to a reasoned hypothesis, is that land, in its widest definition (that is, total natural resources), constituted a safety valve. This is merely one way of begging the question by proposing a new one. Besides, it is easy to demonstrate that as new natural resources were discovered the world population multiplied to take advantage of them and that the old problems were quickly transplanted to a new locality. It can readily be shown that the monopolization of these resources prevented their widest social utilization and that the pressure of labor difficulties was no less intense in new communities than in the old. Witness the Coeur d'Alene strike in Idaho in the same year as the Homestead strike in Pennsylvania. But the natural-resources–safety-valve theory will require a thorough statement and exposition by one of its adherents before an examination can be made. The manufacture of such a hypothesis will be a tough problem, in view of the fact that, ever since the development of the factory system in America, labor unrest has resulted in violently explosive strikes rather than a gentle pop-off of steam through any supposed safety valve. The question will have to be answered: If any safety valve existed why did it not work? Since it did not work, how can it by any twist of the imagination be called a valve at all?

Another turn of the argument is a revival of the supposition of Carter Goodrich and Sol Davison (further expounded) that while no great number of industrial laborers became homesteaders, yet the safety valve existed, because it drained off the surplus of the eastern farm population that otherwise would have gone to the cities for factory jobs. So, free land was a safety valve because it drew *potential* industrial labor to the West.[4]

Again, the question immediately arises: Why did this potential safety valve not work? Was it really a safety valve at all or was it merely a "whistle on a peanut roaster"? There can be no confusion of definitions involved. There is only one definition of the term: "An automatic escape or relief valve for a steam boiler, hydraulic system, etc." Under the catch-all "etc." one may just as well include "labor unrest." Obviously the safety valve is not for the benefit of the steam, water, or labor that escapes from the boiler, hydraulic system, or factory. It is to prevent the accumulation of pressure that might cause an explosion.

A safety valve is of use only when pressure reaches the danger point. This is where the trouble comes with the labor safety valve in all of its interpretations. It certainly was not working at the time of the Panic of 1837, or in the depression following the Panic of 1873, when over a million unemployed workmen paced the streets and knew that free lands were beyond their reach. It was rusted solid and immovable during the bloody railroad strikes of 1877 and the great labor upheaval of the 1880's. When the old-time Mississippi River steamboat captain "hung a nigger" on the arm of the safety valve when running a race, it can be positively asserted that his safety valve as such did not exist. This belief would doubtless be shared by the possible lone survivor picked maimed and scalded off a sycamore limb after the explosion.

No responsible person has ever tried to deny that at all times in America some few of the more fortunate laborers could and did take up land. But this seepage of steam which went on almost constantly did not prevent the pressure from rising when too much fuel was put under the boiler, and the seepage almost stopped entirely whenever the pressure got dangerously high. It was not till the 1830's, when the factory system in America began to bloom and the labor gangs were recruited for the building of canals and railroads, that any situation arose which would call for a safety valve. The shoemaker or carpenter of colonial days who turned to farming did not do so as a release from an ironclad wage system, as millions between 1830 and 1900 would have liked to do if they could. It was an era of slipshod economy and easy readjustment, where no great obstacle was put in the way of misfits. Even if one admits that a scarcity of free labor for hire was one of the minor reasons for the late development of a factory system, and that the choice of close and cheap land kept down the supply, yet a far greater reason was the scarcity of manufacturing capital. When the factory system began, it was easy to import shiploads of immigrant laborers. The same could have been done a generation or two earlier if there had been the demand.

But perhaps a more substantial argument is needed to answer so attractive a hypothesis as that of the potential safety valve. At first glance this new idea has some charm. Certainly the western farms did not create their own population by spontaneous generation. If not eastern industrial laborers, then undoubtedly eastern farmers must have supplied the initial impulse, and each eastern farmer who went west drained the eastern potential labor market by one. But the question is: Did *all* the migration from east to west amount to enough to constitute a safety valve for eastern labor? Did not the promise of free land, and such migration as actually occurred, simply lure millions of Europeans to American shores, seeking farms or industrial jobs, the bulk of the newcomers remaining in the East to make possible a worse labor congestion than would have existed if everything west of the Mississippi River had been nonexistent? The answer is so simple that it can be evolved from census data alone. The post-mortem can now be held. If a sufficient domestic migration did take place with the desired results, then there *was* a safety valve, and there is no corpse of a theory to examine. If not, then the theory is dead and the body can be laid to rest.

The first question to be answered is: How large a surplus of farm population developed and where did it settle between 1860 (just before the Homestead Act) and 1900 (by which date the last gasp of steam is admitted to have escaped from the safety valve)? Here close estimates must substitute for an actual count, for before 1920 the census did not distinguish between actual farm and nonfarm residence. But the census officials did gather and publish figures on the numbers of persons employed for gain in the different occupations, and, wherever comparisons can be made, it is noticeable that the ratio of farm workers to all other persons receiving incomes has always been relatively close to the ratio between total farm and nonfarm population. On this basis of calculation (the only one available and accurate enough for all ordinary needs), in forty years the farm population only expanded from 19 million to 28 million, while the nonfarm element grew from somewhat over 12 million to 48 million, or almost fourfold. Villages, towns, and cities gained about 18 million above the average rate of growth for the nation as a whole, while the farm increase lagged by the same amount below the average. These figures are derived from a careful analytical study of occupations, based on census reports, which shows the number of income receivers engaged in agriculture creeping from 6,287,000 to 10,699,000, while those in nonfarm occupations soared from 4,244,000 to 18,374,000.[5]

Small as was the growth of agricultural population, it must be noted further that over 35 per cent of the farms in 1900 were tenant-operated,[6] and 43 per cent of all farm-income receivers were wage laborers.[7] This leaves only 22 per cent as owner-operators. But even though 25 per cent is conceded, this would allow only 7,000,000 people in 1900 living on farms owned by their families, except for some sons who were also wage laborers or tenants. But the total national population increase was nearly 45 million in forty years. Though the zealot may choose to ignore the fact that at least *some* of the farm workers owned their own land even in 1860 and may accept the figure for 1900 as growth alone, yet he has put but a small fraction of the increased population of the United States on such farms anywhere in the nation, and hardly enough to consider in the West. This is not the way safety valves are constructed.

A further analysis of the data reveals that only 3,653,000 farms in 1900 were operated, even in part, by their owners. But at the same time at least 21 million farm people were tenants and wage laborers and their families on the total of 5,737,000 farms in the nation.[8] These laborers were rarely any better off financially (often worse) than the toiling multitudes in the cities. These were not persons who had found release either from the farms or the cities of the East on land of their own in the West. The bulk of them were still east of the Mississippi River. These were not *potential* competitors of the city workers. They were *actual* competitors, for the hard living conditions of each group had a depressing effect on the economic status of the other. Neither element had the opportunity, the finances, the experience, or the heart to try their luck in the West.

These incontestable facts and figures play havoc with the assumption that "perhaps most" of the eastern boys who left their "ancestral acres" migrated "to the West to acquire and develop a tract of virgin soil." [9] There just was not that much of an increase in the number of farms between 1860 and 1900. Only 3,737,000 units were added to the 2 million of the earlier year, and 2 million of the total in 1900 were tenant-operated.[10] How large a proportion of the eastern boys who left their fathers' farms could have become by any possibility the owners of the fraction of the increase in farms that lay in the West?

Here the potential-safety-valve advocates spoil their own argument. One of them stresses the great fecundity of eastern farmers, "a dozen children being hardly exceptional." [11] At only the average rate of breeding for the whole nation, the 19 million farm population of 1860, with their descendants and immigrant additions, would have numbered about 46 million by 1900. But barely 60 per cent of that number were on farms anywhere in the country at the later date, and only 7 million could have been on farms owned by themselves or their families. If farmers were as philoprogenitive as just quoted, then by 1900 the number of persons of farm ancestry must have been closer to 60 million than 46 million and the increase alone would amount to at least 40 million. But the growth of farm population was only 9 million, and, of these, little more than 2 million could have been on farms owned by their families. If it could be assumed that all the augmentation in farm population had been by migrating native farmers, by 1900 there would have been 31 million of farm background (as of 1860) residing in the villages, towns, and cities; 9 million would have been on new farms or subdivisions of old ones; of these, nearly 7 million would have been tenants or hired laborers and their families, depressing industrial labor by their threat of competition; and about 2 million would have been on their own farms, whether "virgin soil" of the West or marginal tracts in the East. But it would be taking advantage of the opponent's slip of the pen to trace this fantasy further. The law of averages is enough in itself to annihilate the safety valvers' contention. By the use of this conservative tool alone it will be realized that at least twenty farmers moved to town for each industrial laborer who moved to the land, and ten sons of farmers went to the city for each one who became the owner of a new farm anywhere in the nation.

As to the farms west of the Mississippi River, it is well known that many of them were settled by aliens (witness the West North Central States with their large numbers of Scandinavians). Here is a theme that might well be expanded. The latest exponent of the potential-labor–safety-valve theory declares that "potential labor was drained out of the country, and to secure it for his fast expanding industrial enterprise, the manufacturer must import labor from Europe." [12] Anyone must admit that a fraction of the surplus farm labor of the East went on new farms. But how does this additional immigrant stream into the cities affect the safety valve? The immigrants may not really have increased the industrial population. It has often been contended that, instead, the resulting competition restricted the native birth rate in equal proportion to the numbers of the newcomers. Apparently this must remain in the realm of speculation. Be this as it may, the immigrants, with their background of cheap living, acted as a drag on wages, thus making the lot of the city laborer all the harder. This is not the way that even a *potential* safety valve should work.

But, returning to the West, there is a further fact to be considered. The total population west of the Mississippi River in 1860 was about 4,500,000. In 1900 it was just under 21 million.[13] Surely the "fecund" westerners must have multiplied their own stock to about 12 million by the latter date. In the same forty years some 14 million immigrants came to America.[14] By 1900, with their descendants, they must have numbered half again as many, or 21 million, for it has not been contended that immigrant competition lowered the immigrant birth rate. On this point the census data are not altogether satisfying. Foreign-born persons and their American-born children (counting only half of the children of mixed American and alien parentage) numbered 23,673,000. No doubt the survivors of the foreign born counted in the Census of 1860, together with their later children, would reduce the alien accretion since 1860 to the 21 million estimate. If anyone can prove that this should be cut still a few more million, he will not greatly change the estimates that follow.

The western states, in proportion to their total population, had proved amazingly attractive to the immigrants. Though over 19,087,000 of the 1900 count (including those with only one foreign-born parent) lived east of the Mississippi River, 7,112,000 were in the states (including Louisiana and Minnesota) to the west of the same line. In the eleven Mountain and Pacific States they were 47.6 per cent of the total population, the figure reaching 61.2 in Utah, 57.3 in Montana, and 54.9 in California. Nevada also had a majority. Kansas and Missouri alone of the West North Central group had less than 40 per cent of alien parentage, while the percentage in North Dakota was 77.5, in Minnesota 74.9, and in South Dakota 61.1. In round numbers Minnesota had 1,312,000, Iowa 958,000, California 815,000, Missouri 741,000, Nebraska 503,000, Texas 472,000, and Kansas 403,000. Aside from Texas the numbers, as well as the percentages, in the West South Central States were low.[15]

In 1860 the trans-Mississippi West contained 653,000 persons of foreign birth,[16] but the number of their American-born children was not given. Even if the survivors and the children numbered over a million, by 1900 those twenty-two states still had 6 million of post-1860 immigrant stock. If the estimate for the increase of the pre-1860 element is too low, so, it can be countered, were the totals of the Census of 1900. Grandchildren were not counted, and mature immigrants of the 1860's could have had a lot of grandchildren by 1900. All the descendants of the pre-1860 immigrants were included in the estimate of 12 million for the increase of the inhabitants of 1860, whereas all after the first descent are excluded from the post-1860 immigrant posterity. On the other hand, let it be conceded that 12 million by internal expansion and 6 million by immigration, or 18 million in all, is too much. This would leave only 3 million of the West in 1900, or one-seventh of the total, accounted for by migration from the eastern states. The calculator can afford to be generous. Subtract 2 million from the internal expansion and another million from the alien stock, and add these to the migrants from the eastern states. Suppose, then, that 6 million of the West's population of 1900 was of pre-1860 eastern United States origin, and three times that many foreigners and their children had come into the East to replace them. It all simmers down to the fact that the West acted as a lure to prospective European immigrants, either to take up lands, to occupy vacated city jobs, or to supply the demands of a growing industry. In any case the effect was just exactly the opposite of a safety valve, actual or potential.

Now the question is in order as to how many of those eastern boys who left their "ancestral acres" and migrated "to the West" actually were able "to acquire and develop a tract of virgin soil." As will soon be demonstrated, only 47.1 per cent of the western population of 1900 lived on farms. By the same ratio, a mere 2,826,000 of the exaggerated number of the eastern stock (as listed above) were farm residents. There were barely more than 2 million farms west of the Mississippi in 1900.[17] If two-sevenths of the population was eastern in origin, it may be assumed that the same proportion of the farming was done by them. This would give them less than 572,000 units to operate as owners, managers, tenants, or hired laborers. But in the West, as in the nation as a whole, the ratio of tenants and hired laborers to all farmers was very high. A full 35 per cent of all western farms were occupied by tenants. The high ratio in the West South Central region affects the average for all somewhat, but there were several other states that approximated the worst conditions. The percentage in Nebraska was 35.5, in Kansas 33.9, in Iowa 33.6, in Missouri 30.6, and in South Dakota 21.9.[18] But, also, slightly over 40 per cent of all western farm-income receivers were wage laborers.[19] If these same ratios apply to total population on the farms, then well over 1,130,000 of the eastern element in the West were wage laborers' families; more than 989,000 were on tenant holdings; and less than 707,000 occupied farms owned by themselves. This means that there was only one person on such a family possession for each twenty-five who left the farms of the nation in the preceding forty years. But perhaps this number is a little too small. No doubt a good number of the hired laborers were also the sons of the owners. Also, though many of the wage workers in the West lived with their families in separate huts on the farms, another considerable number were single men (or detached from their families) who boarded with the owner. How much this situation affected the given figures is uncertain. But here is something more substantial. Only 65 per cent of the farms, or less than 372,000 in all, were owner operated. Here, then, is the number of those tracts of "virgin soil" taken up and kept—one for each forty-eight persons who left their "ancestral acres" in the East, or possibly one family farm for each ten families. What a showing for the potential safety valve!

One point remains: Urban development in its relation to safety-valve theories. Between 1790 and 1860 the percentage of persons in cities of 8,000 or more inhabitants grew from 3.3 to 16.1; the number of such places from 6 to 141; and their population from 131,000 to 5 million. Over half of this growth took place after 1840. The city was already draining the country. But this was only the curtain raiser for the act to follow. In the next forty years the number of cities was multiplied to 547, their inhabitants to 25 million, and their percentage of the total population to 32.9. They had grown more than twice as fast as the nation at large.[20] The same rule applies to all municipalities of 2,500 and over, as their population expanded from 6,500,000 to 30,400,000.[21] The cities may have bred pestilence, poverty, crime, and corruption, but there is no evidence that they bred population that rapidly. Immigration alone cannot explain the phenomenon, for, if the entire number of immigrants after 1860 is subtracted from the non-farm population of 1900, the remainder still represents twice the rate of growth of farm population.

It is conceded that the bulk of the immigrants settled in urban localities, and it has been demonstrated that the great bulk of the surplus of farm population did the same. For that matter, outside the Cotton Belt, the majority of the westward-moving population did not settle on farms. When the eastern city laborer managed to pay his fare or "ride the rods" westward, he, like the migrating farmer, was likely to establish himself in a mining camp, town, or city, where, as in the Coeur d'Alene region of Idaho, he found that he had exchanged drudgery in an eastern factory for equally ill-paid drudgery (considering living costs) in a western factory or mine. The urbanized proportion of the population west of the Mississippi River, where 1,725,000 new farms had been created,[22] very nearly kept pace with the national average. In 1900, when almost half (47.1 per cent) of America's people were living in incorporated towns and cities, the ratio west of the Mississippi River was over three-eighths (38.1 per cent). Minnesota exceeded, while Missouri, Iowa, and Nebraska nearly equaled, the national ratio. The combined eleven Mountain and Pacific States rated even higher than Minnesota, with 50.6 per cent of their population in incorporated places. It was only the Dakotas and the West South Central States that were so overwhelmingly rural as to keep the trans-Mississippi West below the national ratio.[23] On the basis of the gainfully employed, always a better measure, the West showed a still higher proportion of nonfarm population. The census figures for 1870, 1890, and 1900 are used in Table 10–1 to illustrate this point.[24]

In each decade, the far-western regions were well below the national ratio of agricultural to town and city labor, and to 1890 they were far below. In 1870, outside the West South Central States and Iowa, the figure averaged 44.3 per cent for seventeen western states compared with 47.4 per cent for the United States. In the next twenty years, when free land was presumed to be the greatest lure of the West, the towns gained on the farms till the latter included only 46.5 per cent of the western total in spite of the still preponderantly rural character of the West South Central division. Then in 1890, according to the legend, the gate to free land flew shut with a bang, and the urban-labor safety valve rusted tight forever. Yet, the increase in agricultural population in the next ten years was nearly a fourth larger than the average for the preceding decades. Whereas the city had been draining labor from the farm before 1890, now that the theoretical safety valve was gone the western farm was gaining on the western city. Good land—free, cheap, or at speculators' prices—

TABLE 10-1

Persons Ten Years of Age and Over Gainfully Employed in the West, 1870, 1890, and 1900

AREA	1870 TOTAL THOUSANDS	AGRICULTURE THOUSANDS	PER CENT	1890 TOTAL THOUSANDS	AGRICULTURE THOUSANDS	PER CENT	1900 TOTAL THOUSANDS	AGRICULTURE THOUSANDS	PER CENT
United States	12,506	5,922	47.4	22,736	8,466	37.2	29,286	10,438	35.7
Trans-Miss. West	2,199	1,170	53.2	5,811	2,703	46.5	7,717	3,642	47.1
W. N. Central	1,157	648	56.0	2,988	1,432	47.9	3,693	1,707	46.2
W. S. Central	628	417	66.4	1,487	933	62.7	2,322	1,472	63.4
Mountain	134	50	29.9	501	127	25.3	663	192	28.8
Pacific	280	65	23.2	836	212	25.4	1,039	271	26.1

undoubtedly was more abundant before 1890 than afterward. Before that date, without cavil, this land had helped keep down *rural* discontent and unrest. A small percentage of surplus farmers, and a few other discontented ones in periods of hard times, had been able to go west and take up new farms, but many times that number had sought refuges, however tenuous, in the cities. Whether this cityward migration left the more intelligent and energetic or the duller and more indolent back on the farm is relatively immaterial so far as the release of pressure is concerned. Such evidence as has been uncovered shows no decided weight one way or the other.

This much is certain. The industrial labor troubles of the 1870's and 1880's, when this *potential* safety valve was supposed to be working, were among the most violent ever experienced in the nation's history. Steam escaped by explosion and not through a safety valve of free land. On the other hand, down to 1890 the flow of excess farmers to the industrial centers was incessant and accelerated. When hard times settled down on the farms of the Middle West, as in the 1870's, Grangers could organize, antimonopoly parties arise, and greenbackers flourish; but the pressure was eased largely by the flow of excess population to the towns. No doubt the migrants would have done better to stay at home and create an explosion. Instead, they went to town to add to the explosive force there. Farm agitation died down when a few reforms were secured, and the continued cityward movement retarded its revival.

However, after 1890 this release for rural discontent began to fail. The cities were approaching a static condition and were losing their attraction for farmers. This condition continued until between 1930 and 1940 there was virtually no net shift of population between town and country.[25] In the 1890's when the city safety valve for rural discontent was beginning to fail, the baffled farmer was at bay. Drought in the farther West and congestion in the cities left him no direction to go. He must stay on his freehold or tenant farm and fight. Populism in the 1890's was not to be as easily diverted or sidetracked by feeble concessions as had been Grangerism in the 1870's. In the forty years after 1890, the farmers, balked increasingly in their cityward yearnings, began to take far greater risks than ever before in their efforts to conquer the arid regions. Four times as much land was homesteaded as in the preceding decades.[26] Great things were accomplished in the way of irrigation and dry farming; but also great distress was encountered, great dust bowls were created, and great national problems of farm relief were fostered.

Generalization alone does not establish a thesis, but already there is a substantial body of facts to support an argument for the city safety valve for rural discontent. Nevertheless old stereotypes of thought die hard. Quite often they expire only with their devotees. It has been proved time after time that since 1880, at least, the old idea of the agricultural ladder has worked in reverse. Instead of tenancy being a ladder up which workers could climb to farm ownership, in reality the freeholder more often climbed down the ladder to tenancy. Yet there are people in abundance who still nourish the illusion that their old friend remains alive. There is no reason for assuming that in the present instance the truth will be any more welcome than it has proved to be in the past. There never was a free land or even a western safety valve for industrial labor. There never was one even of the potential sort. So far did such a valve fail to exist that the exact opposite is seen. The rapid growth of industry and commerce in the cities provided a release from surplus farm population. The safety valve that actually existed worked in entirely the opposite direction from the one so often extolled. Perhaps the growth of urban economy also, on occasion, was rapid and smooth enough to absorb most of the growing population without explosive effect. Once the people concentrated in the cities, there was no safety valve whatever that could prevent violent eruptions in depression periods. Of this, the diehards also will remain unconvinced. The persons who mournfully sing that "The old gray mare, she ain't what she used to be" seldom are ready to admit that she never did amount to much.

The post-mortem on the theory of a free-land safety valve for industrial labor is at an end. For a century it was fed on nothing more sustaining than unsupported rationalization. Its ethereal body was able to survive on this slender nourishment as long as the supply lasted. But when the food was diluted to a "potential" consistency, it was no longer strong enough to maintain life. Death came from inanition. The body may now be sealed in its coffin and laid to rest. Let those who will consult the spirit rappers to bring forth its ghost.

Notes

1. John R. Commons *et al.*, eds., *A Documentary History of American Industrial Society* (Cleveland: 1910), Vol. 7, p. 301.

2. Frederick Jackson Turner, *The Frontier in American History* (New York: 1920), pp. 259, 275.

3. Joseph Schafer, "Was the West a Safety Valve for Labor?" *Mississippi Valley Historical Review*, XXIV (1937), 299–314.

4. Edward Everett Dale, "Memories of Frederick Jackson Turner," *Mississippi Valley Historical Review*, XXX (1943), 356. See also Carter Goodrich and Sol Davison, "The Wage-Earner in the Westward Movement," *Political Science Quarterly*, LI (1936), 115, where the expression "*potential* wage-earners" is first, or at least previously, used.

5. P. K. Whelpton, "Occupational Groups in the United States, 1820–1920," *American Statistical Association Journal*, XXI (1926), 339–340.

6. U. S. Bureau of Foreign and Domestic Commerce, *Statistical Abstract of the United States* (1931), p. 647.

7. George K. Holmes, "Supply of Farm Labor," U. S. Dept. of Agriculture, Bureau of Statistics, *Bulletin 94* (Washington: 1912), pp. 14–15.

8. *Statistical Abstract*, 1931, p. 647.

9. Dale, *op. cit.*, p. 356.

10. U. S. Census Office, Eighth Census, 1860, *Agriculture*, 222; *Statistical Abstract* (1931), p. 647.

11. Dale, *op. cit.*, p. 356.

12. *Ibid.*

13. *Statistical Abstract*, 1931, pp. 8–9.

14. *Ibid.*, p. 95.

15. Twelfth Census, 1900, *Population*, I, p. clxxxii.

16. Eighth Census, 1860, *Population*, p. 623.

17. *Statistical Abstract*, 1931, p. 646.

18. Twelfth Census, 1900, *Agriculture*, I, p. lxix.

19. Holmes, *op. cit.*, pp. 17, 19.

20. *Statistical Abstract*, 1941, p. 6.

21. U. S. National Resources Committee, *Population Statistics: 3, Urban Data* (Washington: 1937), p. 8.

22. There were 319,335 farms in the West in 1860, out of a national total of 2,044,077. Ninth Census, 1870, *Wealth and Industry*, p. 340.

23. Twelfth Census, 1900, *Population*, I, p. lxii.

24. Calculated from Ninth Census, 1870, *Population and Social Statistics*, pp. 670–671; Eleventh Census, 1890, *Population*, II, pp. 306–337; Twelfth Census, 1900, *Population*, II, p. cxxxv.

25. *Statistical Abstract*, 1941, p. 671.

26. *Ibid.*, 1931, p. 134.

✢ 11 ✢

Norman J. Simler

THE SAFETY-VALVE DOCTRINE
RE-EVALUATED

The members of the Mississippi Valley Historical Association do
not have to be reminded that the Turner thesis in general, and the
safety-valve doctrine in particular, reigned virtually unchallenged
until the 1930's. The reaction to the thesis set in during the middle
of that decade, and the attack on the validity of the safety-valve
doctrine continued apace until Professor Shannon read his famous
"post-mortem" over the apparently inert body in 1945.

The purpose of this chapter is to review briefly this controversy
and to comment upon the principal arguments advanced on both
sides of the debate in such wise as to lend some credence to what
appears now to be a thoroughly discredited doctrine. To this end I
shall examine the criticisms of Carter Goodrich and Sol Davison,
Fred Shannon, and Murray Kane, as well as the tireless defense of
Joseph Schafer. I intend to show that the participants on both
sides were asking and attempting to answer questions which only
obscured the real issues at stake and, as a consequence, rendered
many of the results of the controversy unnecessarily confused. At
the same time, I believe that it is possible to find a more fruitful
approach to this whole problem.

Norman J. Simler is Professor of Economics at the University of Minnesota,
and the author of *Impact of Unionism on Wage Income Ratios in the Manufacturing Sector of the Economy.*
    Reprinted from *Agricultural History,* XXXII (October 1958), 250–257, by
permission of the author and the publisher.

I

Goodrich and Davison examined contemporary newspapers, searched the records of emigration societies, and evaluated other evidence from western sources.[1] The results of their research led them to remark that although the theory held that "wage-earners took a significant part in the movement to the western lands. . . . Yet in the descriptions of the actual process of settlement . . . the migrants are almost never identified as wage-earners, though there are frequent references to the presence of farmers . . . [and] immigrants. . . ."[2] They concluded that, because worker migration was apparently small relative to the total labor supply in the East, "too few wage-earners left the industrial centers to exert any marked effect on their labor situation,"[3] meaning, presumably, the eastern labor situation. Moreover, they argued that "the real doubts of the soundness of the doctrine arise not from anything that has been said against it, but from the sheer absence of direct evidence in its support. The suspicious thing is that wage-earners are so rarely mentioned in the descriptions of actual settlement. . . ."[4]

Now, methodological criticisms aside,[5] one may legitimately object on other grounds. For instance, to the extent that foreigners would have migrated across the Atlantic even if the "West" were not there (in search of higher wages or, in general, "better opportunities"), the movement of this foreign component to the frontier would act as a kind of safety valve, relieving adverse wage-and-employment pressure on those native Americans who stayed in the East. In the same way, to the extent that eastern farmers and/or their sons who might otherwise have drifted into the eastern labor pool moved west, this displacement would also act as a kind of safety valve.

Goodrich and Davison, however, anticipated this type of criticism for they specifically said: "Our concern is with *eastern* wage-earners, not immigrant or western ones, and with eastern wage-earners who *became western farmers*"[6] and, presumably, not western wage-earners. This kind of counter-argument runs through the whole of the controversy under review, and one wonders why the defenders of the doctrine allowed themselves to be trapped into agreeing that the question can be narrowed like this. Schafer, for instance, agreed that "The precise question under examination is this: Did wage-earners enter into the westward movement to such an extent as to constitute the frontier a 'safety valve' for labor?" [7] Having chosen to meet his critics on their own grounds, he tried to show that almost "one-third of the middle western farmers, around 1880, had earned their farms as common or skilled laborers." [8]

But Goodrich and Davison easily demolished this argument by pointing out that the source material for Schafer's evidence could not reveal whether as former wage-earners these were immigrant, eastern, or western ones, or whether they were industrial workers, hired hands on farms, or itinerants, for the only relevant category was (by mutual consent) eastern industrial wage-earners! They could therefore in good faith "continue to question the presence of any very substantial number of eastern industrial wage-earners in the great stream of migrants that occupied the lands of the West." [9]

It seems that as soon as the theory becomes stated in such a narrow fashion, it becomes virtually impossible to salvage it whole. While it may be a physical truth that steam rises to the top of a boiler and therefore the safety valve must be located at the top, it does not follow that in order to relieve adverse wage-and-employment pressure in a labor market the workers at the "top" (the native American wage-earners) have to be the ones who must "escape" to the West. The "safety valve" in a labor market could be equally well located at the "side" (eastern farmers and/or their sons?) or even at the "bottom" (immigrants?). Any analogy, of course, necessarily "limps," and the "safety valvers" in overlooking this and clinging to a literal translation of a physical fact into the world of economics damaged their own case unnecessarily.

The precise point at issue here requires that the discipline of history employ the discipline of economics. For that reason, it is necessary that we use the concepts, terms, and technical apparatus of economic analysis. If this proves a strain on memory or a bit of hard chewing, it is nonetheless requisite to the task at hand.

It is my contention that the evidence produced by Goodrich and

Davison does not constitute a valid derogatory criticism of an economic safety valve, whatever it may imply for an actual physical specimen of one. In particular, the "fact" that worker migration was small relative to both the total eastern labor supply and the total movement west is meaningless as far as ascertaining its effect on eastern wage rates and employment opportunities is concerned until the elasticity of demand for eastern labor is specified. A given percentage decrease in the labor supply will exert upward pressure on wage rates in inverse proportion to the absolute magnitude of the elasticity of demand for labor. Thus, given a sufficiently low elasticity coefficient, the critics' evidence and conclusions could actually support the economic theory of the safety valve rather than invalidate it. One searches the literature in vain for any recognition of this important point.

Moreover, since an economic safety valve does not have to be located at the "top" of the labor market in order for it to perform its economic function, to the extent that the West made westerners out of immigrants who might otherwise have become easterners, made western farmers out of eastern farmers who might otherwise have become eastern wage-earners, and made western wage-earners out of eastern wage-earners, one cannot really deny that it failed to perform this function. Yet the whole controversy narrowed down to the economically irrelevant question of whether or not the "steam" came out the "top," and not to the broader and economically more significant issue of whether the "steam" escaped at all from anywhere in the market, or even of whether it was really allowed to build up in the first place. To reply to this latter point merely by pointing a finger at the periodic waves of unemployment and worker discontent is to overlook an important question: What would these phenomena have been like in the absence of the West? No one would contend that the economic safety valve worked perfectly; but to argue that because it did not function flawlessly it did not function at all is a *non sequitur*.

II

Professor Shannon argued that the safety valve had not been a plausible doctrine since the advent of the factory system[10] and that it was at best a mere "whistle on a peanut roaster." [11] He cited the small amount of land taken up under the provisions of the Homestead Act, suggesting that the financial and technical difficulties involved in transforming an eastern wage-earner into a western farmer were too formidable to have permitted a sufficiently large migration of this type to have occurred, thereby precluding any favorable effects on eastern wage rates and employment opportunities.[12] Now this merely argues that relatively few eastern wage-earners became western farmers. As has just been pointed out, this "fact" is devoid of economic meaning unless it is related to the elasticity of demand for labor in the East; as it stands, it neither confirms nor denies the safety-valve doctrine in its economic aspect.

Shannon went one step further when he contended that the total migration from East to West of all kinds of people—immigrants, eastern workers, farmers, tradesmen, professional people, and the like—was simply not sufficient to constitute a safety valve for eastern wage-earners. The essence of the evidence adduced in support of this contention lay in the fact that between 1860 and 1900 the ratio of the increase of farm population to the increase of total United States population was only one-fifth.[13] The clear implication is that this ratio was "too low" for the West to have constituted an economic safety valve for eastern labor. Now in the absence of any allusion to the elasticity of demand for eastern labor and of any recognition of the significance of marginal movements of economic variables, one wonders why Shannon was so sure of himself on this count. He went on to show, apparently in the belief that it was economically relevant, that only a very small fraction of the increase in the western farm population represented an increase in the number of owner-occupied farms, the overwhelming bulk of the increase in farm population being absorbed as tenant-farmers and hired-hands.[14] To the extent that people left the East what difference does it make, as far as the effects on eastern wage rates and employment opportunities are concerned, what occupations they pursued in the West?

Both critics and defenders of the safety-valve doctrine seem to have been bewitched by the belief that easterners had to become western farmers in order for favorable effects in the eastern labor market to occur, and then Shannon reduced this to an absurdity by making it appear necessary that the increase in owner-occupied farms in the West was the relevant variable. To the extent that Shannon recognized that eastern wage-earners migrated to become western wage-earners he did so only to point out that, more often than not, the workers involved found they "had exchanged drudgery in an eastern factory for equally ill-paid drudgery . . . in a western factory or mine." [15] While this may or may not have been the case, it is simply irrelevant to the question at issue; for the workers, after all, did leave the East!

The most damaging meaningful argument that Shannon (or anyone else, for that matter) made against the doctrine as a whole was the one which reversed the theory and made the city the safety valve for rural discontent, especially during and after the so-called depression of the 1870's.[16] From data for the period between 1860 and 1900 he deduced that "some 20,000,000 persons had left farms to settle in urban areas, many of them in the great industrial centers of the East . . . [and concluded that] it was the city . . . which furnished at least a partial 'safety valve' for [the discontented farmers]." [17] However, Shannon's farm exodus of 20 million must be interpreted as a gross, not a net, migration: between 1860 and 1900 the "continental United States" population rose by 44.6 million, the "urban" areas receiving only 54 per cent of this increase. That is, not everyone forsook life in the country for that in the city. If it were indeed true that 20 million discontented farmers left the "rural" areas, then over 40 million people must have taken their place, for the population of this sector increased from 25.2 million in 1860 to 45.8 million in 1900.[18] It is, therefore, misleading to conclude that the location of the "safety value" shifted from farm to city in the latter third of the century.

This, however, does not entirely dispose of the matter. Shannon went on to argue that "once caught in the industrial toils, [erstwhile farmers] seldom returned. . . . The years of agricultural distress in the 1870's and 1880's were accompanied by an ever-increasing roll of unemployed in the cities." [19] In fact, he said, since "no person has denied that there were a million men unemployed in the North alone in 1865 [discharged soldiers?], and none has demonstrated that the number ever became perceptibly or permanently smaller. . . . Where then was the siren call of the free lands?" [20] Space does not permit a detailed theoretical and empirical analysis of the reasons for and the actual extent and severity of the post-Civil War depression, particularly in its wage-and-employment aspects. With respect to this latter point, however, several comments can be made in the space remaining.

Shannon said that there were never fewer than a million men unemployed throughout this period, and, in any case, "it cannot be denied that unemployment was a major economic ailment in every decade from 1865 to the close of the century. . . ." [21] But I wonder whether this statement can pass muster. Unemployment statistics gleaned from the scanty records of the latter third of the nineteenth century are notoriously unreliable. However, Rendigs Fels has reported:

. . . the only serious effort to estimate unemployment during the seventies was made by Carroll Wright. . . . In June 1878, which was presumably as bad a time as any, [he] took a kind of census which showed only 28,500 people unemployed in Massachusetts out of a normal working force in [manufacturing and] "mechanical industries" of 318,000. . . . Applying the ratio of unemployed in Massachusetts to the whole country, Wright estimated total unemployment in the United States at 570,000.[22]

This estimate yields an unemployment rate of 9 per cent. By modern standards this may not seem impressively low, but we must not judge the late nineteenth century by our own "full employment" norms.

Crude as Wright's methods must have been, they are nevertheless confirmed by other data which show that, while the contraction of the seventies was severe in monetary statistics, in terms of output (and by inference, employment) it was "singularly mild." [23] For instance, Edwin Frickey's indexes of manufacturing output and of production in the transportation and communication industries,[24] as well as Warren M. Persons' index of mining output,[25] all fell off slightly to troughs in 1876 and then rose to record levels by 1879. Moreover, Martin's figures reveal that real national income in 1879 was two-thirds greater than a decade before and one-third greater on a per capita basis.[26] On the other hand, during the seventies the index of wholesale prices declined 32 per cent, and both the cost-of-living index and the index of average daily wages in all non-agricultural employments fell by 13 per cent,[27] indicating that the trend of real wages was perhaps no worse than stable. It is probably safe to conclude that price and wage flexibility during this period of contraction intensified the decline in the values of monetary variables (i.e., intensified the deflation) but mitigated the fall in the values of real variables (i.e., mitigated the recession).[28] The distinction is an important one.

A deflation of this magnitude necessarily impinged heavily on the debtor groups, e.g., the farmers. Farms that were marginal became submarginal, and their owners were squeezed through the wringer of liquidation. Nevertheless, the fact that agricultural output doubled between 1866 and 1878 implies that low prices were profitable to the many farmers who could obtain cheap land and/or who remained liquid.[29] It seems to me, therefore, that the picture painted by Professor Shannon portrays both the industrial and the agricultural situations in an unnecessarily gloomy way.

III

Let me now turn briefly to the critique of Murray Kane. He narrowed the issue beyond that of eastern wage-earners simply becoming western farmers to eastern wage-earners who did so in times of panic and depression.[30] Moreover, as far as he was concerned, in order for the safety-valve doctrine to win out, it was necessary not only that "many" workers migrated but that the "majority" of them did so:

. . . for only in so far as the majority . . . of the population could reach the frontier during a particular period of panic or depression, can it be truly said that the frontier acted as a safety valve for the discontent of the country.[31]

Kane, of course, went on to show—no one has ever really questioned it—that the "majority" of wage-earners did not migrate to the West during any particular period of depression, nor, for that matter, during any particular period of prosperity. But again this reduces the whole question to an absurdity. No responsible economist has ever argued that, in order to induce favorable wage-and-employment effects in a labor market, the majority of the labor supply has to be exported out of the market. The values of economic variables are determined at the "margin," and, even in the most "discontinuous" of economic worlds, this never implies that more than a "few" of the economic quantities involved must "move." Kane admitted that there were individual and small-group migrations of wage-earners, "but these migrations were insignificant in number when considered in relation to the total number of the other elements of the population, which took part in the respective westward migrations. . . ." [32] But as I have argued before, it simply is not necessary that large numbers of wage-earners, or even potential wage-earners, leave a labor market in order to relieve downward pressure on wage and employment. Even the fact that "the minor number of mechanics who did migrate during the prosperity period remained in their traditional occupations," [33] or in any event did not become farmers, is adduced by Kane against the safety-valve doctrine. The point that these eastern mechanics became western ones and, in the process, relieved pressure on those remaining in the East is overlooked.

IV

Joseph Schafer, the principal defender of the doctrine during this period, contented himself with efforts to rebut the allegations of the critics, meeting them, in each case, on the opponents' well-chosen grounds. By and large, these efforts were doomed to failure or, at least, did not persuade the critics to abandon the attack. In one place, however, Schafer argued:

. . . the settlement of the frontier . . . was not merely agricultural; it involved the building of towns and cities, mills, factories, transportation systems, and it called for the full complement of mechanics and laborers demanded as a condition of advancing civilization.[34]

Now this statement is as close as Schafer ever got to recognizing a broad and economically meaningful construction of the question at issue.[35] That he himself did not really accept such a construction is shown by his using the quoted statement as a prelude to his main point: "these mechanics [and laborers], to a considerable extent, [later] became farmers on their new environments. . . ."[36] An economically meaningful interpretation of the doctrine does not require that such wage-earners eventually become farmers.

V

The safety-valve doctrine has had a very peculiar history. To begin with, it seems to me, it received an unfortunate name, and some of the misleading implications of a physical safety valve have been noted in this chapter. Moreover, in the controversy under review both proponents and opponents confused, or at least failed to distinguish clearly between, two different, but related, safety valves: a "social" safety valve and an "economic" safety valve. I have no quarrel with what I take to be the critics' position on the social safety valve—that the West, by and large, offered no easy avenue of "escape" for propertyless wage-earners caught up in the "industrial toils" of the East; for, as the critics have correctly pointed out, relatively few eastern wage-earners actually became western property owners. Rather, the West was a safety valve, a social safety valve, if you will, largely for the non-laboring propertied classes, forestalling for a number of generations the industrialization of the American farmer and other small-property owners. As Professor Hacker has put it: "the fluidity within the American society was largely confined to the middle class: petty-bourgeois property owners . . . [and/or their sons] had real opportunities to improve their economic and social positions by movement upward,"[37] thanks, in large part, to their ability to move west.

But to grant this is not to deny the existence of an economic safety valve. I do not think it a drastic oversimplification to say that from the point of view of those who succeeded in becoming property owners in the West, it was the social safety valve that was operating; while from the point of view of those who remained in the East, the West was an economic safety valve. This chapter has been focused on this latter point, which, it seems to me, has been too long neglected or, at least, improperly analyzed.

In agreeing to confine the issue to whether sufficient numbers of eastern wage-earners succeeded in becoming western farmers, both proponents and opponents at once clarified and confused the issue. The social safety valve was thereby placed in sharp relief, but its economic counterpart was almost lost sight of. And when the question was narrowed still further to whether the "majority" of eastern wage-earners during industrial depressions became occupying owners of western farms, the economic safety valve was pushed to the brink of absurdity, while its social counterpart was put in even clearer focus. This is, of course, a hindsight judgment, for, as we have seen, all the participants succeeded in confusing the two.

Yet amid all the confusion washed up by the waves of controversy certain undeniable economic facts shine through. The American economic complex was (and is) radically different from the European. The United States had a whole continent, rich in natural resources, to exploit. Labor, especially skilled labor, was historically a scare resource relative to the other cooperant factors. It is clear that people, and this includes the laboring classes, possessed a high degree of mobility. The West, after all, did get populated and it clearly did not get that way by a process of "spontaneous generation." Historians in other contexts speak of wave after wave of migrants and marvel at the rapidity with which the process of filling up the continent was carried to completion.[38] To be sure, a significant portion of this pulsating stream consisted of immigrants and the non-laboring propertied classes of the East. But that workers, too, displayed an astonishing degree of mobility cannot be denied. Worker mobility was sufficiently great to make necessary the creation of national trade unions and in itself to constitute a sufficient (although not unique) reason for the emergence of such organizations; while, at the same time, the problems that such mobility created were continuous and prickly thorns in the sides of the leaders of the labor movement.[39]

To assert that the West was the only, or even the most important, factor making for the undeniably generally favorable labor market conditions of the time is patently incorrect: the historical relative scarcity of labor, and the growth in worker productivity made possible largely because of a rapid rate of technological change and the growing stock of real capital, individually and collectively dwarf whatever economic safety-valve effect there was. But to deny therefore that the West, that the presence of alternative opportunities, had a non-negligible impact on the eastern labor market is just as clearly incorrect. Running through the (at times) acrimonious controversy reviewed here is this false dichotomy: either the West was a very important factor in the eastern labor market or it was no factor at all.

To judge the importance of the West in this economic context one must not only look at what was happening on the supply side of the market. Here, one would have to admit that the labor-supply function decreased over time independently of the reasons for which eastern workers, or potential eastern workers, left the market; whether they became western wage-earners or western farmers is economically (but not socially) irrelevant. In addition, one must at least evaluate the absolute magnitude of the elasticity of demand for labor and the extent of the dynamic upward shifts in the labor-demand function. If both demand and supply displayed such dynamic shifts—I would guess that demand increased relatively more than supply decreased—then the market position of workers became more favorable. To the extent that the West was a factor in this context, the economic safety valve was operating. To assert that the West was no factor at all is simply a misreading of historical fact. Given the relative shifts in the market functions over time, the wage elasticity of the functions is crucial. The more inelastic with respect to wages they are, the more favorable for the market position of the workers become the relative shifts in the functions.

These theoretical considerations appear to have been completely overlooked by all the participants in the controversy. It is a major contention of this paper, therefore, that, as far as meaningful economic analysis is concerned, the participants were asking and attempting to answer the wrong (or at least unimportant and, at times, irrelevant) questions. It would appear that a more fruitful approach to this whole problem could be constructed by first distinguishing clearly between the two safety valves, the economic and the social, along the lines suggested in this chapter.

Notes

NOTE: This article was read before the Mississippi Valley Historical Association, Minneapolis, Minn., on April 25, 1958.

1. Carter Goodrich and Sol Davison, "The Wage-Earner in the Westward Movement I," *Political Science Quarterly*, L (June 1935), 161–185; and "The Wage-Earner in the Westward Movement II," *Political Science Quarterly*, LI (March 1936), 61–116.

2. *Ibid.*, Vol. I, p. 161.

3. *Ibid.*, Vol. II, p. 115.

4. *Ibid.*, Vol. I, p. 166.

5. Schafer correctly pointed out that Goodrich and Davison tried "to prove a negative by means of negative testimony, employing mainly the [dangerous] *argumentum ex silentio.*" See Joseph Schafer, "Concerning the Frontier as Safety Valve," *Political Science Quarterly*, LII (September 1937), 408.

6. Carter Goodrich and Sol Davison, "The Frontier as Safety Valve: A Rejoinder," *Political Science Quarterly*, LIII (June 1938), 268–269. The *italics* are in the Goodrich and Davison "Rejoinder."

7. Joseph Schafer, "Some Facts Bearing on the Safety-Valve Theory," *Wisconsin Magazine of History*, XX (December 1936), 216.

8. Schafer, *op. cit.*, p. 418.

9. Goodrich and Davison, "Rejoinder," p. 270.

10. Fred A. Shannon, "The Homestead Act and the Labor Surplus," *American Historical Review*, XLI (July 1936), 651.

11. For a summary of Professor Shannon's remarks at the 1937 meeting of the Mississippi Valley Historical Association, see George F. Howe, "The Thirtieth Annual Meeting of the Mississippi Valley Historical Association," *Mississippi Valley Historical Review*, (September 1937), 198.

12. Shannon, "The Homestead Act and the Labor Surplus," pp. 638–646, *passim*.

13. Fred A. Shannon, "A Post-mortem on the Labor-Safety-Valve Theory" (Chapter 10).

14. *Ibid.*, pp. 33–34.

15. *Ibid.*, p. 36.

16. *Ibid.*, pp. 38–39; for a summary of Professor Shannon's remarks in this connection at the 1944 meeting of this Association see Harold W. Bradley, "The Thirty-Seventh Annual Meeting of the Mississippi Valley Historical Association," *Mississippi Valley Historical Review*, XXXI (September 1944), 230.

17. Bradley, *op. cit.*, p. 230.

18. United States Bureau of the Census, *Historical Statistics of the United States, 1789–1945* (Washington: 1949), p. 25.

19. Shannon, "The Homestead Act and the Labor Surplus," p. 649.

20. *Ibid.*, p. 650.

21. *Ibid.*, p. 651.

22. Rendigs Fels, "The Long-Wave Depression, 1873–97," *Review of Economics and Statistics*, XXXI (February 1949), 72; and "American Business Cycles, 1865–79," *American Economic Review*, XLI (June 1951), 345. Wright's estimates are in the *Tenth Annual Report of the Bureau of Statistics of Labor*, Massachusetts Public Document No. 31 (January 1879), 6–13.

23. Fels, "American Business Cycles," p. 345.

24. Edwin Frickey, *Production in the United States, 1860–1914* (Cambridge: 1947), pp. 54, 117.

25. Warren M. Persons, *Forecasting Business Cycles* (New York: 1937), pp. 170–171.

26. Robert F. Martin, *National Income in the United States, 1799–1938* (New York: 1939), p. 6.

27. *Historical Statistics*, LX, 234–235.

28. Fels, "American Business Cycles," p. 347; and Rendigs Fels, "The Effects of Price and Wage Flexibility on Cyclical Contraction," *Quarterly Journal of Economics*, LXIV (November 1950), 608.

29. Fels, "American Business Cycles," p. 331.

30. Murray Kane, "Some Considerations on the Safety Valve Doctrine," *Mississippi Valley Historical Review*, XXIII (September 1936), 169–171.

31. *Ibid.*, p. 171.

32. *Ibid.*, p. 174.

33. *Ibid.*, p. 187; see also his "Some Considerations on the Frontier Concept of Frederick Jackson Turner," *Mississippi Valley Historical Review*, XXVII (December 1940), 379–400.

34. Joseph Schafer, "Was the West a Safety Valve for Labor?," *Mississippi Valley Historical Review*, XXIV (December 1937), 309.

35. Goodrich and Davison, however, did in one place admit that "the abundance of western land drew away many thousands of *potential* wage-earners who might otherwise have crowded into [eastern] factories. . . . Though here the 'safety valve' was the farmer's rather than the worker's, we need not doubt that its operation tended to hold up the level of industrial wages." See "The Wage-Earner II," p. 115. Unfortunately, they never pursued this pregnant lead.

36. Schafer, "Was the West a Safety Valve for Labor?," p. 309.

37. Louis M. Hacker, *The Triumph of American Capitalism* (New York: 1940), p. 203.

38. See, for example, Frank Thistlewaite, *The Great Experiment* (Cambridge, England: 1955), Chapters V and VIII, *passim.*

39. See, for example, Lloyd Ulman, *The Rise of the National Trade Union* (Cambridge, Mass.: 1955), Parts I and II, *passim.*

✢ 12 ✢

George G. S. Murphy and Arnold Zellner

SEQUENTIAL GROWTH,
THE LABOR-SAFETY-VALVE DOCTRINE,
AND THE DEVELOPMENT OF
AMERICAN UNIONISM

I

"Let those who will consult the spirit rappers to bring forth its ghost." [1]

Such was Professor Shannon's firm caveat as he laid Frederick Jackson Turner's safety-valve doctrine to rest after a post-mortem performed with some gusto. The warning seems to have had the effect intended. Although Turner's frontier concept continues to influence the work of American historians and not a few economists, the labor-safety-valve doctrine seems generally to have been accepted as dead and buried.[2] We have little taste for ghosts or spirit rapping, but we would like to argue that the safety-valve doctrine, even if suffering from neglect, retains more than a spark of vitality.

This chapter attempts to present an "up-to-date" version of the labor-safety-valve doctrine which has its roots in Turner's work.[3]

George G. S. Murphy is Professor of Economics at the University of California, Los Angeles, and the author of *Soviet Mongolia: A Study of the Oldest Satellite*.

Arnold Zellner is H.B.G. Alexander Professor of Economics and Statistics at the University of Chicago and the author of papers in economic statistics and econometrics which have appeared in *Econometrica, Journal of the American Statistical Association,* and other periodicals.

Reprinted from the *Journal of Economic History*, XIX (September 1959), 402–421, by permission of the authors and the publisher.

To achieve this objective it is vitally important to develop the safety-valve doctrine within the context of certain aspects of the American growth process, in particular a Turnerian type of frontier process.

Turner's frontier process involves what we shall call sequential economic growth. That is, development in the American economy in the nineteenth century was in part a function of a sequence of decisions made by individuals in the market place and by governments (local, state, and federal) regarding the *time-rate* of exploitation of new slabs[4] of resources and the *size-rate* of the exploitation process. It so happened that private and public decisions made directly and indirectly led to a rapid annexation of many large slabs of resources to the more developed and still developing sections of the country. The set of such private and public decisions, their formation, their implementation, and their influence on human values and character, socioeconomic institutions, and growth constitute the core of Turner's process.[5]

It must be stressed that in America *many* of the new slabs of resources, although not all, afforded broad production possibilities with high marginal productivities of both capital and labor.[6] This important feature of the American frontier process cannot be too strongly underlined; *in fact it may be important enough to make the American frontier process unique.*[7] Without it, in any case, the process of sequential growth could not have taken place.

The process in the United States also involved the *free* exploitation of frontier areas in the sense that people were free to migrate, free to engage in the opportunities offered by successive frontier areas, and free to attempt to rise economically and socially. As a corollary to this people were relatively free to determine the speed of exploitation. Continued existence of such freedoms and opportunities and the fulfillment of the latter on a broad scale had important implications for economic incentives, factor mobility, and the successful operation of the process. The fact that once people moved to exploit the rich and varied resources they set in motion a social process which tended to reinforce economic freedoms is one of its important endogenous aspects.[8]

Thus over a space of many decades new areas were annexed to the older areas of the United States and many of them grew to rival the older areas in the complexity of their economic and social forms and the extent of their economic development. Three very broad features of the process as it developed in the United States illustrate this generalization: the temporal-spatial distribution of population, the urban distribution of population, and the relative regional importance of manufacturing activity.

The temporal-spatial distribution of the population of the United States by census regions is shown in Figure 12–1.[9] As regards population the New England and South Atlantic groups of states have been declining in relative importance since 1790. Successively the Middle Atlantic, the East South Central, the East North Central, and the West North Central groups of states have "grown into the economy" population-wise. Still growing into the economy are the Pacific and Mountain States, which, however, accounted for but minor fractions of the total population of the United States in the nineteenth century. The fact that this process of growing-in for the East North Central and West North Central groups of states terminated near the end of the nineteenth century is of particular importance.[10]

A somewhat similar picture, though different in one important feature, emerges with respect to the distribution of the total urban population of the United States by census regions. (See Figure 12–2.) The older regions, New England, Middle Atlantic, and South Atlantic, show declining relative importance, while the relative importance of the East North Central and West North Central urban populations grew until late in the nineteenth century. While the West South Central region showed increased relative importance with regard to total population, its relative importance with regard to urban population showed no such rise during the latter part of the nineteenth century. This we believe is due to the fact that this region's production possibilities at that time were quite limited relative to those of other areas which were growing into the economy.[11]

The relative regional importance of manufacturing activity over the last part of the nineteenth century is summarized in Table 12–1. At the time of the Census of 1869, the New England and Middle Atlantic regions accounted for 64 per cent of the total value of manufactured products produced in the United States. By 1889, just twenty years later, this figure had dropped to 53 per cent. Gains of course were registered in other regions, no-

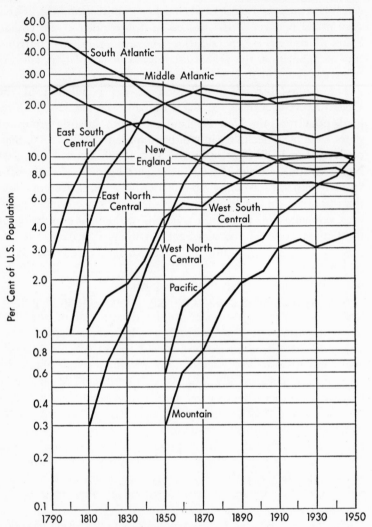

Figure 12–1. Percentage Distribution of United States Population
by Regions, 1790–1950*

* From *United States Census of Population: 1950*, Vol. I, p. ii.

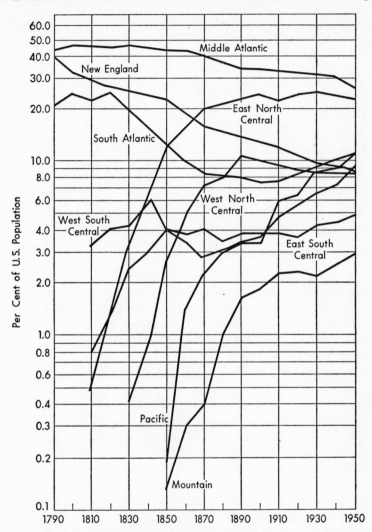

FIGURE 12–2. Percentage Distribution of United States Urban
Population by Regions, 1790–1950*

* Percentages calculated from data in *United States Census of Population: 1950*, Vol. I,
pp. 17–18.

TABLE 12-1

*Percentage Distribution of the Value of Products of Manufacturing
Establishments in the United States by Regions, 1869–1899* *

REGION	1869	1879	1889	1899
New England	24.45	20.90	16.46	14.71
Middle Atlantic	39.53	38.98	36.55	35.60
East North Central	18.38	22.15	25.00	24.95
West North Central	6.38	6.43	8.68	8.57
South Atlantic	5.39	5.36	5.53	6.33
East South Central	2.54	2.43	2.74	2.86
West South Central	0.91	0.92	1.48	2.18
Mountain	0.65	0.45	0.62	1.65
Pacific	1.77	2.33	2.95	3.17
Total	100.0	100.0	100.0	100.0

* Calculated from data in R. A. Easterlin, "Estimates of Manufacturing Activity," in
Population Redistribution and Economic Growth, United States 1870–1950 (Philadelphia:
The American Philosophical Society, 1957), 692–693.

tably the East North Central region which by 1889 had become
relatively more important than New England had been at any
time in the period 1869–1899. Here indeed is a case of a region
flowering into a complex industrial section, a process which had
occurred earlier in eastern sections.

This sequential growth process had effects on economic institutions in general, for instance on agricultural and business institutions.[12] This chapter is concerned to assess its influence on labor
alone.[13] In particular it is argued that this process, as it operated in
America, was largely responsible for (1) keeping the percentage
of the labor force unionized small, (2) preventing that portion
which was unionized from exerting continual social leverage of
any significance, and (3) keeping what Hobsbawm has called
leaps and explosions connected with both unionized and total
labor to a surprisingly low incidence rate.[14] This followed from
the fact that sequential growth (1) involved extremely favorable
effects on the level and rate of growth of per capita income and
employment, (2) created and preserved a large measure of horizontal and vertical socioeconomic mobility, and (3) created a legislative climate quite favorable to liberal labor legislation. *Taken
together*, these three elements produced the results above.

II

It seems commonplace to state that a single addition of rich natural resources to the stock already being utilized raises labor's (and capital's) marginal product and that in a full-employment economy this results in real income per worker being higher than it would otherwise be, given the rate of increase in the supply of labor. As a corollary, given the rate of increase in the supply of labor, *successive* additions of rich resources with many production possibilities to those already being exploited provide a rate of increase in real income per worker which is greater than would be the case had no such additions been made. In America the slabs of resources annexed to the older regions were rich and possessed broad production possibilities. Mere additions of frontier areas possessing narrow production possibilities, say limited to a single export crop, might produce high per capita income under certain conditions[15] but would not support industrialization.[16] The presence of an export crop may be a necessary condition for industrialization of a new region, but it is hardly alone a sufficient one, for suitable production possibilities are also required. The fact that many frontier areas in America satisfied both conditions meant that their contribution to the growth of per capita income and employment was substantial and operative over a series of decades.

American economic growth, of course, did not take place under conditions of continuous full employment. The seriousness of historical interruptions to the growth process during the period of the American frontier depended largely upon the behavior of what is usually termed autonomous investment, that is investment called forth by trend factors.

It seems clear that sequential growth is an important example of such trend factors with special features of its own. Whereas technological innovation may act as an important prop and stimulus to autonomous investment, there are several important differences between this and sequential growth. With expansion into a region with broad production possibilities, much of the investment which takes place is a repetition of a similar investment process which took place earlier in older sections of the country. Much of the uncertainty which surrounds the appearance and carrying through of investment made in response to technological innovation is not present.

Furthermore, investors in the new regions have the benefit of the older regions' experience on which to draw. That is, there is a stock of "once-and-for-all" investments, to use H. J. Bruton's[17] phrase, associated with the growing into the economy of a new region. These include the laying down of a transportation system, a road system, a set of public buildings, urban development, and the like. Since these developments are expected to occur with some certainty, although there may be some uncertainty regarding the timing, other supplemental investment projects are undertaken with great rapidity in anticipation of the exploitation of the stock of "once-and-for-alls." All of this provides a substantial boost to autonomous investment which seems more shock proof than similar spurts provided by technological innovation.

In addition, the investment stimulated by technological innovation may be impeded by the presence of technical interrelatedness of capital equipment which may make all-or-nothing decisions mandatory in an economy without frontier areas. In a country with successively developing frontier areas, these areas may offer an avenue of escape from the problem of interrelatedness.[18]

Finally, if, as Simon Kuznets has suggested, there were limitations on growth arising from the saving side, insofar as the exploitations of new natural resources substituted for capital-using innovations to overcome diminishing returns, a possible growth limiting factor was partially offset.[19] In summary, the process of sequential growth provided a substantial contribution to the growth of so-called autonomous investment which contribution acted to prevent extremely serious and prolonged interruptions in the growth of per capita income and employment.

In pointing to these propositions we do not imply that increase in the stock of natural resources was the only factor responsible for raising the marginal productivity of labor and maintaining a rapid growth of autonomous investment. Of course many technological innovations and growth in the stock of capital had similar effects on labor's marginal productivity and the growth of autonomous investment. But the American economy was distinguished by the presence of technological innovation, plus a growing stock of capital, plus successive geographic frontiers all in conjunction with one another. This set of key factors produced the nineteenth century's highest level of per capita income and rate of increase in per capita income. (See Table 12–2.)

TABLE 12–2

Pre-World War I Percentage Change Per Decade of National Product, Population, and National Product Per Capita for Eleven Countries

COUNTRY	INITIAL PERIOD	TERMINAL PERIOD	PERCENTAGE CHANGE PER DECADE		
			NATIONAL PRODUCT [*]	POPULATION	NATIONAL PRODUCT [*] PER CAPITA
United States	1869–78	1904–13	56.0	22.3	27.5
Japan	1878–87	1903–12	49.2	11.6	33.7
Canada	1870–79	1905–14	47.1	17.8	24.7
Germany	1860–69	1905–14	35.6	11.5	21.6
Sweden	1861–68	1904–13	34.8	6.8	26.2
Denmark	1870–78	1904–13	32.7	11.3	19.3
Russia	1870	1913	27.7	15.7	10.4
United Kingdom	1860–69	1905–14	25.0	11.1	12.5
France	1841–50	1901–10	18.6	1.9	16.3
Italy	1862–68	1904–13	15.7	7.0	8.1
Ireland	1860–69	1904–13	11.6	−5.4	17.9

[*] National Product in constant prices.

Source: Simon Kuznets, "Quantitative Aspects of the Economic Growth of Nations," *Economic Development and Cultural Change*, V (October 1956), 13.

This fact is of some importance. Since the United States' level of per capita income and rate of growth were so high relative to those experienced elsewhere we conjecture that if there were any place in the Western world where actual levels of income and rates of growth of income which workers experienced did not deviate greatly from those to which they aspired, then it was in the United States.[20]

Before the 1880's, the decade in which the process of sequential growth was coming to an end,[21] we would guess that these deviations were not of sufficient magnitude to produce any serious Hobsbawmian "leaps" in American union membership or "explosions" in total labor activity. In what E. J. Hobsbawm calls the Labroussian period, sometime before 1840, when social discontent could take most vigorous forms, there does not seem to have been extreme unrest in post-revolutionary America in contrast to Europe. After 1840 two great "leaps" were those of 1886, when the labor movement tripled, and 1936–1937, when it almost doubled. The former leap took place when the trend influence of the frontier was virtually non-existent. The "explosions" of 1886 and those connected with the Industrial Workers of the World are examples which seem to dwarf anything which went before in American labor history.[22] Hobsbawm remarks:[23]

Perhaps the most useful assumption is that, under the nineteenth- and early twentieth-century conditions, the normal process of industrial development tends to produce explosive situations, i.e., accumulations of inflammable material which only ignite periodically, as it were under compression.

Recalling the latent strain of violence in the American labor movement which has been occasionally revealed in its more recent history, it is surprising that before the close of the frontier process labor history was so peaceful. The American population was a highly selected one due to the process of immigration; it is amazing that the stresses and strains of industrial change caused it to react so little! There are indeed isolated cases of violence before the frontier process closed, the Molly Maguires are an excellent example of this. Such cases show what truly combustible material the American labor force contained. But until the nature of American labor disturbances has been subjected to careful quantitative analysis in the way Hobsbawm indicates, we must rely on first impressions. It is ours that the 1880's mark a real watershed for American labor.

In passing we might ask whether it is mere coincidence that each of the leaps and explosions which occurred in and after 1886 took place in a decade during which the rate of growth of national product per capita was very low compared to that of the directly preceding decade. (See Figure 12–3.)

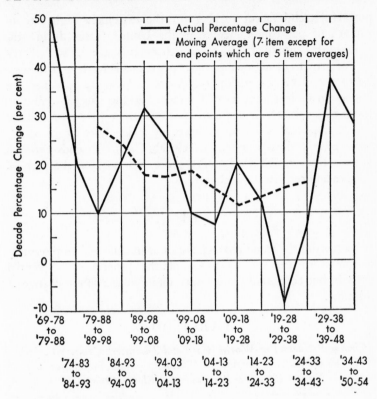

FIGURE 12–3. Decade Percentage Change in United States
Net National Product (1929 prices) Per Capita, 1869–1954 *

* S. Kuznets, "Quantitative Aspects of the Economic Growth of Nations," *Economic Development and Cultural Change*, V (October 1956), 85.

Finally could the termination of the process of sequential growth be an important element in explaining the apparent downward drift of the decade rates of growth in national product per capita shown in Figure 12–3? The figures in the Table 12–3 indicate that compared with ten other countries relative retardation in the United States was more serious than in any other country, except Germany.[24] These findings, tentative though they may be, appear to be compatible with the hypothesis that the termination of the frontier process constituted the cessation of the action of a powerful trend factor making for the extremely high rate of growth of per capita income in the United States during the nineteenth century. In the twentieth century the United States' rate of growth of national product per capita is far from the highest of the eleven countries considered in Table 12–4. What this implies to us is a long-term downward adjustment of aspiration levels to levels which begin to approach those of a more settled and "completed" society, a society in which lines begin to become clearly drawn and in which labor seeks its ends through organizations which are founded more and more on the premise "once a laborer, always a laborer."

III

Not only did the trend characteristics of income and employment change with the disappearance of the process of sequential growth, but economic opportunity underwent a subtle change at this time.

TABLE 12–3

Change Between Pre-World War I and Twentieth Century Periods in Decade Rates of Growth of National Product, Population and National Product Per Capita for Eleven Countries*

	CHANGE IN PERCENTAGE CHANGE PER DECADE		
COUNTRY	NATIONAL PRODUCT	POPULATION (PERCENTAGE POINTS)	NATIONAL PRODUCT PER CAPITA
United States	−22.2	−7.3	−11.1
Japan	−11.3	1.7	−12.0
Canada	−5.7	3.1	−7.7
Germany	−15.7	−1.7	−13.3
Sweden	3.0	−0.2	3.0
Denmark	−2.1	0.6	−2.6
Russia	5.4	−3.4	8.2
United Kingdom	−7.8	−5.5	−1.5
France	−7.5	−1.3	−5.9
Italy	6.5	0.0	6.1
Ireland	5.6	11.0	−6.9

* Calculated from data in Tables 12–2 and 12–4.

TABLE 12–4

*Twentieth Century Percentage Change Per Decade of National
Product, Population, and National Product Per Capita
for Eleven Countries* *

COUNTRY	INITIAL PERIOD	TERMINAL PERIOD	PERCENTAGE CHANGE PER DECADE		
			NATIONAL PRODUCT [a]	POPULATION	NATIONAL PRODUCT [a] PER CAPITA
United States	1894–1903	1950–54	33.8	15.0	16.4
Japan	1893–1902	1950–54	37.9	13.3	21.7
Canada	1895–1904	1950–54	41.4	20.9	17.0
Germany [b]	1895–1904	1950–54	19.9	9.8	8.3
Sweden (Gross Domestic Product)	1894–1903	1950–54	37.8	6.6	29.2
Denmark (Net Domestic Product)	1894–1903	1950–54	30.6	11.9	16.7
Russia— U.S.S.R.[c]	1900	1954	33.1	12.3	18.6
United Kingdom [d]	1895–1904	1949–53	17.2	5.6	11.0
France [e]	1901–10	1949–53	11.1	0.6	10.4
Italy	1894–1903	1950–54	22.2	7.0	14.2
Ireland—Eire [f]	1894–1903	1949–53	17.2	5.6	11.0

a 1929 prices.
b Average of pre-World War I territory for 1895–1904 to 1905–14 (weight 1); 1925 territory for 1913 to 1935–41 (weight 2.5) and Western Germany for 1936 to 1950–54 (weight 1.6).
c Average of Russia for 1900 to 1913 (weight 1.3) and the U.S.S.R. for 1913–54 (weight 4.1).
d Excluding southern Ireland.
e Including Alsace-Lorraine.
f Average of Ireland for 1894–1903 to 1904–13 (weight 1) and Eire for 1911 to 1949–53 (weight 4).
* S. Kuznets, "Quantitative Aspects of the Economic Growth of Nation," *Economic Development and Cultural Change* (Oct. 1956), V, 10.

So long as sequential growth continued then investment, job, and status opportunities were continually recreated in association with reappearing stocks of "once-and-for-alls." At successive frontier areas, in Turner's words,[25]

. . . were mill sites, town sites, transportation lines, banking centers, openings in law, in politics—all the varied chances for advancement afforded in a rapidly developing society where everything was open to him who knew how to seize the opportunity.

Furthermore such opportunities continued over many generations. While American economic growth still continues to burgeon out into fresh areas, the "once-and-for-alls" which are thus created constitute a relatively small addition to the total pool of economic opportunity. New regions now can have relatively little effect upon a mature and powerful economy. Where before there were frontier opportunities and opportunities within the expanding economy of the older regions now the latter alone have importance.[26]

It should be noted in passing that the opportunities correlated with the exploitation of "once-and-for-alls" were of a special kind. As pointed out already, investment opportunities were less risky than opportunities associated with innovational investment in a settled society. Frontier areas permitted, also, greater social and political manipulation of investment and job opportunities. To the unsuccessful they permitted fresh chances and often an easy escape from the penalties of failure.

Paul Gates mentions that frontier areas also conferred, as it were, a "capital stake" on those who wished to exploit the opportunities there:[27]

In practically every town, large or small, the local squire, the bank president, the owner of numerous mortgages, the resident of the "big house," the man whose wife was the leader of "society," got his start— and a substantial start—as a result of the upward surge of land values in the nineteenth century.

It is true that many such opportunities aggrandized eastern interests, but it seems clear that easterners did not pre-empt all opportunities made available! Furthermore while economic rents were also generated by economic advance in the settled areas, the status advantages of many of the opportunities at the frontier (together with the associated economic rents) could only be enjoyed by those who resided there. So long as sequential growth continued another related process could be maintained. Continuous streams of immigrants with lower aspiration levels than native-born Americans arrived in the country to take relatively non-favored jobs. As Ruth Mack has pointed out, this provided a boost, as it were, to push native Americans upwards in the socioeconomic scale.[28] Thus those with the lower aspirations engaged in the less preferred occupations while those with the higher were guaranteed more preferred occupations. Such a social mechanism could hardly be conducive to union growth! Clearly this process could not continue for many decades after the frontier areas were occupied and "completed," and indeed fears about a declining real income created strong pressures for the ending of uncontrolled immigration.

In face of the opportunities for vertical and horizontal mobility presented by sequential growth, it is difficult to see how any labor movement of any real significance could emerge. It is not strange to find Alfred Marshall attributing the weakness of American unions to the American workingman's "restless enterprise, his constant opportunities for bettering himself by changing his abode and his occupation, and the abundance of land on which he could settle as an independent owner." [29] Ray Ginger has pointed out that indeed it might not even be necessary to have people rise vertically in the social scale to delay formation of a labor movement; horizontal mobility alone might account for difficulties in forming unions.[30]

Once the full exploitation of "once-and-for-alls" had been completed, it seems reasonable to conclude, on a priori grounds, that social mobility declined. It must be admitted that such a conclusion goes against the general drift of recent opinion. Oscar Handlin writes, for instance, "Investigations have shown the dubious quality of the generalization that the rate of growth of social mobility has declined in recent decades." [31] Both Ely Chinoy and William Petersen,[32] who have reviewed the literature on the subject, also are inclined to support this view. Chinoy remarks, for instance:[33]

It seems clear, then, that neither inferential analysis based upon historical study nor direct analysis of mobility of groups of individuals can yet indicate whether there has been any change in the rate of vertical mobility in American society.

But as Ray Ginger has pointed out, there is really very little substantial evidence on the subject.[34] Furthermore, and more important to the arguments of this chapter, Chinoy repeats a common mistake in dealing with the Turnerian frontier process. He argues that the closing of the frontier could not have appreciably diminished agricultural opportunities because the debate on Turner's safety-valve doctrine has clearly revealed how few eastern wage-earners became owner-operators of a western farm before 1890. The evidence on this score is, of course, strong.[35]

But Turner viewed the frontier as creating economic opportunity on a broader front than the agricultural one. In other words he was concerned with opportunities associated with reappearing stocks of "once-and-for-alls" as well as those in agriculture. Thus, so long as we are not concerned with agricultural opportunities alone then we still seem to have a proposition that appears intrinsically plausible, that is: "For many years, the frontier and free land provided significant elasticity." [36] However, it is a proposition which still awaits factual proof or disproof.[37]

Our position is then that sequential growth, itself operating within the context of the growing Atlantic community,[38] gave a solid foundation to the rags-to-riches saga. Migration continued westward. The centroid of population moved westward. Cities were constructed to the West. Fortunes were made in the West. Political and social reputations were made in the West. We should not be surprised that a system of values emerged which was appropriate to this movement. Joseph Schafer goes so far as to say:[39]

It is certain, however, that the effect of what has been called the safety valve has been largely psychological, operating alike upon laborers, employers and the general public.

American social history indicates quite clearly that the "belief" in a safety valve had a potent effect upon social action in America. Similarly, when conditions in industry began to crystallize and vertical and horizontal mobility to decline, when the frontier process could no longer assimilate fresh immigrations, then the belief in unlimited opportunity did decline. It is not necessary for every gambler to make a fortune to keep people gambling. But when the odds get too loaded only the truly irrational still believe in the game.

It is not improbable, however, that other factors were also responsible for the workingman's sense of diminished economic opportunities. We recognize that we are engaging in a rather crude sociology-of-workers' attitudes. For instance it may be, as Selig Perlman suggests, that with the progress of the industrial order the rising threshold of skills necessary for vertical social ascent helped to generate job consciousness.[40] If data on social mobility show anything, they certainly demonstrate that a real barrier exists *now* between "hand" and "head" workers.[41] Skilled trade union leadership could also help to generate job consciousness. All these effects married to a period, the 1880's, when aspired-to and actual levels of income diverged significantly, could explain the emergence of the sense of diminished opportunity. One thing seems to be of prime importance; until the ending of the frontier process it seems unlikely that the other factors such as vigorous union leadership or a sense of inadequacy on the part of the worker could have stemmed the average American's belief in limitless opportunity for himself and his children. But with the ending of the frontier, instead of there being isolated accumulations of explosive material, to use Hobsbawm's terminology, the whole labor situation became fraught with potential danger.

Sequential growth also had a special qualitative effect on the trade union movement. It not only presented to union organizers a fluid mass of workers believing in unlimited status, job, and investment opportunity, but it continually robbed unions of leadership. Alfred Marshall has portrayed the loss to the labor movement of capable individuals within the context of non-frontier industrial society.[42]

We believe it was Turner's insight that this drain of potential leadership was greater when industrial change was ramified by the frontier process. He also thought that the "goers" were not so much those who were willing to challenge existing institutions as those who found life intolerable in those institutions but did not wish to fight them. If he was right, and we need knowledge from social psychology to tell us, the type of men he had in mind probably would make up the second strata of leadership. These men would be those unwilling to become martyrs, as it were, to engage in full battle with the going order, but nonetheless able, intelligent, and ambitious men. Such men under sequential growth were offered the chance to stay in society to achieve their per-

sonal goals provided they moved. It may be that international migrants are heavily composed of such personalities. Given barriers
to movement, the leaders in the struggle against existing institutions might have found their second-in-commands, their chiefs of
staff, and their company commanders. It seems not unlikely that
the frontier acted as a social margin to draw off the younger and
abler persons in much the same way as new industries with their
shortrun high gains create a like type of margin for labor and
entrepreneurial ability. Thus the mere counting of migrants does
not reveal the whole story. Economic historians may have
counted the troops but missed the drain of officers!

This drain on the labor movement created by vertical and horizontal mobility did not work irrespective of the cycle. It is especially unreasonable to expect workers to migrate during periods
of unemployment; why move from being employed in Boston to
being unemployed in Chicago?[43] It is precisely the frustration
connected with the denial of opportunity to work over a long
period, on top of a large deviation of the level of actual from
aspired-to income, which sets the scene for Hobsbawm's "leaps"
and "explosions." But the influence of the frontier in addition to
robbing unions of their leaders and rank and file was felt in the
matter of the cycle. Insofar as it shortened and modulated business cycle contractions, it contributed to shortening and alleviat-
ing critical situations for labor as a whole.

IV

The spectrum of opportunities presented by sequential growth
thus, in our view, had a definite effect on the labor movement.
That opportunities existed and actually came to fruit also affected
the supply of effort which in turn had an effect on the general
economic climate.[44] It should also be stressed that the general legislative climate in America afforded labor other routes than union
activities to achieve its ends. For instance, American labor gained
the franchise far earlier than their English counterparts. There
was early federal acceptance of both the ten-hour and the
eight-hour day. The fact that American labor so frequently engaged in political activity before the emergence of the American

Federation of Labor may thus be not so much a tribute to the immaturity of job-consciousness and of union immaturity as to the fact that political activity paid off. Americans lived in a mild legislative climate in the nineteenth century. Even organized labor did not suffer great legislative disabilities from Hunt versus Commonwealth until the massive use of the injunction. As Selig Perlman notes, trade unions felt so secure in the 1870's and 1880's that their leaders advocated legal incorporation.[45] It is not hard to believe, as Turner did, that the process of sequential growth had something to do with this mild legislative climate. However, it would take us too far afield to pursue this question.

If all these features are taken into account then, it appears that there is substantial evidence for the truth of the safety-valve doctrine. And in addition to the labor movement other economic institutions developed within a special American environment. This is a broader theme than that with which this paper is concerned, but it may be that such developments are the better understood if viewed within the context of sequential economic growth, itself taking place within, and having influence upon, a growing Atlantic community. We believe this to have been Turner's intuition at its best; an intuition which permits a sounder approach to economic history than ones which stress only the theme of the "Frontier" or only the theme of "the growing industrial order."

Notes

NOTE: We are indebted to Douglass C. North and to Herbert Kisch for helpful comments and criticisms. Naturally, all errors of fact and interpretation are our own. An earlier version of this chapter was presented to the Western Economic Association in August 1958.

1. Fred A. Shannon, "A Post-mortem on the Labor-Safety-Valve Theory" (Chapter 10).

2. Some economic historians had misgivings. See, for instance, Herbert Heaton, "Other Wests than Ours," *The Tasks of Economic History*, papers presented at the Sixth Annual Meetings of the Economic History Association, Baltimore, Md., Sept. 13–14, 1946, p. 61; see also Norman J. Simler, "The Safety-Valve Doctrine Re-evaluated" (Chapter 11).

3. *The Early Writings of Frederick Jackson Turner*, edited by Fulmer Mood (Madison: The University of Wisconsin Press, 1938); F. J. Turner, *The Frontier in American History* (New York: Henry Holt and Co., 1937);

F. J. Turner, *The Significance of Sections in American History* (New York: Henry Holt and Co., 1932); F. J. Turner, *Rise of the New West, 1818–1820* (New York and London: Harper and Brothers, 1906); F. J. Turner, *The United States, 1830–50, The Nation and Its Sections* (New York: Henry Holt and Co., 1935). Since the present chapter is not a study in doctrine, we do not quote Turner's works extensively to substantiate the claim that the version of the labor-safety-valve doctrine which we present is rooted in his works.

4. The notion of a "slab" of resources does not entail any functional concept of a region but is merely meant to connote a given quantity of resources distributed in space and added to the resource base of American economy by the historical accidents of frontier advance.

5. Turner did not reject the view that the development of the American economy was shaped in part by its membership in a growing Atlantic community. Indeed he stressed the frontier because it helped him to explain why American historical development differed from that of *other industrial* nations of the Atlantic community.

6. Such broad production possibilities were partly created by contemporaneous changes in the world economy. Benjamin H. Higgins, *Economic Development: Principles, Problems and Policies* (New York: W. W. Norton and Company, 1959), p. 189, distinguishes between geographic and economic frontiers. The former is an area where increasing returns occur without changes in technology, demands, or population size. The latter is an area where increasing returns occur after a change in one of these factors. It is clear from Turner's writings that he was not thinking solely in terms of a moving geographic frontier but was aware of the effects of changes in the factors Benjamin H. Higgins mentions. It is difficult to judge which of the factors was of greatest historical importance. Some economic historians have investigated the role of international demands in the development of frontier-type economies. An interesting example is S. Daniel Neumark, *The South African Frontier* (Stanford: Food Research Institute, Stanford University, 1957). The reviews of the book suggest that the problem is a complex one to handle. See Bert F. Hoselitz, *Current Economic Comment*, XX (May 1958), 68–70, and W. K. Hancock, "Trek," *Economic History Review*, X (April 1958), 331–339.

7. B. H. Higgins, *Economic Development: Principles, Problems and Policies*, ch. vi, p. 192, writes: "In one respect, however, the American case is absolutely unique. For the westward movement does not tell the whole story of frontier development in the United States, there have been movements north and south from the center as well. . . . No other country can match the remarkable speed of urban growth throughout its entire area, in wave after successive wave, that has occurred in the United States. In Canada urban development has been confined to a narrow strip within a few hundred miles of the United States border; and great cities are found only in Ontario and Quebec. Australian frontier development built no cities away from the coast. In Europe, the major cities have grown up side by side over several centuries; there has been no progressive opening up of new frontiers, followed by urban growth, such as occurred in this country. The story of Chicago, Detroit, Kansas City, St. Louis, Dallas, Houston, and Los Angeles is a purely American-style story. It is surely not unreasonable to suppose that this continuous opening up of new areas and the concomitant urban growth has been a major factor, both in providing investment opportunities and in

keeping alive the 'log cabin to riches,' folklore and the enterprising spirit that goes with it."

8. American economic development under sequential growth can be contrasted to Russian economic development before the Plan Era. Generally speaking Russian frontier advance did not bring in areas of broad production possibilities. Alexander Baykov, "Economic Development of Russia," *Economic History Review*, VII (December 1954), 137–149, assigns greater importance to the nature of Russian resources than to institutional factors in explaining Russia's fall into relative backwardness in the nineteenth century.

9. Census groupings of states are used for convenience and are only an approximation to a "slab." Charts such as these have previously been employed by R. A. Easterlin.

10. These are not the only areas which "grew in" to the economy. Subsections of the broad census regions in the East did so at an earlier period historically.

11. Robert Baldwin, "Patterns of Development in Newly Settled Regions," *Manchester School of Economic and Social Studies*, XXIV (May 1956), 161–179, has suggested that two regions equally rich in resources and initially specializing in the production of a staple for export may develop quite differently if there are important differences in the staples' production function. He has in mind differences between plantation cotton growing with economies of scale and wheat production in which there are few such economies. His argument seems to depend on the assumption of extremely low factor mobility, especially low labor mobility. Whether this constitutes a better explanation of why the West South Central region's urban population and manufacturing activity (see Table 12–1) failed to grow in relative importance requires further investigation.

12. Economic growth within a settled society has many similarities to that within a frontier society. This has been pointed out by T. S. Ashton, *An Economic History of England, The 18th Century* (London: Methuen and Co. Ltd., 1955), p. 232, who refers to an interesting article by W. A. Mackintosh, "Some Aspects of a Pioneer Economy," *The Canadian Journal of Economics and Political Science*, II (November 1936), 457–463. But we believe that there are still important differences economically between what Hoselitz has termed "expansionist" growth and "intrinsic" growth [*Canadian Journal of Economics and Political Science*, XX (November 1955), 416–431], particularly when the former takes place in a climate of broad production possibilities.

13. In assessing the influence of sequential growth process on labor we believe that we are keeping to the essential spirit of Turner's views on the social elasticity provided by the frontier process.

14. E. J. Hobsbawm, "Economic Fluctuations and Some Social Movements since 1800," *Economic History Review*, V (August 1952), 1–25.

15. Harold A. Innis has studied the development of basic staples in the Canadian economy in order to throw light on general economic growth in that economy. J. S. Duesenberry, "Some Aspects of the Theory of Economic Development," *Explorations in Entrepreneurial History*, III (December 1950), 63–102, describes the income generation process involved. Under special conditions both the new regions and the old regions benefit from the growth of the new regions.

16. It is interesting to note that Douglass C. North, when criticizing W. W. Rostow's position on the "Take-off" period of American economic

development, suggested as an hypothesis—one the reverse of Rostow's—that "the opening up and development of new areas capable of producing primary goods in demand in existing markets induced the growth of industrialization." *Manchester School of Economic and Social Studies*, XXVI (January 1958), 74. This hypothesis clearly depends on the implicit assumption that broad production possibilities exist in the new areas. See also Douglass C. North, "International Capital Flows and the Development of the American West," *The Journal of Economic History*, XVI (December 1956), 494.

17. H. J. Bruton, *A Survey of Recent Contributions to the Theory of Economic Growth* (Cambridge: Center for International Studies, Massachusetts Institute of Technology, 1956), mimeographed.

18. See in particular M. Frankel, "Obsolescence and Technological Change in a Maturing Economy," *American Economic Review*, XLV (June 1955), 296–319; D. F. Gordon, "Obsolescence and Technological Change," *American Economic Review*, XLVI (September 1956), 646–652; and M. Frankel's reply to D. F. Gordon's note which follows in the same issue.

19. This is not to underrate the importance of international capital flows in the development of the American economy.

20. We assume that it is not so much the actual level of income or its rate of increase which is critical in evoking unionization or other types of workers' response to their economic situation as the size of the deviation between the wages workers earn and those to which they aspire (and similarly the deviation between the rate of growth which they actually enjoy and those to which they aspire).

21. Turner believed that his frontier process had largely ceased to work by the decade of the 1880's. As Turner grew older, 1890 as a turning point in American history gradually assumed less importance in his thought.

22. Strike data only go back until 1880. See Florence Peterson, *Strikes in the United States, 1880–1936*, Bureau of Labor Statistics, Bulletin No. 651, 1938. The 1872 strike involved 100,000 workers which was an exceptionally large number for American labor disturbances prior to the 1880's. This fact suggests that labor history was relatively peaceful. Similarly there are few data on unions before 1881. Preliminary estimates show, however, that the percentage unionized in the 1880's was very small, probably much less than 1 per cent.

23. E. J. Hobsbawm, *Economic History Review*, V (August 1952), 15.

24. Estimates of national product, as the reader will be aware, are not as accurate as could be desired even for the twentieth century. The problem of deflating the national product in current prices to obtain national product in constant prices is particularly thorny, especially when the time period under consideration is a long one. Kuznets is hesitant about inferring retardation from the downward drift of the moving average rates. See Simon Kuznets, "Quantitative Aspects of the Economic Growth of Nations," *Economic Development and Culture Change*, V (October 1956), 35 ff. Moses Abramovitz, "Resource and Output Trends in the United States since 1870," *American Economic Review*, XLVI (March 1956), 5–23, has similar reservations. In his view the downward drift of national product figures is not large enough and persistent enough to establish retardation in the growth rate. But until better data and improved methods are available, we cannot entirely disregard what the best estimates have to tell us!

25. F. J. Turner, *The Frontier in American History*, p. 271.

26. However, compare Carter Goodrich and Sol Davison, "The Wage-Earner in the Westward Movement," *Political Science Quarterly*, LI (March 1936), 116.

27. Paul Wallace Gates, *Frontier Landlords and Pioneer Tenants* (Ithaca: Cornell University Press, 1945), p. 2. Reproduced from the *Journal of the Illinois State Historical Society* (June 1945), by permission.

28. Ruth Mack, "Trends in American Consumption and the Aspiration to Consume," *American Economic Review*, XLVI (March 1956), 64. This argument is also made by William Petersen, "Is America Still the Land of Opportunity?" *Commentary*, XVI (November 1953), 481.

29. Alfred Marshall, *Economics of Industry* (London: Macmillan and Co. Ltd., 1932), p. 392. Since Marshall wrote this, the debate on Turner's safety-valve doctrine has shown that agricultural opportunities were not very great.

30. Ray Ginger, "Occupation Mobility and American Life," *Explorations in Entrepreneurial History*, VI (May 1954), 234–244.

31. Oscar Handlin, "A Note on Social Mobility and the Recruitment of Entrepreneurs in the United States," *Explorations in Entrepreneurial History*, VIII (Winter Supplement, 1954), papers presented to the Third Working Conference on Social Mobility and Social Stratification, Amsterdam, December 16–18, 1954, p. 3.

32. Ely Chinoy, "Social Mobility Trends in the U.S.," *American Sociological Review*, XX (April 1955), 180–190. William Petersen, *Commentary*, XVI (November 1953).

33. Ely Chinoy, *American Sociological Review*, XX (April 1955), 190.

34. Ray Ginger, *Explorations in Entrepreneurial History*, VI (May 1954), 235.

35. See especially Fred A. Shannon, "A Post-mortem on the Labor-Safety-Valve Theory" (Chapter 10).

36. The quotation is from Ruth Mack, "Trends in American Consumption and the Aspiration to Consume," *American Economic Review*, XLVI (March 1956), 64. She also stresses the importance of immigration, the supply of effort, and economic expansion.

37. Despite a growing literature, the economic data available have not yet been fully exploited on the subject of mobility. There are, however, some difficult conceptual problems involved. See S. M. Miller, "The Concept of Mobility," *Social Problems*, III (October 1955), 65–73.

38. This paper does not deal with the effect of sequential growth on the economic development of the Atlantic community, although it was probably very important.

39. Joseph Schafer, "Concerning the Frontier as Safety Valve," *Political Science Quarterly*, LII (September 1937), 420. See also Murray Kane, "Some Considerations on the Safety Valve Doctrine," *Mississippi Valley Historical Review*, XXIII (September 1936), 188.

40. Selig Perlman, *A Theory of the Labor Movement* (New York: A. M. Kelley, 1949), p. 239.

41. See especially Natalie Rogoff, *Recent Trends in Occupational Mobility* (Glencoe, Ill.: Free Press, 1953). William Petersen, *Commentary*, XVI (November 1953).

42. Alfred Marshall, *Memorials of Alfred Marshall* (London: Macmillan and Co. Ltd., 1925), 227–255.

43. It seems plausible to believe that the facts should show that the behavior with respect to migration of those employed and those not employed should be quite different during a depression period.

44. There is circularity in this proposition, as Ruth Mack points out, but it still seems correct.

45. Selig Perlman, *History of Trade Unionism in the United States* (New York: The Macmillan Company, 1929), p. 152.

Index